CONTENTS

List of illustrations	5
Preface	9
Acknowledgements	10
David N. Robinson OBE MSc (1927–2017)	11
Foreword, David N. Robinson OBE MSc	12

PROLOGUE

1.	Introduction	13
2.	Timeline – Claxby, Nettleton and Walesby	15
3.	Geology	16
4.	Archaeology	20
5.	Landowners and Prospectors	24

CLAXBY MINE

6.	In the Beginning	25
7.	Underground	29
8.	Ventilation	33
9.	Surface Works and Buildings	35
10.	Railway Siding and Incline	40
11.	Calcining	44
12.	The Miners	45
13.	Accidents	49
14.	The Strike of 1872	53
15.	1871 Census	54
16.	Production	57
17.	Closure and After	58
18.	Claxby Parish Church	59

NETTLETON TOP MINE

19.	Early Proposals	61
20.	In the Beginning	63
21.	Underground	66
22.	Surface Works and Buildings	70
23.	The Aerial Ropeway	75

NETTLETON BOTTOM MINE

24.	Development	79
25.	Underground	83
26.	Surface Works and Buildings	87

NETTLETON MINES AND MINERS

27.	Opencast Working	89
28.	The Chalk Quarry	92
29.	Holton le Moor Sidings	95
30.	Locomotives and Rolling Stock	97
31.	The Miners	103
32.	Accidents	108
33.	Compressed Air Picks	109
34.	Production	109
35.	Lysaghts Sports and Social Club	113
36.	Economies and Closure	115

THE WALESBY SHAFT and POSTSCRIPT

37.	A Study of the Walesby Shaft	117
38.	Postscript	121

Notes and References	125
Bibliography	130
Index	131

LIST OF ILLUSTRATIONS

Nettleton, Back o' the Farm with opencast mining underway on the hillside 11

Fig 1.1. Ironstone workings in Lincolnshire 14

Fig 3.1. Britain's iron ore deposits 17
Fig 3.2. The extent of the Claxby ironstone field 18
Fig 3.3. Geological cross section, Nettleton 19
Fig 3.4. Geomorphology at Claxby 19
Fig 3.5. Claxby Ironstone. A close up of the 'gunshot' grains within the stone 20
Fig 3.6. Claxby Ironstone, with bivalve shell 20
Fig 3.7. Examples of fossilised shells and belemites found at Nettleton 21
Fig 3.8. Claxby Parish Church 21

Fig 4.1. Archaeology 23

Fig 6.1. The broken nature of the ground along the hillside around Claxby Mine 25
Fig 6.2. The 'Proposed site of iron works' at Holton le Moor 26
Fig 6.3. Copy of the plan showing the area leased by the Yarborough Estate to William Firth in 1866 26
Fig 6.4. Extract from plan dated 1867 showing the land required for works and tramways at Claxby Mine 27

Fig 7.1. Pillar and stall working at Claxby Mine 29
Fig 7.2. Claxby Mine, to show phases of mining with entrances and ventilation shafts 30
Fig 7.3. The site of Drift No 2 in April 1998 31

Fig 8.1. The top of the Claxby Mine ventilation shaft prior to infilling, 1955 32
Fig 8.2. The site of the original upcast shaft for Drift No 1 32

Fig 9.1. The surface works and buildings in 1887 33
Fig 9.2. Conjectured layout of the surface works and buildings when the mine was in operation 34
Fig 9.3. Section of rail found at Claxby Mine 35
Fig 9.4. The scatter of bricks marking the site of the stables and smithy 35
Fig 9.5. The section of tramplate found at the site of the stables and smithy 35
Fig 9.6. The remains of the retaining wall at the base of the embankment by the tipping stage 36
Fig 9.7. The retaining wall along the east side of the route of the siding 36
Fig 9.8. The powder house, seen here in March 1995 36
Fig 9.9. Claxby hillside with some of the structures that would have been prominent in this open landscape 37

Fig 10.1. The route of the railway siding crossing the fields to the site of the Claxby Mine (OS map, 1890) 38
Fig 10.2. The route of the incline (OS map, 1888) 39
Fig 10.3. The winding drum at Claxby Mine, seen here in 1927 40
Fig 10.4. Conjectured drawing of what the winding house and drum may have looked like in operation 40
Fig 10.5. The wire rope found on the route of the incline in 1991 40
Fig 10.6. The inclined wall following the route of the cable down from the Winding Drum 41
Fig 10.7. The pinch bar found on the mine site 42

Fig 12.1. The miners' houses, the village school and their location in relation to the village 46
Fig 12.2. Claxby Terrace 47
Fig 12.3. Internal layout of 7, The Terrace 48
Fig 12.4. The Mine Manager's House in 2016 49

Fig 13.1. The gravestone of William Keal in Claxby churchyard 51

Fig 16.1. Claxby Mine: ironstone production, 1868 to 1885 59

Fig 18.1. The Ironstone Pit, (OS map, 1888) 60
Fig 18.2. The location of the ironstone pit is identified by the trees in this view from the north 60

Fig 19.1. The trial holes, (OS map1906) 61
Fig 19.2. A drift entrance to a tunnel isolated from the rest of the mine 62

Fig 20.1. Work begins in 1929 to dig the Nettleton Top Mine 63
Fig 20.2. A view from above the first adit with stone being tipped to form the pit bank, 1929 64
Fig 20.3. The pit bank almost complete 64

Fig 21.1. Nettleton Top Mine, underground layout 67
Fig 21.2. A loaded train being taken out of Top Mine, taken in the late 1930s 68
Fig 21.3. The main entrance to Top Mine, shortly after going into production in 1934 69
Fig 21.4. A horse hauling loaded tubs out of the mine 69
Fig 21.5. Carbide lamp and Safety lamp formerly owned by Edward (Ned) Mumby 69

Fig 22.1. The buildings at Nettleton Top (December 1964) 70
Fig 22.2. The extent of the mines yard as shown on the six inch OS map 71
Fig 22.3. Undated map of 'Nettleton Mine' showing the surface buildings 72
Fig 22.4. The range of buildings immediately outside the main entrance to Nettleton Mine 73
Fig 22.5. The tipping operation to empty loaded tubs, taken shortly after the mine opened 73
Fig 22.6. An empty tub being hauled by the endless chain back up to 'ground' level 73
Fig 22.7. The power house, front, with the workshop beyond 74
Fig 22.8. The interior of the power house 74

Fig 23.1. The aerial ropeway seen from the mine 75
    Fig 1. View of one of the trestles 75
    Fig 2. General view of belt conveyor, storage bunker, ropeway station, etc 76
    Fig 3. View of the terminal gear and steel frame of loading station 76
    Fig 4. View at unloading station 77
    Fig 5. Return station frame with inclined tension jib 77

Fig 24.1 Typical section of strata. Borehole No.6 78
Fig 24.2. Nettleton Bottom Mine, drifts and new railway and road 79
Fig 24.3. Building the 1959 entrance 79
Fig 24.4. The interior of the 1957 Drift looking out into the yard 80
Fig 24.5. Nettleton Bottom Valley looking eastwards immediately before mining began 80
Fig 24.6. Nettleton Bottom Mine Drift entrances about 1960 81
Fig 24.7. The geological fault on both sides of the valley of the Nettleton Beck 81

Fig 25.1. The underground layout of Bottom Mine 82
Fig 25.2. A face made safe for the miners to go back to and take another three feet of stone out 83
Fig 25.3. Miners preparing to drive a cross cut tunnel 83
Fig 25.4. The form of sublevel caving mining adopted at Bottom Mine 84
Fig 25.5. An Eimco Rocker Shovel 84
Fig 25.6. Two of the main haulage tunnels inside Bottom Mine 85

Fig 26.1. Two large 75 hp LHU Class locomotives, Bottom Mine, 1967 85
Fig 26.2. The surface buildings to serve the new Bottom Mine. 86
Fig 26.3. Tub in tippler with another waiting its turn 88
Fig 26.4. Top yard sand washer 89

Fig 27.1. Nettleton Bottom opencast quarry, June 1961 90
Fig 27.2. Fowler Challenger 4 tractor with an Onions box scraper 91
Fig 27.3. A Ruston Bucyrus 22 RB face shovel with an Aveling Barford shuttle dumper 91
Fig 27.4. Loco No 8 leaving the opencast workings on the west side of Nettleton Bottom valley 92
Fig 27.5. Underground mine roadway exposed by opencast working 92

Fig 28.1. The chalk quarry 93
Fig 28.2. The method of work within the quarry 94
Fig 28.3. A view of the chalk quarry from the west 94

Fig 29.1. Undated plan of the early layout of Holton le Moor Sidings 95
Fig 29.2. Holton le Moor Sidings before and after the opening of Bottom Mine 96
Fig 29.3. One of the fleet of six AEC Dump Truks 96
Fig 29.4. Holton le Moor Sidings and the Lysaghts Playing Field in about 1960 97

Fig 30.1. Loco No 1 (RH 170374) lowering tubs down to the tippler, probably in 1935 100
Fig 30.2. Prototype Ruston LBU locomotive (RH 318748) on trial at Nettleton in 1952 100
Fig 30.3. Ruston LBU Class locomotive, believed to be works number 432654, Nettleton No 9, in 1959 at Back o' the Farm 100
Fig 30.4. Nettleton loco 14, (RH 435403) 101
Fig 30.5. Nettleton loco 14, (RH 435404) seen here in disguise as Ivor the Engine at the Sittingbourne and Kemsley Light Railway, Kent 102
Fig 30.6. Greenwood and Batley tramming locomotive 102
Fig 30.7. A Greenwood and Batley 4-wheel battery electric trolley, in use with the Admiralty at Chattendon in Kent in 1958 103
Fig 30.8. Greenwood and Batley electric trolley crossing the embankment leading to the Nettleton Bottom mine entrance 104
Fig 30.9. The body of one of the ambulance cars, seen here in use as a garden shed at Nettleton Top 104

Fig 31.1. Bill Portass was horsekeeper in 1961, seen here with horses Monty and Darkie 105
Fig 31.2. The mine manager, Eurig Thomas, right of centre, with Josef Ivicz to his right 106
Fig 31.3. One of the buses hired to provide a service to and from the mine 107
Fig 31.4. Orb Cottages on Cooks Lane at Nettleton, built for miners by Lysaghts in 1944

Fig 32.1. The Ambulance Room underground shortly inside Nettleton Bottom mine 109
Fig 32.2. Mine rescue demonstration at a Gala in 1966 109

Fig 33.1. The miners basic tools, the pick and shovel 110
Fig 33.2. Two miners using pneumatic compressed air picks 110
Fig 33.3. The trial of a coal cutting machine, probably early in 196 110

Fig 34.1. Private owner wagons at Holton le Moor Sidings 111
Fig 34.2. Nettleton Mines: Ironstone Production, 1934 to 1961 112

Fig 35.1. The clubhouse in 1995 113
Fig 35.2. A tug o' war competition under way on the playing field 113
Fig 35.3. Cannonball and its carriages on the Lysaghts Playing Field 114
Fig 35.4. Lysaghts Club Snooker Trophy 114

Fig 36.1. A last day photograph of the men working underground 116

Fig 37.1. Extract from a plan showing the area leased by the Frodingham Iron and Steel Co 118
Fig 37.2. The concrete capped vertical shaft with the spoil heap beyond 119

Fig 37.3. The view westwards from above the site of the mouth of Shaft No 1 119

Fig 37.4. The bottom of the shaft and the start of Heading No 2 120

Fig 38.1. Nettleton Mine visit, Heritage Open Days, 17 September 1995 121

Fig 38.2. The, now closed, tunnel to take the public footpath, now the Viking Way, underneath the embankment in Nettleton Bottom valley, seen here in January 2015 121

Fig 38.3. Wolds Walks leaflet and heritage trail, first published 2002 122

Fig 38.4. Nettleton Village Hall, Drop In Day, 10 January 2015 122

Fig 38.5. Claxby Mine, Geology Walk, Heritage Open Days 11 September 2016 123

Fig 38.6. Former miners at the launch of the touring exhibition display 123

Table 1: National Census of Population, Normanby, Claxby and Nettleton 45

Table 2: Claxby Ironstone Mine – Accidents, mainly recorded in newspapers 50

Table 3: Mine Employees – 1871 Census 55

Table 4: Ironstone, sand and limestone taken, Claxby Mine, 1868–1884 58

Table 5: Locomotives and rail trollies, Nettleton Mines 98

Table 6: Ironstone Production, Nettleton Top and Bottom Mines, 1934–1969 111

PREFACE

Lincolnshire is not a county that springs to mind when thinking about underground mining. Indeed, it is likely that relatively few of today's residents will realise that such mining took place here. For many years the subject of mining in Lincolnshire has fascinated me and I have been researching and writing about it now for around thirty years. In truth, there was little here that was different from the mining techniques and infrastructure used elsewhere, although this has been a big advantage with research into the early mines. In an industry where the last mines closed around forty-five years ago there are still ex-miners and their families whose memories can be recorded. And it is important that these should be noted and that the story be told.

The Nettleton and Claxby mines were just below the highest point in the county, 550 feet above sea level, from where the ore bed sloped gently down to the east. But it is interesting to note that the miners were working underground at a higher level than the vast majority of county people lived. There is only a small handful of villages and hamlets, together with several isolated farms, which lie around or above the 330 feet level, Ludford and Kelstern for example, in the immediate area and a few others in the Kesteven Uplands, to the south and west of Grantham. Some of the latter, Stainby and Gunby for example, were also places from where iron ore deposits were quarried.

Finally, in the last thirty years I have been going into underground mines, both working and long closed, all over the UK. Every time I come out I am very grateful and relieved to emerge into the daylight and give thanks that most of my working life was spent in the open air. I have to record my admiration and respect for all those who have toiled long and hard doing dirty and dangerous work, often for years on end, in underground mines.

Stewart Squires, November 2017

ACKNOWLEDGEMENTS

My principal tributes must be made to two men, both well known historians of Lincolnshire, the late David Robinson of Louth and the late Rex Russell of Barton upon Humber. It was David's article on the Nettleton Iron Mine in *Lincolnshire Life*, of April 1971, that sparked my interest in mining in Lincolnshire. Rex and I worked together to produce our first study of the Claxby mine, published in 1999. Both men through their leadership and knowledge inspired a generation of historians. Their extensive and thorough research was done without the access to the internet, which is such an advantage to us today. So, for example, all Rex's newspaper references about Claxby and Nettleton were discovered by looking through original newspapers or the long study of microfiche copies. I have been able to add to this with the help of the online British Newspaper Archive.

My research on this began in earnest back in the early 1990s and by 1995 I was able to collect enough information for publication of some initial notes. Research continued and I was able to give talks and to lead guided visits to all three mine sites, which I have continued to do for over twenty years.

The incentive and opportunity to bring research to a head came about in 2014 as a result of an initiative by the local community in Nettleton and Claxby, jointly with the Down Your Wold project of the Lincolnshire Wolds Countryside Service. Events have included displays, a drop in day to hear about the project, record memories, identify people on photographs and copy documents; guided walks to the sites of all three mines; television and radio interviews; and talks at a variety of venues.

The interest and enthusiasm of local people provided oral history, duly recorded for posterity, notes and memories, photographs, plans, documents and objects; all of which helped to tell the story of the Nettleton Mines in particular. So I have many more people to thank:

Members of the Nettleton and Claxby Mines Community Steering Group: John Cocoran; Dr John Esser; Elizabeth Jefferson; Trevor Lyle; Jon Sass; ably supported by Helen Gamble and Sam Phillips-Meiklejon of the Lincolnshire Wolds Countryside Service.

Former mine workers and others who I have interviewed, some a long time ago and who have since passed on, or who have recorded their working memories more recently: John Carter; Ken Clark; John Corcoran; Charles Dent; Eric Farmery; Derek Favill; David Jackson; David King; Patrick Loftus; Bill Maund; Jack Mumby; Kenneth Sharp; Bill Shaw; Eurig Thomas; Les Wilkinson; Joe Willisch; Fred Wright; the family of the late John Harradine.

Landowners: Chris Bourne; John Brant; Jonathan Brant; Motley Brant; Andrew Vincent

Caroline Adamson, whose research on my behalf in 2001 included transcribing Yarborough documents in the Lincolnshire Archives which, since then, have not been available for inspection due to their extremely fragile state.

Ken Redmore, Society for Lincolnshire History and Archaeology, who has drawn many of the plans for the book and, as Chairman of the Publications Committee, has supported and guided me through the process of book production.

Ros Beevers, Society for Lincolnshire History and Archaeology, for her work on the book design

Archaeology: John Aggett, David Start

Geology: Paul Hildreth; Peter Rawson; David Robinson, Peter Worsley

Locomotives and machinery: Adrian Booth, author, *Greenwood and Batley Locomotives 1927-80*; Derek Broughton; Simon Chapman, Cleveland Ironstone Mining Museum; David Garland, Signalling Record Society; Dave Billmore, James Hay and Tim Hudson, Narrow Gauge Railway Society; David Ingall; Sidney Leleux; Michael Lewis; Sophie Lindley, Brotherton Library, University of Leeds; Andrew Neale, author, *Ruston and Hornsby Diesel Locomotive Album*; Robin Waywell, Industrial Railway Society;

Others who have given advice, information, photographs and other vital support: David Allen, Booklaw Publications Carole Barnes; D Bailey; Alan Dennis; David Elford; Barry Graham-Rack; Richard Oliver; Linda Oxley; Chris Padley; Katherine Perry; Helen Pitman; Midge and Roy Thomas; Peter Thorpe, National Railway Museum; Rob Wheeler.

And last but by no means least, the following organisations: British Geological Survey; Caistor Heritage Trust; Lincolnshire Archives; Lincolnshire Historic Environment Record; Lincolnshire Wolds Countryside Service; National Museum of Wales.

Dr John Esser

A member of the Community Steering Group, John contributed his knowledge of and enthusiasm for the local geology to our research. In addition he was a gifted photographer and several of his photographs appear in this book. John died in August 2017.

DAVID N. ROBINSON OBE MSc (1927–2017)

The publication of this book has been made possible by David Robinson's generous donation of a large number of books to SLHA. These books, many of which have considerable value, mostly relate to historical aspects of Lincolnshire, and they are being sold to Society members or through the Jews' Court bookshop.

David was delighted with this arrangement. As a former President of the SLHA, he was keen to make a lasting contribution to the Society and this book on ironstone mines in the Wolds exactly matches one of his principal areas of interest. In a real sense this book forms a tribute to David's scholarship and the contribution he made to our understanding of the Lincolnshire Wolds and their underlying geology. It is therefore a matter of great regret that David, who died in July 2017, was not able to see the book published.

Nettleton, Back o' the Farm, with opencast mining underway on the hillside in 1959. The ironstone face is being worked in the left background. The land to the right is being restored. (Photo by David Robinson)

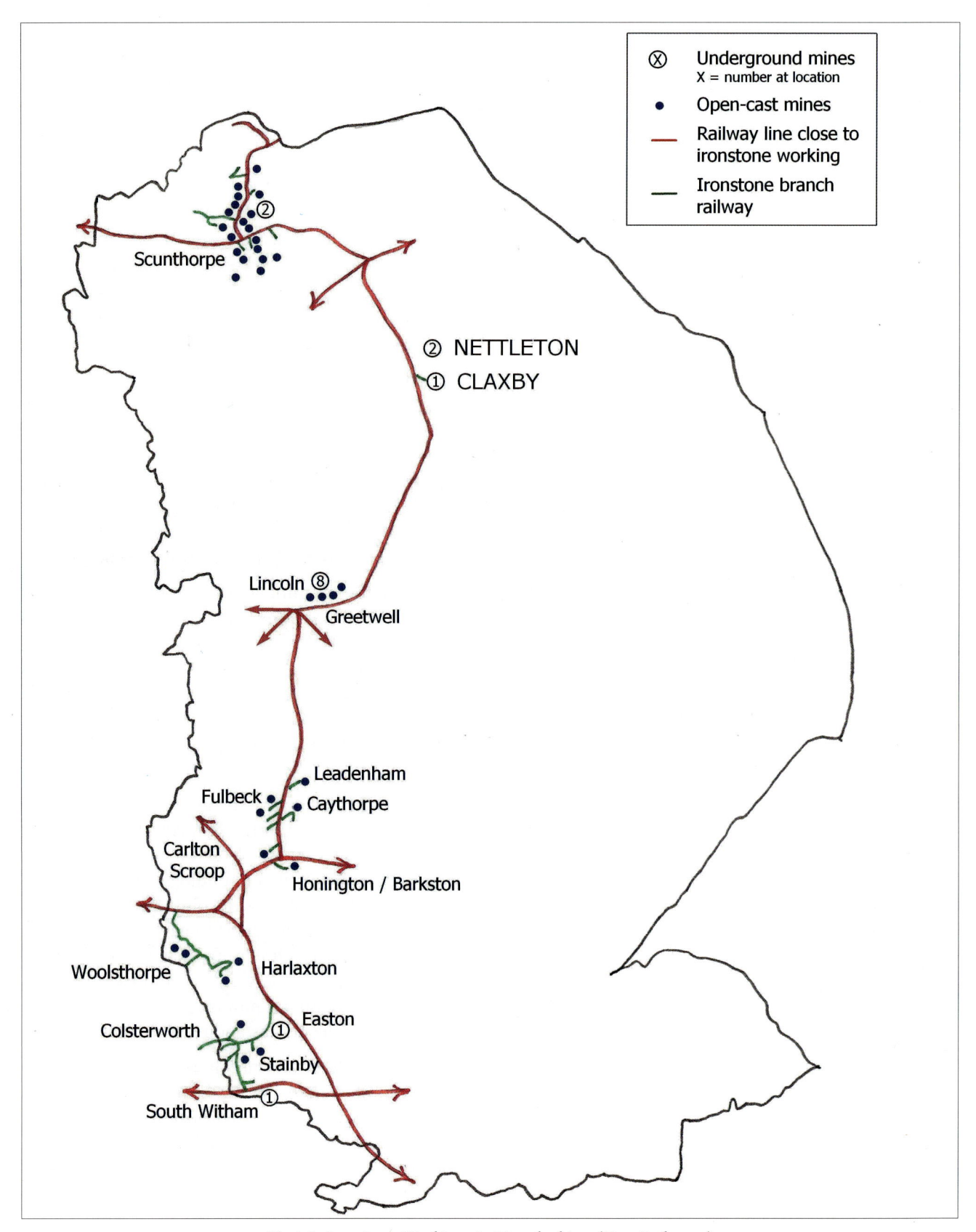

Fig 1.1. Ironstone Workings in Lincolnshire. (Ken Redmore)

2. Timeline: Claxby, Nettleton and Walesby

Early 1860s	Workable quantities of ironstone discovered at Claxby.
1867	Work on the Claxby Mine is underway
1868	Claxby Mine goes into production, operated by the West Yorkshire Iron & Coal Co. The stone goes by rail to their ironworks at Ardsley, near Leeds.
1868	Prospecting proves workable quantities of ironstone at Nettleton.
1871–73	Twenty houses built in Claxby for mine workers and the village school is extended to cope with extra children.
1872	Many deaths and injuries force the Revd Sumner of Nettleton to write to the papers describing the mine as 'that gloomy cave of disaster' and seeking safety improvements.
1873	'About 250 men' employed at Claxby, the peak year for production of almost 70,000 tons.
1875	'Under 100' men employed at Claxby.
1885	Claxby Mine closes.
1905	Workable quantities of stone identified again at Nettleton Top.
1919	The Walesby Shaft is dug to determine the economy of starting a new mine here. Geological difficulties rule it out.
1929	Work on digging Nettleton Top Mine begins by the Mid Lincolnshire Iron Co.
1934	Nettleton Top Mine goes into production.
1937	'About 160 men' employed at Nettleton Top Mine.
1944	Mid Lincolnshire Iron Co taken over by John Lysaghts of Scunthorpe.
1944	Orb Cottages, Cooks Lane, Nettleton, built for miners by John Lysaghts.
1957	Work on opening up Nettleton Bottom Mine begins.
1959–68	Ironstone taken by quarrying the hillsides around Nettleton Top Mine.
1960	Nettleton Bottom Mine opens.
1960	Nettleton Chalk Quarry opens to provide chalk for use in the smelting process at Scunthorpe.
1961	Lysaghts becomes a branch of the GKN Steel Co Ltd.
1961	Nettleton Top Mine closes.
1967	The year of peak production, almost 280,000 tons by 180 men.
1968	The mines become part of the British Steel Corporation.
1968	Nettleton Bottom Mine closes.
1971	The Nettleton Chalk Quarry closes.

3. Geology

The standard text giving a full understanding of the geology of the county is *The Geology of Lincolnshire*[1] and the reader is directed to it to learn more on this subject.

Britain's iron ore deposits are shown on Fig 3.1. This shows the principal ore fields with, most dramatically, the ore fields of the Jurassic period which have been worked for the stone stretching from Middlesbrough to Banbury, taking in the Frodingham Ironstone and Northampton Sand workings on the way. They were formed between 170 and 190 million years ago. The Claxby Ironstone, by contrast, is of the Cretaceous period, which followed the Jurassic, and was deposited about 132 to 135 million years ago. The extent of the Claxby Ironstone Field is shown in Fig 3.2 together with the locations of the mines at Nettleton, Claxby and the Walesby Shaft within it. The eastern boundary, shown in Fig 3.2 by a pecked line, is nominally said to be the Caistor High Street although this is an arbitrary line as unexplored deposits extend beyond it. Here, Caistor High Street refers to the road along the western edge of the Wolds, linking Caistor and Horncastle. It has a prehistoric origin.

The Lincolnshire Wolds combines a dramatic western scarp, rolling chalk capped uplands with steep sided dry valleys and a former sea cliff on the eastern edge. From being under a sub-tropical sea, then covered by ice, to eventually becoming the highest ground between Yorkshire and Kent, the landscape that we see today has undergone immense change. The rolling chalk uplands form the main and highest point of the Wolds. The soils here are thin and flinty and during the autumn months, after ploughing, the colour variations within the fields are clearly visible.

The western edge of the Wolds, between South Ferriby and North Willingham, is very different. Here the steep edge is marked in places by the remains of the ironstone mining and areas of rough, damp grassland, which is an increasingly scarce habitat in Lincolnshire. At the foot of the scarp slope, Ancholme Clay is overlain by blown sand, deposited towards the end of the last Ice Age.

The Claxby Ironstone, as it is known, averages about three metres in thickness and occurs between the Spilsby Sandstone and the Tealby Clays. It was deposited in shallow coastal seas on the margin of the North Sea Basin. *(Fig 3.3)* The main outcrop is along the Wold escarpment between Caistor and Claxby. It has been worked not only at Claxby but also, between 1929 and 1969, at the nearby Nettleton Top and Nettleton Bottom Mines. The ore has relatively low iron content, 25% to 35% iron, and has a high silica content, which meant more lime had to be used in the smelting process.[2]

The geology of the west facing escarpment between Claxby and Nettleton is reflected in the landscape. The thin layer of soil covers successive layers of Spilsby Sandstone, Claxby Ironstone, Lower Tealby Clay, Tealby Limestone, Upper Tealby Clay, Roach Stone, Carstone, Red Chalk (known also as the Hunstanton Formation), and White Chalk, together spanning the whole of the latest Jurassic and Early Cretaceous time. This is known as the Tealby Series. The relatively hard limestone and ironstone beds are separated by softer, less durable mudstones, clays and sands forming an unstable mix and there is much evidence of landslips along the bottom of the slope. *(Figs 3.3 and 3.4)*

The sequence of conditions under which these rocks were deposited had a shallow shore for the ironstone which deepened to the Tealby Limestone, and then shallowing again to the Roach Stone. The ironstone thins out to the north and south.

The ironstone consists of a coarse iron rich oolite (sedimentary rock formed from tiny, spherical, fish-egg like grains). *(Fig 3.5)* Fossils are common with bivalves (including large pecten shells), oysters, belemites and ammonites being more numerous towards the top of the beds. *(Figs 3.6 and 3.7)* The large pecten shells, up to 200 cm, eight inches, across, gaped when they died in the iron rich seas. The soft parts rotted and were replaced by oolitic iron which closed the shell by the deposits above. The best specimens from the mine were kept in the first aid drawer of the underground ambulance room *(Fig 32.1)* for the benefit of visitors.

Other minerals were also worked in Nettleton for the benefit of the Scunthorpe steelworks. The overlaying chalk, underneath which was located the

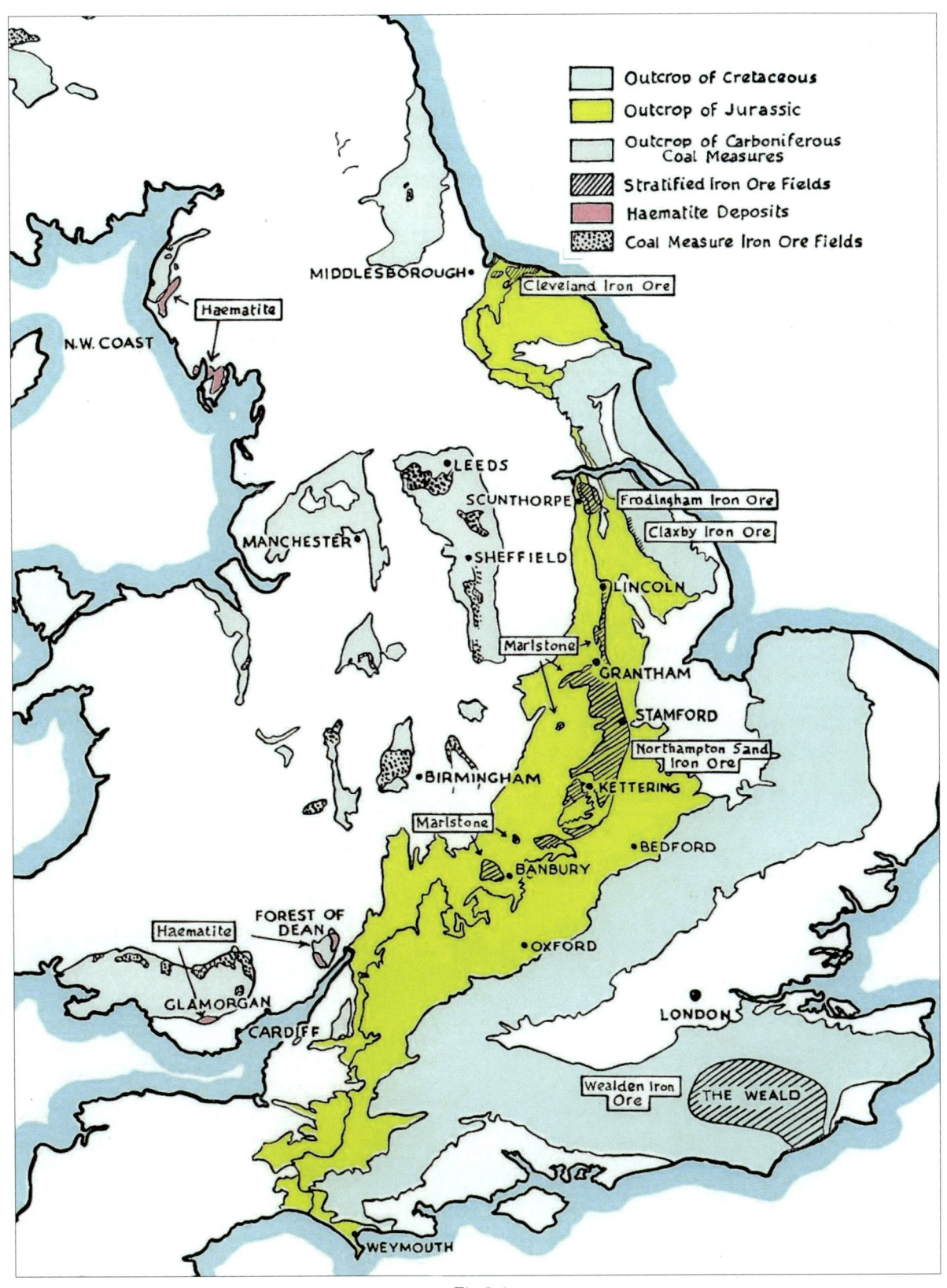

Fig 3.1.
Britain's Iron Ore Deposits (National Council of Associated Iron Ore Producers, 1960)

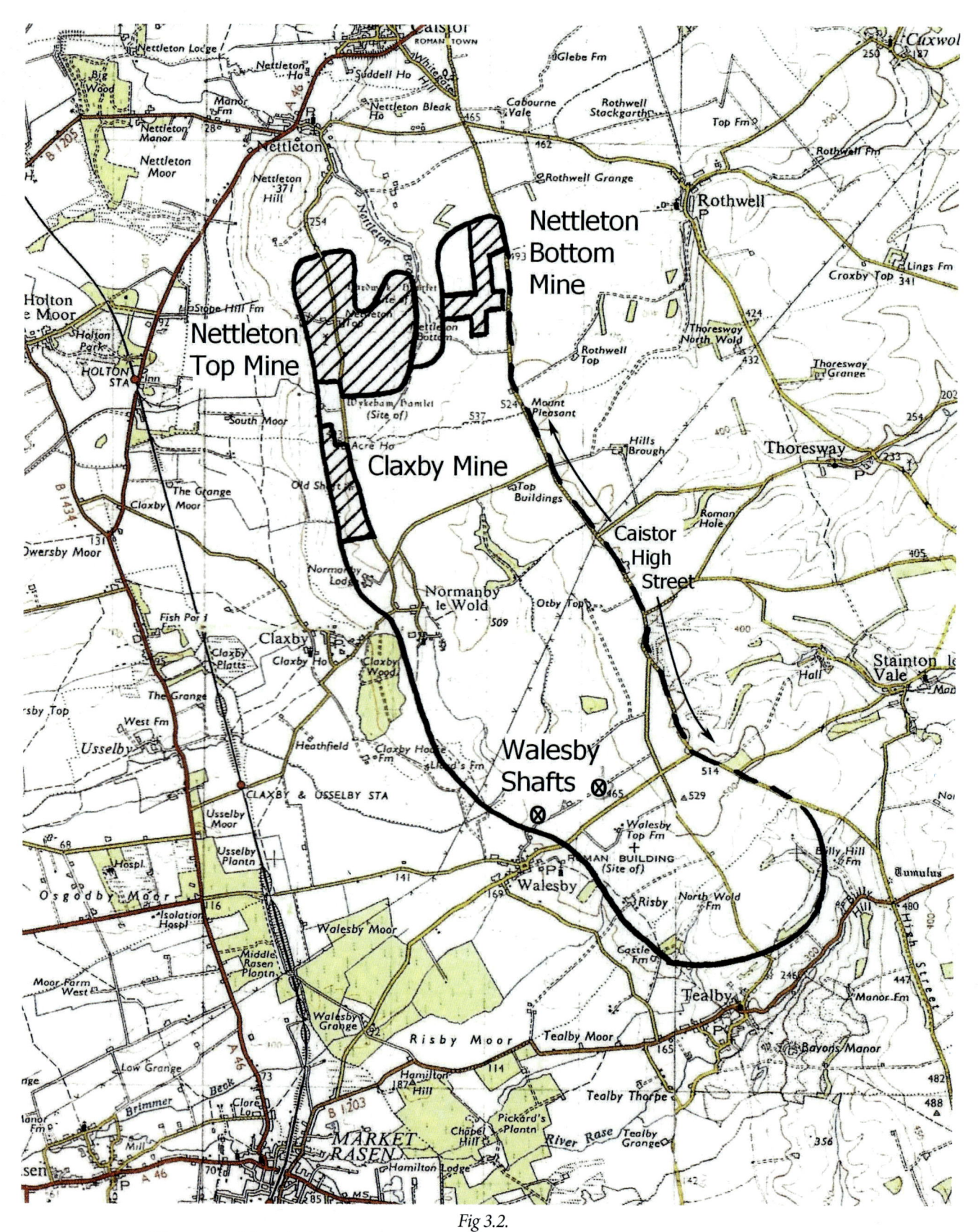

Fig 3.2.
The extent of the Claxby Ironstone Field (Ordnance Survey with annotations by Ken Redmore)

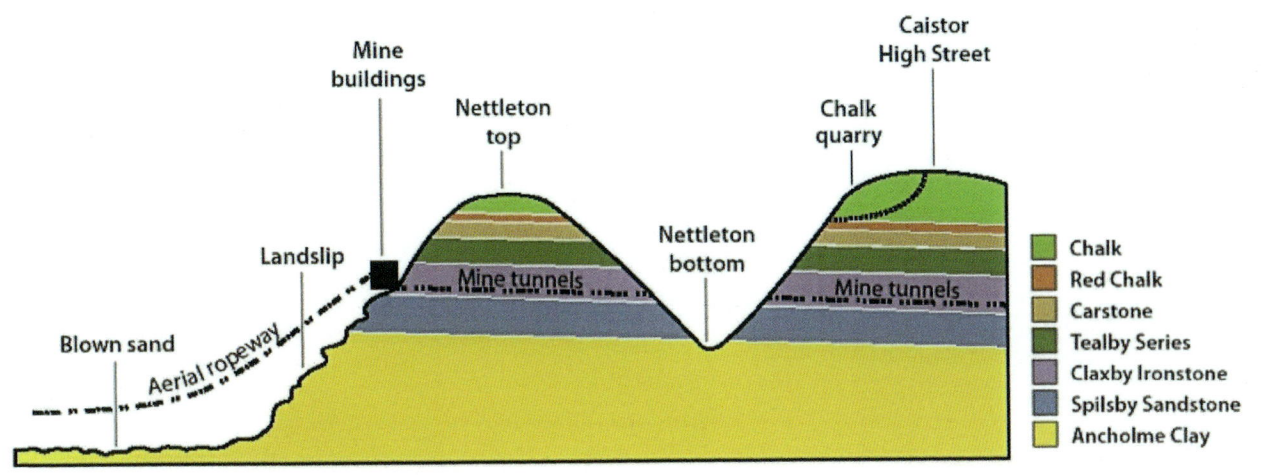

Fig 3.3.
Geological Cross Section, Nettleton. (Lincolnshire Wolds Countryside Service)

Nettleton Bottom Mine, provided lime for use in the smelting process. A chalk quarry opened in 1960 above this mine. From the 1920s it was the practice at Scunthorpe to mix their local Frodingham ore with that from Northamptonshire or Nettleton in the proportion necessary for a self fluxing blast furnace charge. This was because these ores had a high natural lime content which allowed it to be smelted without the addition of limestone. The chalk was used to enhance the lime content to the required proportion for the blast furnace feed.[3]

The west, north and east sides of Nettleton Top Mine, where the Claxby Ironstone outcropped on the hillsides, were worked as opencast quarries. *(Fig 21.1)* On the north side were deposits of high quality plaster sand below the ironstone, which were also worked. These provided for building works in the steelworks with the excess sold on the open market. Indeed, after the mine closed sand working continued for a time with part of the mines yard and a small quarry leased to a local company.

The presence of ironstone had been known in the area for many years, and it was widely used as a building stone. A good example is Nettleton village where many of the older cottages are built of ironstone or iron rich limestone. Nettleton church is of ironstone, the tower

Fig 3.4.
Geomorphology at Claxby (Dr John Esser)

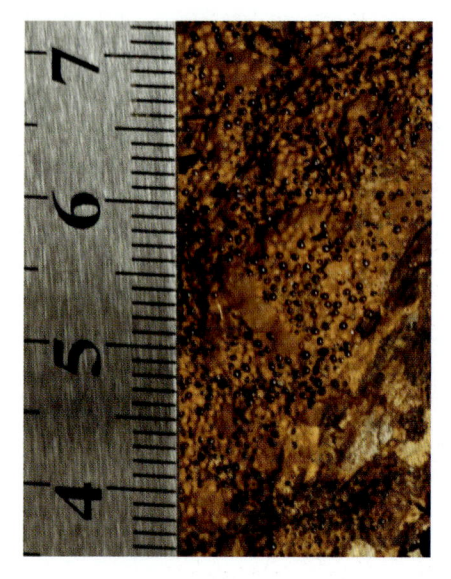

Fig 3.5. (Left)
Claxby Ironstone. A close up of the oolitic grains within the stone. These are fossilized fish eggs. The figures on the scale are centimetres. (Dr John Esser)

Fig 3.6. (Right)
Claxby ironstone, with bivalve shell. The figures on the scale are centimeters. (Dr John Esser)

built in the fifteenth century, although the whole church was rebuilt by James Fowler of Louth in 1874. The earliest surviving use of this local ironstone for building was the tower of Caistor church in the thirteenth century, with the oldest surviving building of the Caistor Grammar School being built of ironstone in 1631.

An examination of Pevsner's book on Lincolnshire buildings[4] shows that there are some 30 other churches in north Lincolnshire that used ironstone in all or part of the building. Examples of the latter are Ulceby (13th–14th century), Linwood (1419) Wyham (1686), North Owersby (1762) and Lissington (1796). Examples of the whole church are Tealby (1871–2) and Brocklesby (14th century). Two others were designed by S. S. Teulon: (North Elkington (1852) and North Ormsby (1848); and two – Humberston (1710) and Yarburgh (1405) – are some 15-16 miles away from the source of the ironstone. *(Fig 3.8).*

This implies the early importance of ironstone for building, probably quarried where the bed outcropped on the hillside. Although not a good building stone because of its poor weathering quality, it did not deter Fowler of Louth from designing the new church at Binbrook of ironstone in 1869.

Evidence of the extent of the Claxby Ironstone bed can be found elsewhere in the Wolds, notably near Donington on Bain. At Benniworth Haven the Bardney to Louth railway line cuts through an exposure.[5] Although never worked for iron ore, this did give rise to some short lived excitement in the 1870s when the line was being built, with subsequent speculation that an iron works might be built at Donington on Bain.

4. Archaeology

There has been no evidence of the ironstone here being worked prior to the late nineteenth century although there are indications of iron smelting having taken place in Roman times. The County Council Historic Environment Records show that Roman and Romano-British pottery scatters have been found in Nettleton, Normanby le Wold and Claxby parishes. The greatest concentration of evidence, in the form of pottery and habitation finds, is in Claxby, mainly to the south of the village as well as around it. Included within the records are five sites where evidence of slag has been found.[1] The amount of evidence for Claxby parish may be a reflection that more research in the form of Field Walking has taken place here than the other parishes. *(Fig 4.1.)*

Four of the HER records referred to above date from 1983 and one from 1965. However a newspaper report in 1892 referred to fragments of slag, pieces of charcoal and pottery indicating that the Romans knew the value of the stone.[2] A similar statement was made in 1913.[3] The Claxby and Nettleton mines were located at the highest point of Lincolnshire. The highest spot in the county, at 550 feet is only two fields to the east of the Normanby Road, the eastern boundary of the workings. Nettleton Top is at 425 feet. Even in such an exposed area there is a history of human activity, usually in association with the sheltered lee provided by the western scarp slope of the Wolds and the deep cut of the Nettleton Bottom valley.

At the sites of both the Claxby and Nettleton mines there is archaeological evidence of former activity both for settlement and farming. The present day Acre House Farm, from which the Claxby mine derived one of the names it was known by, lies about 300 yards to the east of the earlier farmstead it replaced in the mid nineteenth century. The earthworks here might be interpreted as the site of a small deserted medieval hamlet similar to sites nearby at Risby and Otby. Medieval documents show that Newsham Abbey owned land here, a small estate founded in the twelfth century. Post medieval records indicate that the site is most likely to be the remains of a post Dissolution farmstead with the present Acre House being the most recent replacement.[4]

Claxby mine lay underneath the centre of the land of the Grange and the later farmstead and has contributed to the earthworks in the form of pitfalls created following the collapse of underground cavities. There were also two short lived mine entrances nearby. These would be passages dug to the open air to provide air circulation around the mine. They are also likely to have been used by miners to access their workplace underground. There is evidence of tracks here that may have been used by miners but which may also date from earlier times.

The development of the Claxby Mine gave rise to the curious case of the Claxby 'cells'. In June 1869 a newspaper report appeared,[5] here quoted in full.

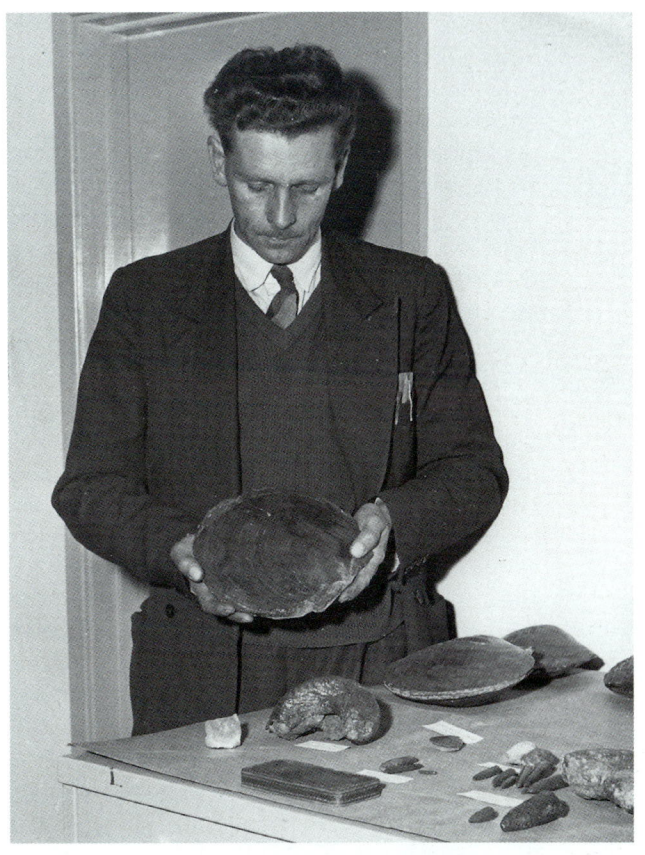

Fig 3.7. (Top)
Examples of fossilised pecten shells and belemites found in Nettleton mine, with Mines Surveyor, John Bassingthwaite. He is holding a pecten shell. (Grimsby Evening Telegraph)

Fig 3.8. (Bottom)
Claxby Parish Church was rebuilt using ironstone, to the design of James Fowler of Louth, in 1871. (Dr John Esser)

Discovery of antique cells at the Normanby Iron mine. – Some interest has been excited in this neighbourhood by the discovery of five cells, or caves, evidently of great antiquity, in the hill at Normanby, in front of the iron mine. About 50 yards to the south of the adit by which the mine is entered, near the brow of the hill, the first of a series of mysterious cells was found by a party of labourers employed in quarrying the ironstone. Four others in the stratum of ironstone (which averages about six feet in thickness), about twenty yards apart, having for floors the green sandstone, were subsequently found. The cells varied in size, being from 10 to 15 feet in width, and 20 to 30 feet in length, and had been reached where there was no subterranean passage by perpendicular shafts about 4 feet square. At this part of the hill a shaft of 25 to 30 feet was necessary to reach the sandstone. The cells were walled with squares of the sandstone of about six inches – a species of masonry that must have been executed with great difficulty in such extremely hard material. No bones were found to indicate that they had been used for sepulture, nor were there any relics to indicate for what purpose or at what time they were made. Unfortunately the workmen paid no respect to these relics of antiquity, and they have all disappeared in the progress of the work. Various conjectures are afloat, but the probability is that they were Saxon places of concealment. Most probably other similar places will yet be found.

No similar places were found and this is their only record. From the description it appears that they were built as concealed chambers rather than being evidence of earlier mining but they remain an enigma to this day. On a steep hillside such as this, and later as at Nettleton Top mine, a flat working area was needed outside the entrances for offices, workshops and tramways. This was created by cutting into the hillside to provide the necessary space, partly by excavation and partly by infill. This is probably what the workers were doing when the cells were discovered.

During the Second World War the Claxby hillsides were used as an army training ground. To date there are only oral accounts of this and the effects are little understood. Live rounds and explosives are believed to have been used and there may be a residue of earthworks created and demolished. This may account for a scatter of what were stones built originally as a wall on part of the mine site but this is a history and archaeology waiting to be researched and interpreted.

At Nettleton almost all of the earthworks that can be seen at Nettleton Top and in the Nettleton Bottom valley are due to the mining activity. Here there are pitfalls and slumps caused by the collapse of voids underground, the shelf cut into the scarp slope to create the mines yard, roadways, railway routes and tunnel mouths. In addition there was also open cast quarrying of ironstone from the hillsides around the west, north and east sides of Nettleton Top Mine.

Here the open cast quarrying did destroy at least part of the sites of two deserted medieval settlements. Both are referred to on OS maps and both have entries in the County Council Heritage Environment Record.[6] Hardwick is to the north side of Nettleton Top Mine and West Wykeham, simply Wykeham on the OS map, on the west side of Nettleton Bottom valley in its upper reaches. No detailed assessment of their sites has been carried out but it may be that, in both cases, quarrying was responsible for destruction of only a part of both. The main part of Wykeham appears to be in a field untouched by quarrying. Evidence of the village is said to be discerned within growing crops from time to time. It is likely that there has been an adverse effect on the remains of both from changing farming practices over a long period of time.

Finally, the archaeological evidence of the nineteenth and twentieth century mining activity has also left its mark in the fields and the wider landscape and it is that archaeology which is the subject of this book.

Fig 4.1. (Opposite page)
Archaeology (Ordnance Survey, 1:25,000 Provisional Series, Sheets TF09 and TF19, 1961 reprint, annotations by Ken Redmore)

PROLOGUE

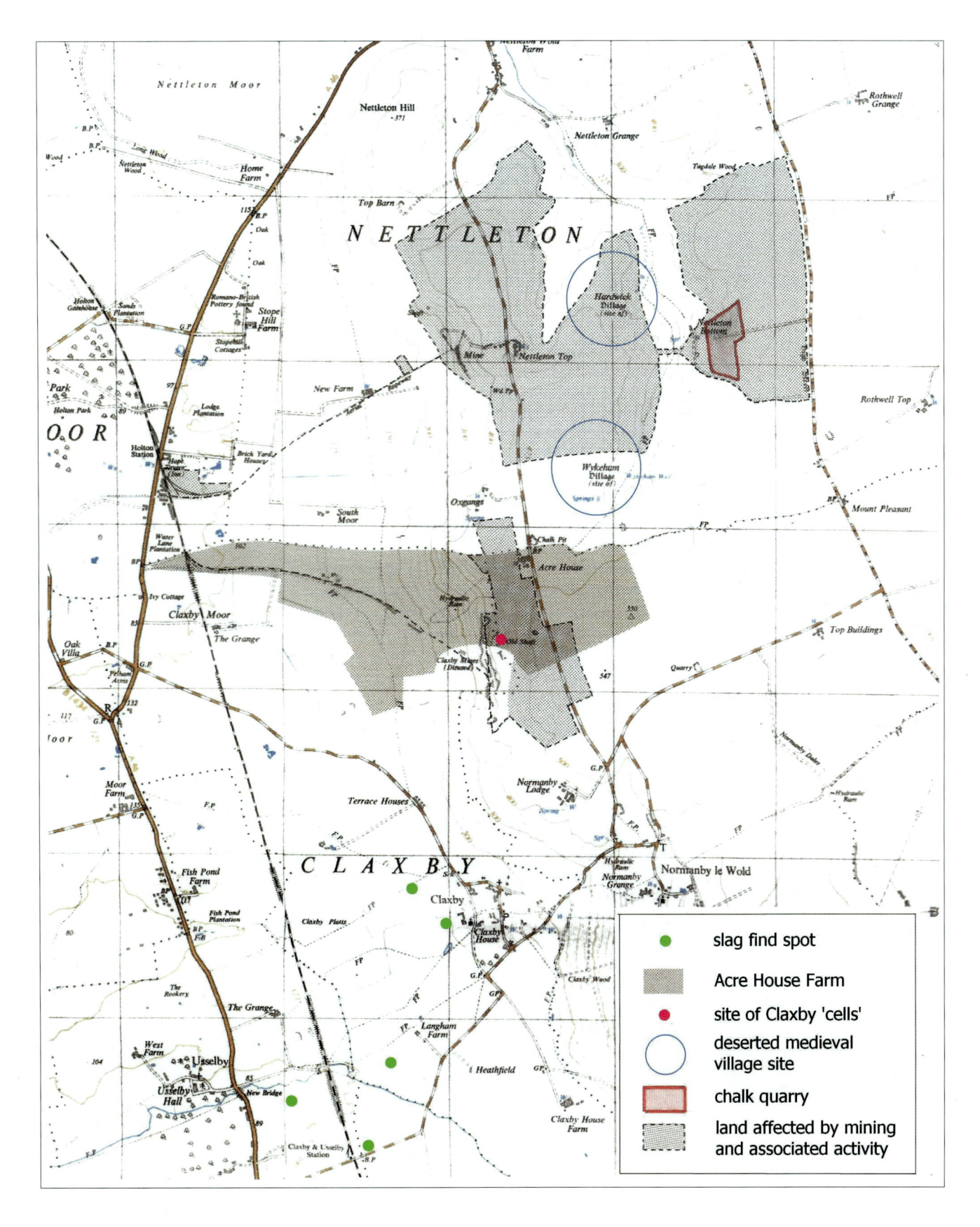

5. Landowners and Prospectors

The extensive Appleby Estate had long been owned by the Winn family and soon after 1839 Rowland Winn, son of the owner, Charles Winn, was appointed to manage their north Lincolnshire estate.[1] In 1854 Rowland Winn found ironstone in a pit made while marling[2] the land near the village of Scunthorpe. The stone was of poor quality but following later discoveries of better quality stone in 1858 he sent for John Roseby, of Whitby, to report on the minerals on the estate.

By the mid 1850s John Roseby was a well known mining engineer, working initially with his father and later his son, the latter William John Roseby, both mining engineers. With his father he had discovered the quality and extent of the Cleveland Ironstone reserves in the late 1840s and, on his own account, beds of stone around Banbury and Oxford. It was the Frodingham stone that brought him to Lincolnshire and his prospecting identified quality stone at Kirton Lindsey and Lincoln along the Lincoln Edge and, in the Lincolnshire Wolds, north and south of Caistor and Donington on Bain. John Roseby and son William were to play a critical role in proving the workable quantities of ore in the Wolds and play a part in the establishment of mining here.

The first reference to the potential for mining in this area of the Lincolnshire Wolds appeared in the *Stamford Mercury* in 1860. The paper reported:

> Lincolnshire has been hitherto considered purely as an agricultural county, but it is likely to turn out very rich in minerals, as in addition to the iron found at Kirton Lindsey, on the estate of R. Winn Esq., of Appleby, another estate in the neighbourhood of Caistor is likely to turn out equally rich. We have just been shown specimens of iron ore likely to yield a very rich percentage ... and we should not be surprised in a few months to see a blast in full operation, as it is not unlikely where there is so much iron that coal may be found as well.[3]

One week later the newspaper confirmed that iron ore

> has recently been discovered on the property of Mr J. T. Chant, druggist, of Caistor. It is not of superior quality to the Appleby and Kirton material, but from the present researches made it is anticipated that the Caistor hills are much more productive.[4]

After another week came a further report:

> All doubt is now set at rest as to the quantity and quality of iron ore dug up in and adjoining Caistor parish. Mr J. T. Chant, in addition to his own land and the lands of R. Owston Esq., of Hundon, has explored the lands at Nettleton belonging to T. J. Dixon Esq., of Holton Park, and also the lands of Sir Culling Eardley Eardley, Bart, and has tested the iron ore found there both chemically and magnetically; ... the result shows that iron greatly abounds ... Mr Chant ... has communicated the above facts to the owners of the lands, who it is hoped will bestir themselves to develop the advantages of such a discovery.[5]

None of these or other reports mention Claxby specifically by name. As is stated in the introduction, much of the underground working was within Nettleton parish. It may be that this report, referring to Nettleton, records the discovery of ore subsequently worked by Claxby Mine.

Fig 6.1.
The broken nature of the ground along the hillside around Claxby Mine in 2015. The view is to the north with the cutting through the centre being the route of the siding. The earthworks for the mine infrastructure are distorted by landslides and soil creep, made worse by crown holes and collapses post closure. (Dr John Esser)

CLAXBY MINE

6. In the Beginning

The least known of all the former underground mines in Lincolnshire is Claxby. It opened in 1868 and closed in 1885. By this time the second mine in the county had opened, at Greetwell on the outskirts of Lincoln. Mining started there in 1873, so for five years the Claxby Mine was the only one in the county. There are physical remnants on the hillside north of the village, but very little has been written of its history. This may be because of the limitations of a lack of public access together with the often very rough nature of the ground which can make it difficult to traverse. *(Fig 6.1)*

Apart from being the precursor of underground mining in the county there is nothing unusual in the history of the Claxby mine or how it was operated. Its fascination lies in the fact that so little is known about it. Yet it must have had a dramatic effect in physical, social and economic terms on this area of rural Lincolnshire, and that in itself makes it well worth investigating. The information that follows has pulled together surviving documents, together with what has been published in the past, and an understanding of ironstone mining practices elsewhere in the same period. All this has been combined with further study and interpretation of the remains on the ground. Certainly, the research has provided a much greater understanding of the site and, in some cases, put a different interpretation on some elements of the site than has been the case previously.

Although known usually today as the Claxby Ironstone Mine, and shown as such on the 1905 County Series, 1:2500 Ordnance Survey Map,[1] a contemporary plan of the workings in the author's collection describes them as ironstone mines worked

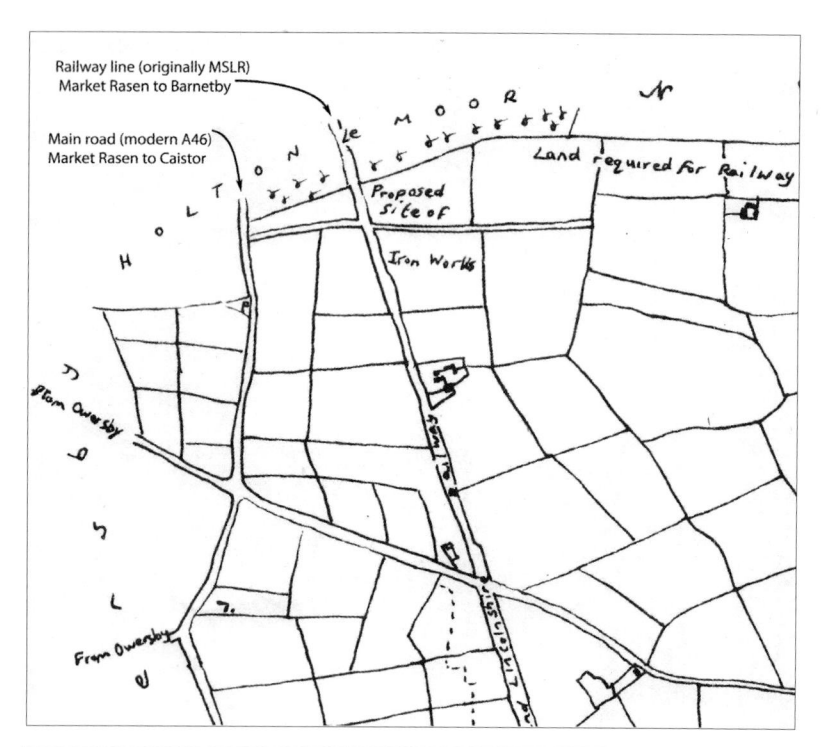

Fig 6.2.
(Left). The location of the 'Proposed site of Iron Works' at Holton le Moor. The A46 level crossing is ½ mile north of this, off the map. (Lincolnshire Archives Ref YARB 5/9/7, with amendment by Ken Redmore)

Fig 6.3.
(Below). Copy of the plan showing the area leased by the Yarborough Estate to William Firth in 1866. The only part of this that was worked was under the fields numbered 1, 2, 2A and a small part of 3 in Normanby parish, 68 in Claxby parish and part of 5 in Nettleton parish. (Lincolnshire Archives, YARB/5/9/6)

Fig 6.4.
(Opposite page). Extract from plan dated 1867 showing the land required for works and tramways at Claxby Mine. This shows the two small quarries (highlighted) that were probably dug to prove the quality and quantity of the ironstone. (Lincolnshire Archives, YARB 5/9/8 with amendments by Ken Redmore)

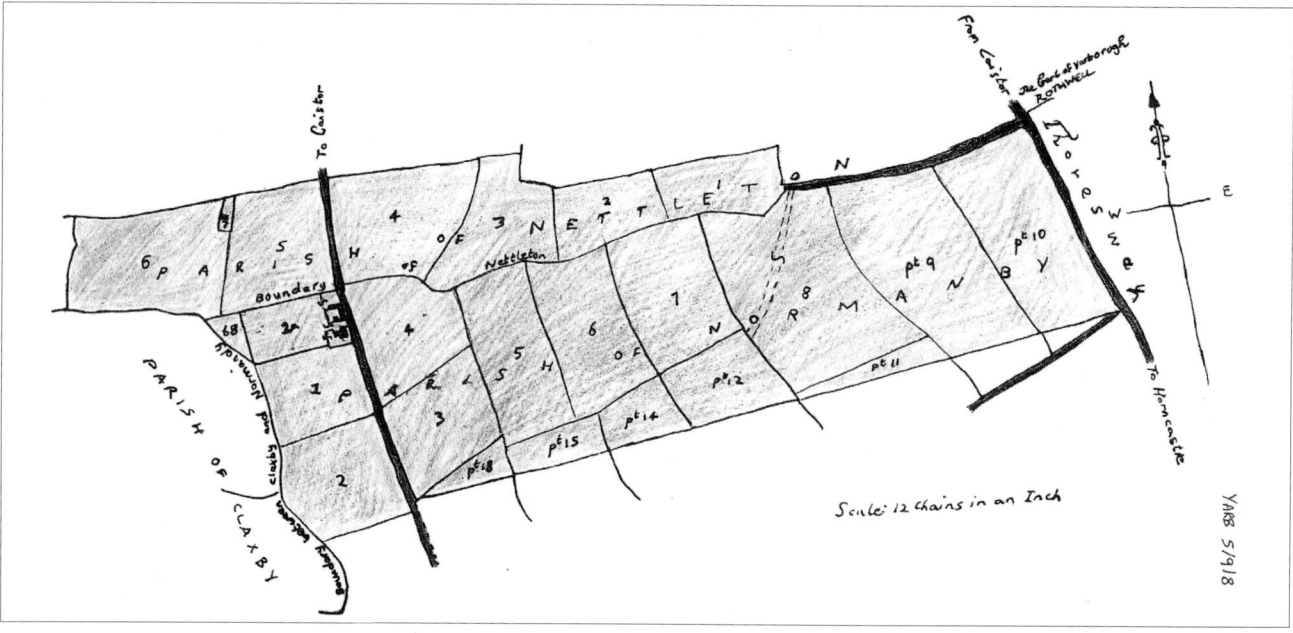

in the parishes of Normanby, Nettleton and Claxby.[2] In fact, the surface buildings were in Claxby, with the underground workings in Normanby and Nettleton, the mine being located around the position where the three parish boundaries come together. Another name that is sometimes used is Acre House Mine, after the adjacent farm on the Normanby to Nettleton road.

The Claxby Mine was on land owned by the Earl of Yarborough. If workable quantities of ore were present on adjacent land it is reasonable to suppose that the Earl was interested. Certainly, as it transpired, he was interested. A draft lease, undated but with provision for a date of 186?, can be found in the Estate papers.[3] It must predate the lease signed in 1866. This was between the Earl of Yarborough

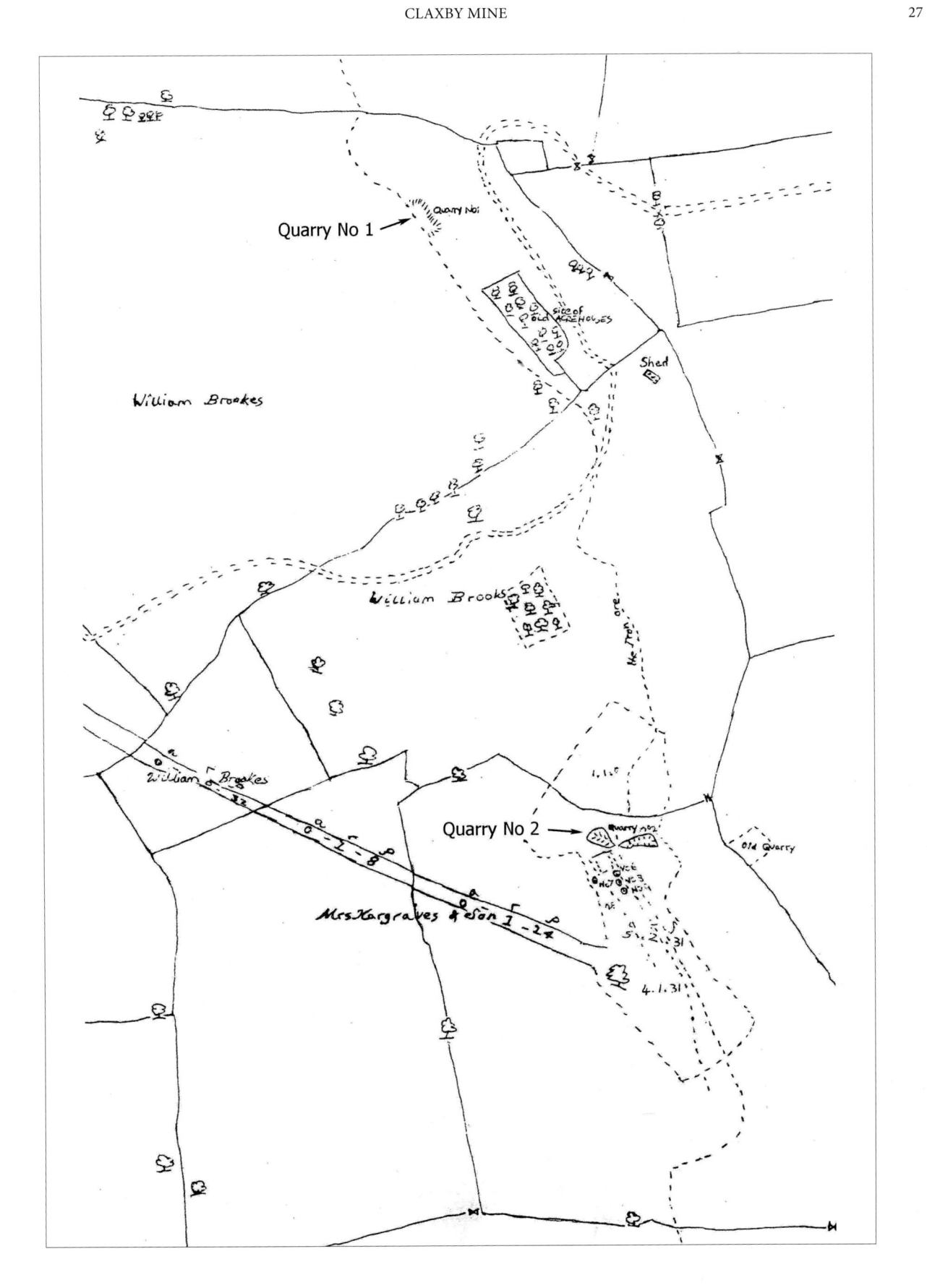

CLAXBY MINE

Quarry No 1

Quarry No 2

site of Old ACREHOUSES

Shed

William Brookes

William Brooks

William Brookes

Mrs Hargraves & son

Old Quarry

as the owner and John Roseby of Appleby, John Woodhead Marsden, mining engineer of Leeds, and Edwin Bray of Tottenham, the latter referred to as a 'railway contractor'.

John Roseby is an interesting character. *(See Section 5. Landowners and Prospectors)*. He was a well known mining engineer responsible for the discovery of ironstone fields in Cleveland and in Oxfordshire and it was he to whom Roland Winn turned to develop the ore fields on the Frodingham and Appleby estates. He became mineral agent for Winn and was expected to devote half his time to the development of the industry in the Scunthorpe area. The plan with the draft lease indicates a site for the 'Proposed Site of Iron Works' in the two fields, one north and one south of what was to become the junction of the railway siding with the railway line south of Holton le Moor station. *(Fig 6.2)*. Such a suggestion was unlikely to appeal to the Scunthorpe interests that Roseby also served.

These negotiations went unfulfilled, however, as agreement was reached with another party and the *Stamford Mercury* reported on 22 November 1867:

> On the 12th inst., the ceremony of taking up the first sod for a new branch railway to connect the iron diggings with the Hull and Lincoln line was performed by Dr Chalmers … (of Caistor)… . The new line will be about two miles long, and will reach the main line a few yards beyond Holton Station. It is expected to be completed in a few weeks, when extensive excavations will be made, and the ore calcined before removal.[4]

This siding was the link to the mine to enable the ore to be taken away for processing. In fact it was 1.3 miles long, not two. In 1867 the West Yorkshire Iron and Coal Company approached the Manchester, Sheffield and Lincolnshire Railway Company to construct the siding from Holton le Moor. They estimated that twenty wagonloads of iron ore would be sent daily to their ironworks at Ardsley. The cost of the siding was estimated at £300, and was borne by the Railway Company.[5] The West Yorkshire Iron and Coal Company was formed in 1866. Its chairman was William Firth. They had an ironworks at Ardsley, near Leeds. By 1901, when they changed their name by dropping the West prefix, they also had collieries at Tingley, near Leeds, together with 268 acres of farmland and 106 houses and cottages at Tingley and Woodkirk. As the ironstone industry expanded in Lincolnshire they worked other quarries elsewhere in the county.[6]

The lease for the mine was granted by the Earl of Yarborough to William Firth for fifty years from 29 May 1866.[7] Described as a 'merchant' and with an address of Burley Wood, in Leeds, his company was the West Yorkshire Iron and Coal Company. The lease included 438 acres of land, from the ironstone outcrop in the west to Caistor High Street in the east. *(Fig 6.3)*. Only a small proportion of this area, around 90 acres, was eventually mined. In addition to the ironstone the lease also included the working of limestone and chalk. A very small quantity of limestone was taken in 1876. There was no right to extract sand in this lease but considerable quantities of sand were also produced throughout the life of the mine. *(See Section 16. Production)*. All the stone produced went to the furnaces of the West Yorkshire Iron and Coal Company.

There were separate agreements for the construction of the railway siding and the land and buildings to the west of the top of the scarp slope. A plan dated 1867 of an early proposed lease survives.[8] *(Fig 6.4)*. William Brooks farmed most of this land, including the railway siding route and the north end of the above ground infrastructure. Most of the site of the south end of the latter, including most of the railway incline, was on land tenanted by Mrs Hargraves & Son. It should be noted that the boundary of the land proposed to be leased is smaller than the more extensive area actually used for the mine here, evidence to suggest that there may have been a successive lease.

On this plan two small quarries are shown. Both lie along the line of the base of the outcrop of the ironstone, which is also identified. One, 'Quarry No 2', is almost at the point where the main mine entrance was constructed and the second, 'Quarry No 1' is to the west of Acre House, just north of where a ventilation adit, Drift No 4, was opened in 1873/4. *(Figs 6.4 and 7.2)*. It is likely that the quarries were dug to prove the quality of the ironstone here and thus the opportunity for a mine. This is similar to the two shafts dug later west of Nettleton Top which helped to prove the quality of the ore there. *(See Section 19. Nettleton Top Mine, Early Proposals)*. In the Yarborough Account Book[9] there is an entry in the Half Yearly Statement

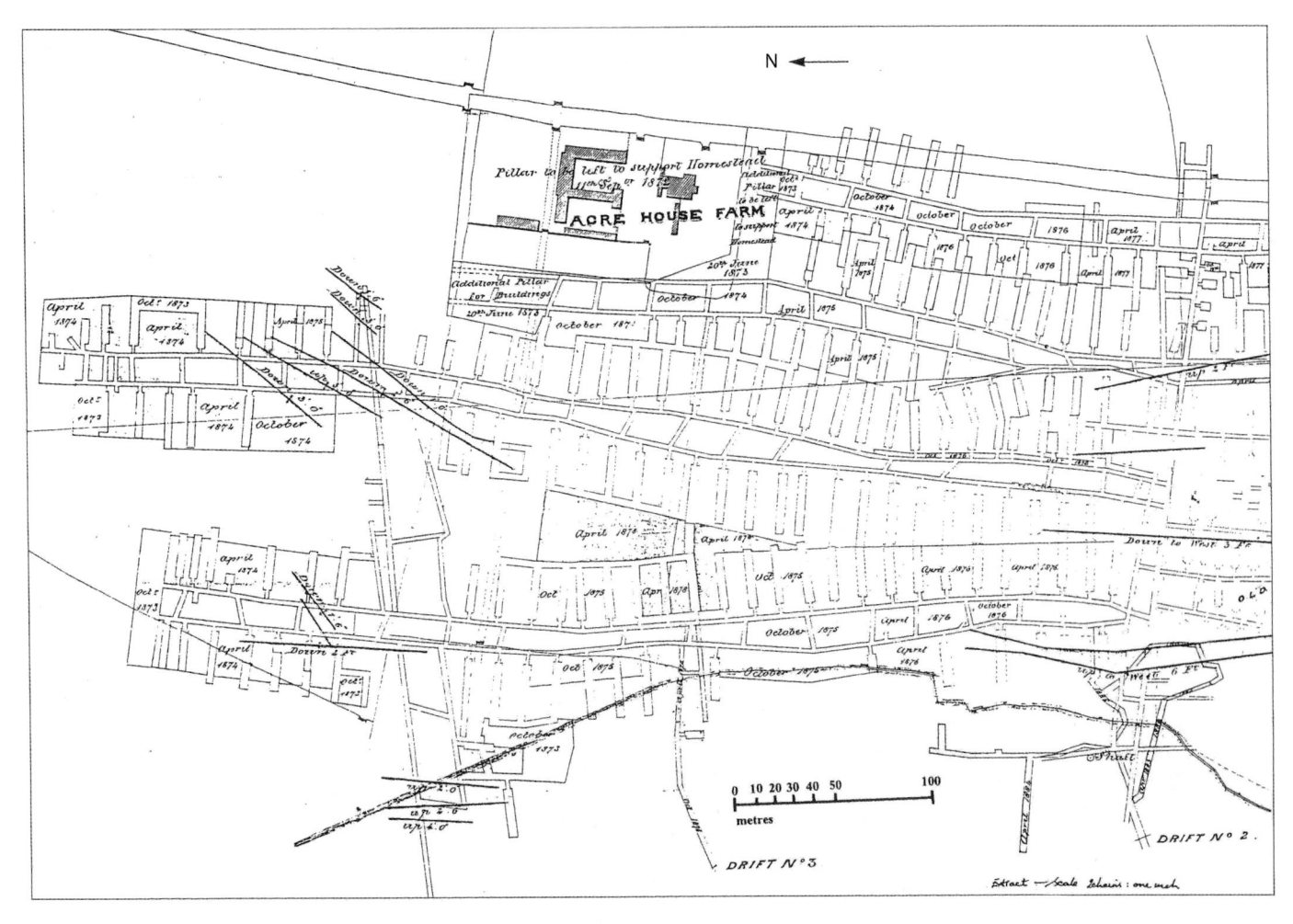

Fig 7.1.
Pillar and Stall working at Claxby Mine. The stalls are the chambers excavated at right angles to the main linear roadways. Pillars are the pillars of stone left between the stalls. Note the succession of tunnels inside Drift No 2. The regular use of the latter must have ceased in 1877 but the later dates of 1883, 1884 and 1885 are shown on the convoluted tunnels excavated later. This probably indicates a need subsequently to get back into this part of the mine following collapses of the earlier tunnels post first closure. The black lines of various lengths are fault lines. Each is annotated to show where the bed rises and falls and the height difference of each fault. (Extract from Plan of Ironstone Mines worked in the Parishes of Normanby, Nettleton and Claxby, Dated 1872 but updated with the workings to 1885, Author's collection)

of Accounts to 1 July 1868 for 'Allowance for damage done in getting ironstone for trial in 1864'. This is on land held by the tenant William Brooks and it was he who was the tenant of the site of Quarry No 1.

Fig 6.4 also shows an 'Old Quarry' to the east of Quarry No 2. This was dug into the carstone and limestone layers at a point immediately below the crest of the scarp slope. Its purpose is not known but it may have been to provide stone for the Acre House farmstead or even to provide stone for road repairs. By the time the mine was in operation this quarry was fenced off to become part of the field to the west and within it was built the powder house, the building within which explosives were stored for mine use. *(See 9. Surface Works and Buildings).*

7. Underground

Underground working was by bord and pillar, also known as 'pillar and stall' *(Fig 7.1)*. A series of

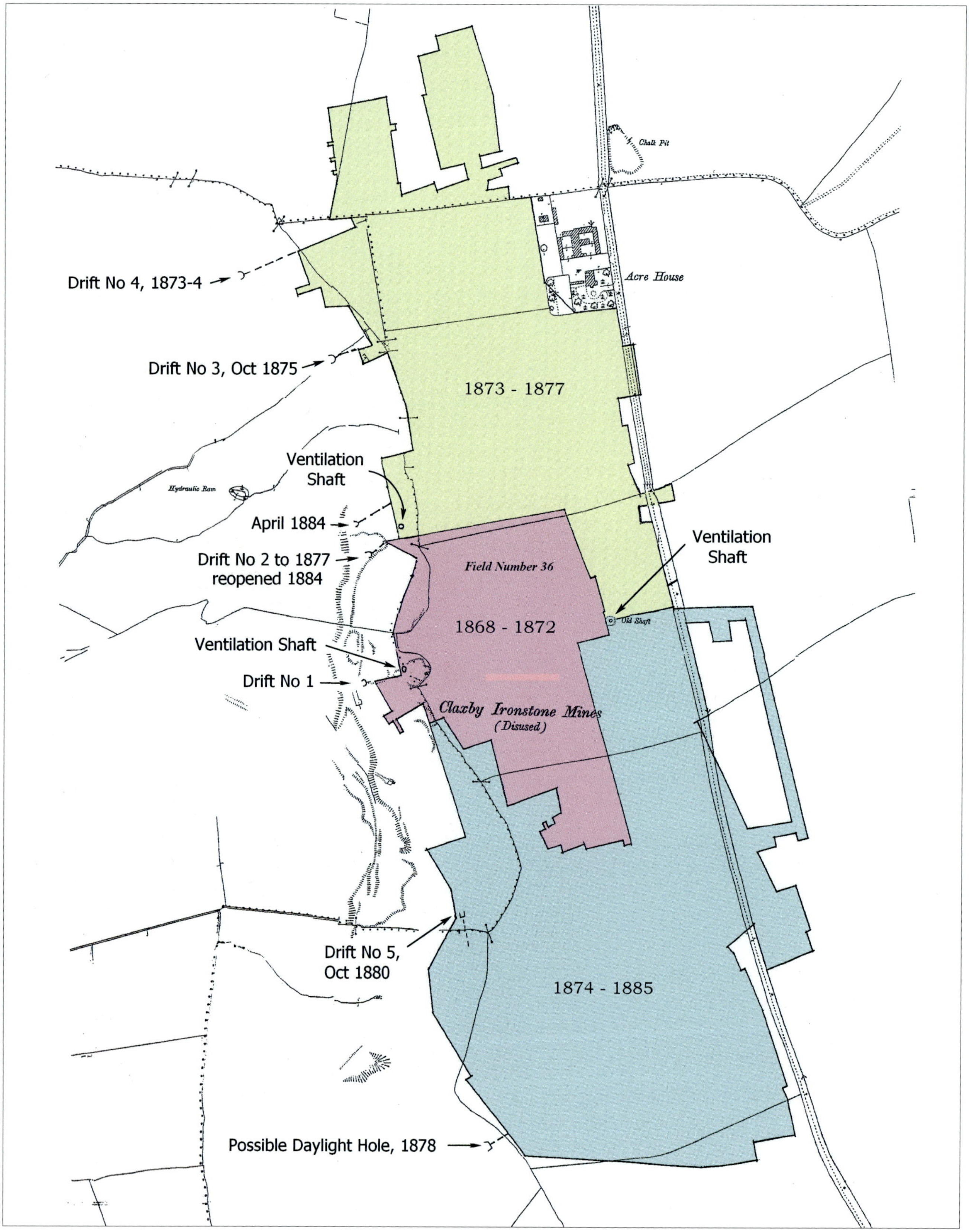
Chalk Pit
Acre House
Drift No 4, 1873-4
Drift No 3, Oct 1875
1873 - 1877
Ventilation Shaft
Hydraulic Ram
April 1884
Drift No 2 to 1877 reopened 1884
Field Number 36
Ventilation Shaft
1868 - 1872
Old Shaft
Ventilation Shaft
Drift No 1
Claxby Ironstone Mines (Disused)
Drift No 5, Oct 1880
1874 - 1885
Possible Daylight Hole, 1878

Fig 7.2. (Opposite page).
Claxby Mine, to show phases of mining with entrances and ventilation shafts. (Extract from the Ordnance Survey, 1:2500, County Series, Second Edition, 1906, Sheets XXXVII.12 and XXXVIII.9. Alterations and annotations by Ken Redmore)

Fig 7.3. (Above).
The site of Drift No 2 in April 1998. The entrance is marked by the tree, right upper centre, with the tramway running alongside the bank curving to the bottom left corner. (Author)

progressively extended paired linear tunnels, with regular cross passages linking them, provided access into and out of the mine as well as for ventilation. The paired tunnels were constructed at an average of around 250 feet apart. From these bords or stalls, chambers around 100 feet by 15 feet were excavated. The bed of stone here was around 10 feet thick, although this also included a bed of clay two feet thick near to the top. The stalls would be around eight feet in height.

In this mine the stalls were reached by a short and narrow entrance passage, known as 'narrow neck' entries. The 'pillar' was the pillar of stone left between the stalls. Subsequently, most of the pillars would be 'robbed', that is removed, although it was rarely possible to remove them all. Around 80% of the ironstone would be extracted using this method. As Fig 7.1 indicates, no stone was removed from below Acre House Farm and its buildings, thus ensuring their stability was not threatened. Indeed, in 1873 an additional pillar was left to the south 'to support Homestead'. Although a few stalls and tunnels were dug under the Nettleton to Normanby road, no robbing took place here to protect the road from subsidence.

The mine was worked in three main phases. *(Fig 7.2)*. These were the central section, 1868 to 1872; the north, 1873 to 1877; and to the south, 1874 to 1885. The one feature they had in common was a ventilation shaft *(discussed in more detail in section 8 Ventilation)*.

The mine had two main entrances, that is, those entrances into which the tramway tracks ran and so became part of what may be considered to be the permanent infrastructure. They were Drifts 1 and 2. *(Figs 7.1, 7.2 and 7.3)*. In addition were Drifts 3, 4 and 5. These were of a temporary nature, to allow for ventilation, and perhaps access on foot, to particular parts of the mine as working progressed. In addition to this a further opening, which may have been what was known at Nettleton Mine as a 'daylight hole' to improve ventilation, is known at the south end. The locations of all of these are shown in Fig 7.2. Such additional drifts were often known as travelling drifts, with the main drifts being horse or haulage drifts. The use of the former avoided the dangers of contact with horses and tubs being drawn into and out of the mine, always a potential source of injuries to men working underground.

Drift No 2 appears to have become unused after 1877 when the northern end of the mine was worked out. In 1884 it was reopened, the reason for which is not known but may have been due to a need to improve ventilation, to enable the reclamation of material prior to closure or to check or ensure the stability of the ground above. The rather convoluted routes of this re-entry, shown in Fig 7.1, are likely to be a result of a lack of maintenance after 1877 coupled with movement of the notoriously unstable hillside here.

A sample of borehole records from the British Geological Survey, together with known heights above OD, and faults shown on the mine plan *(Fig 7.1)* show that Drifts No 1 and 2 were driven into the hillside almost at the top of the ironstone outcrop. Underground faults lift the ironstone bed about six feet some 300 feet from Drift 2, from where the bed is at a generally consistent height on both sides of Normanby Road. This is a similar situation that would be found when the Main Drifts were driven at Nettleton Top and Bottom Mines. *(Fig 24.7)*.

Lighting underground would be largely provided by candles. Miners are likely to have taken their own, both to light their way and to provide illumination in the area within which they were working. They would have been supplied by the owner with the cost deducted from their wages.

Fig 8.1. (Top)
The top of the Claxby mine ventilation shaft prior to infilling, 1955. (John Brant)

Fig 8.2. (Bottom)
The site of the original upcast shaft for Drift No 1. It is now infilled, most recently with stone from the remains of the powder house. (Author)

8. Ventilation

A flow of air was required within the mine to allow miners to work, as well as to clear the dust in the air following the use of explosives. This was achieved in a number of ways and the common factor and principal means was the provision of the vertical shaft which opened into the field above, OS Field Number 36 on Fig 7.2. This shaft was 113 feet deep, brick lined with a stone coping and around 10 to 12 feet in diameter. The opening was protected by a circular earth bank around the top and it probably had a metal grille. The base of the shaft was at mine level. Fig 8.1 shows the top of the shaft at the time it was being infilled in 1955. At this time the top had been covered with a domed brick cap which must have been constructed after closure.

Ventilation was by the 'furnace' method. A fire at the base caused hot air to rise, although there could also have been a natural flow of air without a fire. It may be that a fire was not needed all the time, dependent upon the distance from the foot of the shaft men were working. This would draw air from a mine entrance, via the tunnels and finally through an inclined shaft to the vertical shaft, drawing the air in above the fire itself. This was known as the 'upcast' shaft.

Reference has been made above to the parallel paired tunnels within the mine, together with their connecting links. As the headings progressed they were connected by further links, with the earlier

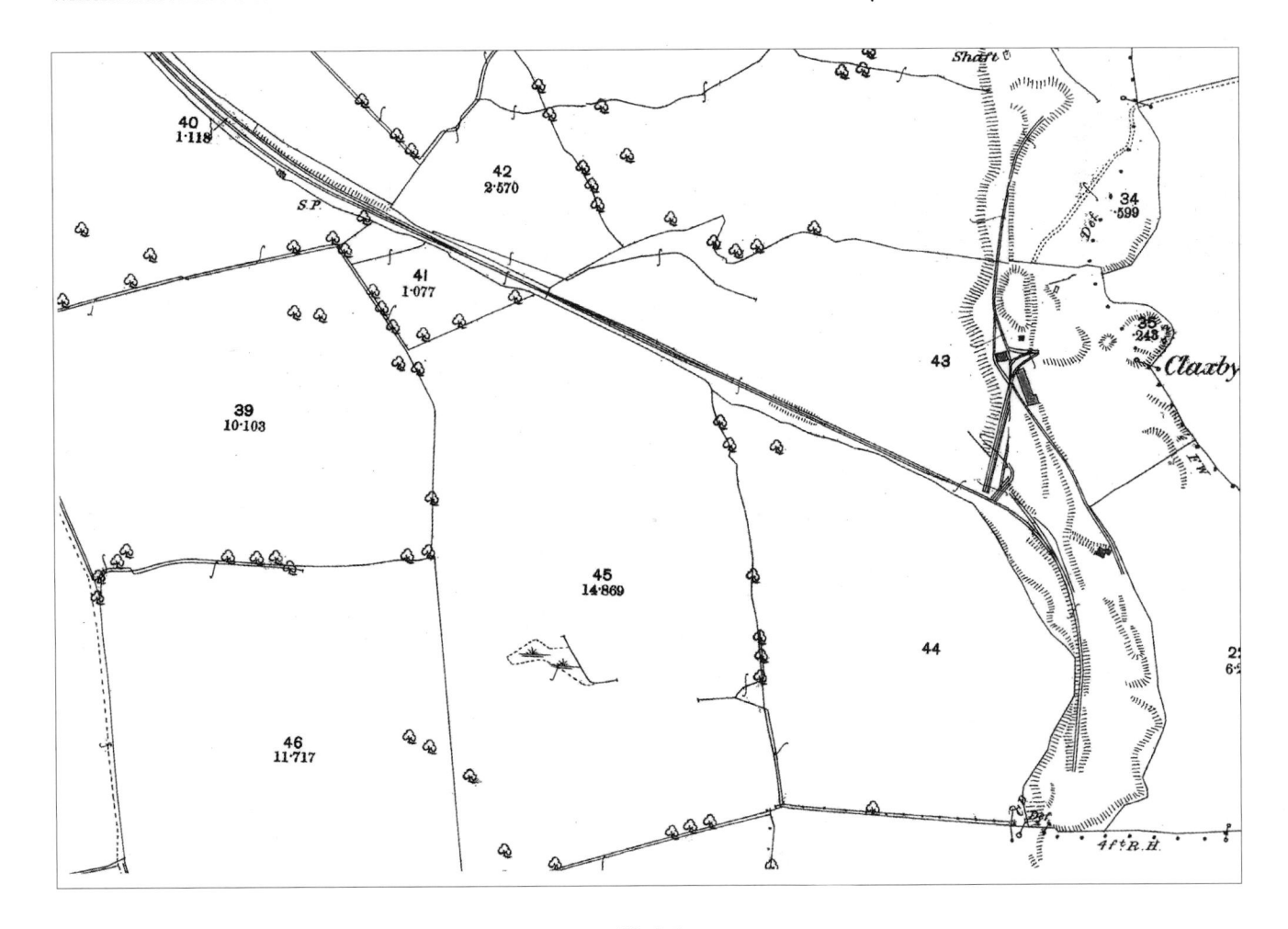

Fig 9.1.
The surface works and buildings in 1887. This map was surveyed and published in 1888 after the mine closed so may not be an accurate record of the layout when it was working. (Ordnance Survey, 1:2500 County Series First Edition, sheets XXXVII.12 (left) and XXXVIII.9 (right)

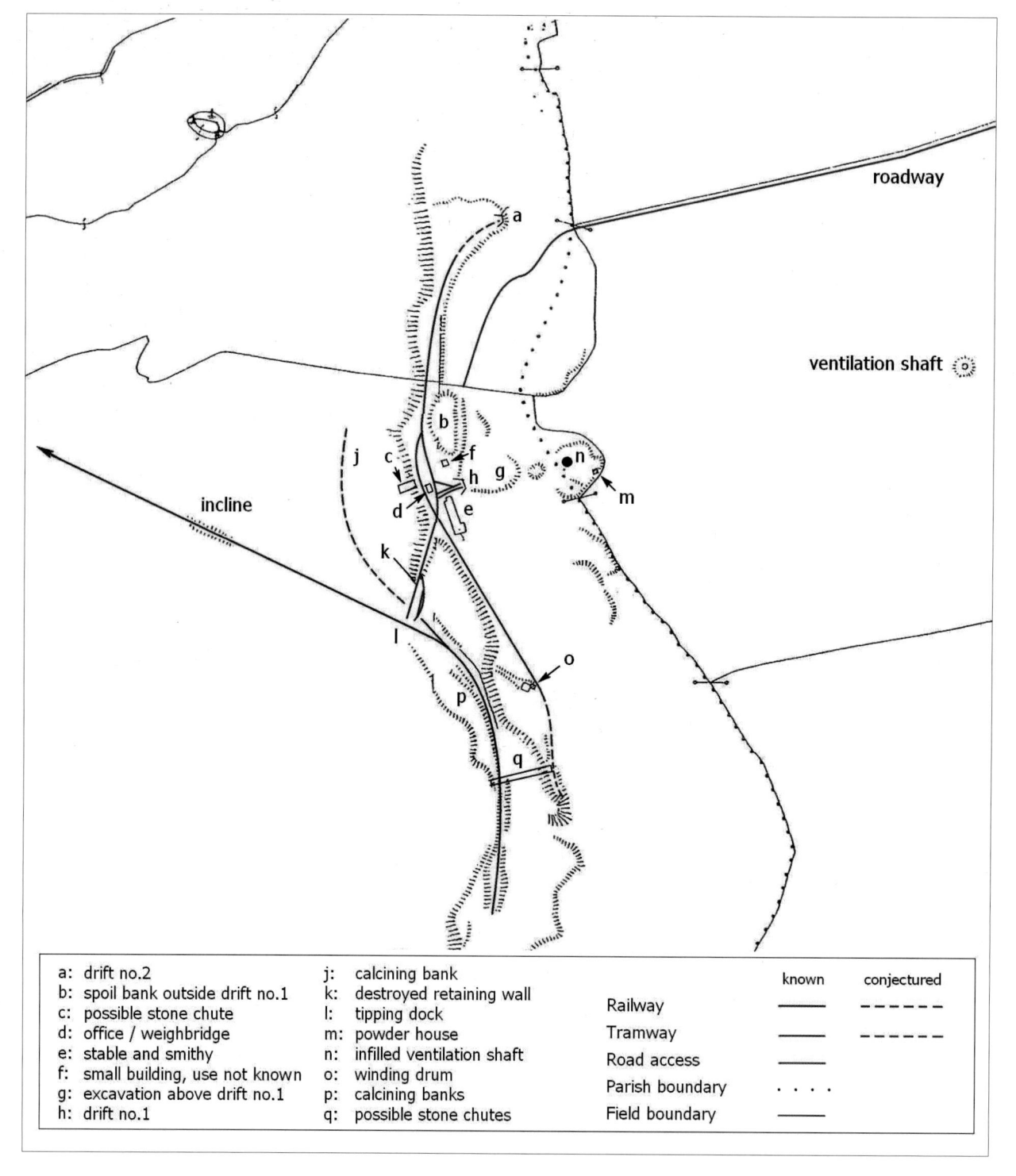

34 IRONSTONE MINING IN THE LINCOLNSHIRE WOLDS

a:	drift no.2
b:	spoil bank outside drift no.1
c:	possible stone chute
d:	office / weighbridge
e:	stable and smithy
f:	small building, use not known
g:	excavation above drift no.1
h:	drift no.1
j:	calcining bank
k:	destroyed retaining wall
l:	tipping dock
m:	powder house
n:	infilled ventilation shaft
o:	winding drum
p:	calcining banks
q:	possible stone chutes

Fig 9.2.
Conjectured layout of the surface works and buildings when the mine was in operation. (Extract from the Ordnance Survey, 1:2500, County Series, Second Edition, 1906, Sheets XXXVII.12 and XXXVIII.9. Alterations and annotations by Ken Redmore)

remains of the calcine banks. *(For information on this see section 11. Calcining)*. Loaded wagons would then be hauled by horse, back to the top of the incline, to be lowered, attached to a cable, down the incline to the sidings below. The speed of the journey was controlled by the winding drum. *(For the operation of this see section 10. Railway Siding and Incline)*.

The road access to the mine came along a hedge line from Normanby Road. On reaching the scarp slope crest it turned southwards, running obliquely down the slope to lessen the gradient and entering the mine site by the side of the small building of unknown use referred to above.

As the roadway entered the mine site it effectively ran through a cutting. The cutting face to the east is created by the natural form of the hillside but that to the west is the result of a spoil bank here, clearly shown on the OS maps. Immediately above and to the east of Drift No 1 is an excavation in the hillside, also shown on the OS maps. *(Fig 9.2)*.

If this excavation and spoil heap had existed prior to the mine being opened their size is such that they can have expected to have been shown on the 1867 map at Fig 6.4. They are not. The instability of this hillside is well known. *(Fig 7.1)*. The excavation and spoil heap, therefore, may well be the result of an attempt to stabilise the hillside above Drift No 1 by reducing pressure on it.

The existence of an earlier hilltop quarry at the top of the hillside to the east of Drift No 1 has been referred to above. *(See Section 6. In the Beginning)*. This was the location of the powder house.[6] Experience at Nettleton mine showed that generally the Claxby ironstone was soft to work but occasional harder patches needed the use of explosives to loosen.

Fig 10.2. (Right)
The route of the incline as shown on the First Edition OS maps. This clearly shows that below the passing loop the line was single track and that the upper section consisted of three rails, the centre rail used in common by both ascending and descending wagons. The signal post at the foot of the incline is shown as a dot to the right of the top of the letter P in the identifying initials SP. (Ordnance Survey with annotations by Ken Redmore)

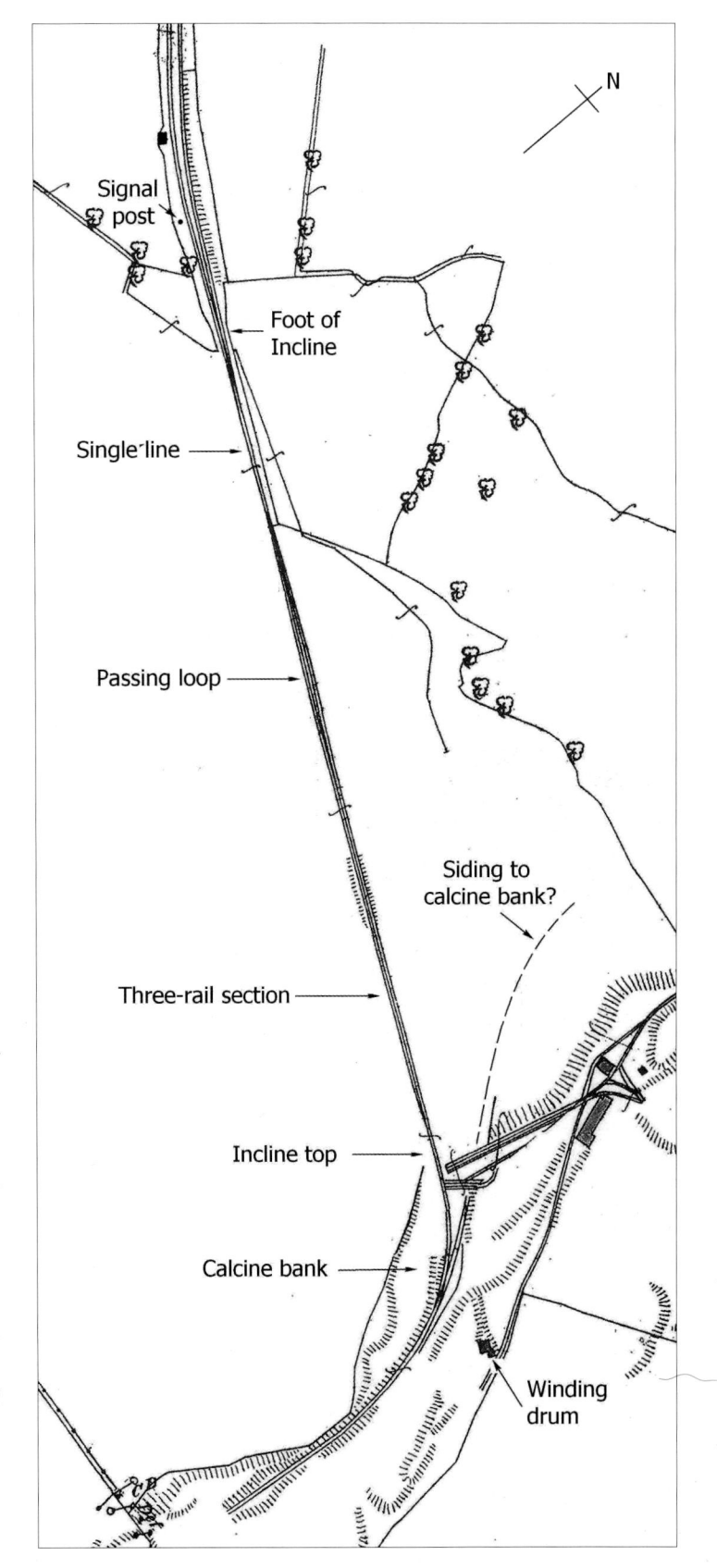

Clockwise from top left:
Fig 10.3.
The winding drum at Claxby Mine, seen here in 1927, still in situ 44 years after the mine closed. It was dismantled in 1934. The person is believed to be Mr Brant. (Authors collection)

Fig 10.4.
Conjectured drawing of what the winding house and drum may have looked like in operation. (Drawing by Anne Keward)

Fig 10.5.
The wire rope found on the route of the incline in 1991. It is about 3 inches in diameter. (Chris Padley)

For safety reasons explosives were always stored on mine sites away from where men and machinery were working. Conventionally, also for safety reasons, they had stout surrounding walls, indeed, often circular, with a sacrificial roof. This would ensure that any blast would go upwards, thus reducing risks. The powder house at Claxby was, by contrast, a chamber excavated into the rock wall of the quarry with a stone faced entrance with a brick lined doorway and an arched brick roof. Any blast here would go horizontally through the doorway. However, it was around 50 feet above and 250 feet to the east of Drift No 1. *(Figs 9.2 and 9.8)*.

Little now remains of the powder house. There is a scattering of stone and brick at the site but part may remain buried in the hillside. The nearby former upcast shaft for Drift No 1 appears to have some of the rubble in it suggesting that following post 1995 subsidence it was used as a source of infill material.

Fig 9.9 gives an impression of what the mine site may have looked like when the mine was working with substantial structures erected on the hillside.

10. Railway Siding and Incline

The standard gauge railway siding, marked as a tramway on the 6 inch OS map, ran from Holton-le-Moor Station to the foot of the hillside below the mine, a distance of almost a mile. *(Fig 10.1)*. It was single track but approaching the foot of the hill divided into two to create parallel sidings. This loop ended at the foot of the hill and the line continued up the incline for a further 380 yards. A short passing loop was incorporated at a point halfway up the hill.

Fig 10.6.
The inclined wall following the route of the cable down from the Winding Drum, up the slope to the right, down to the siding. Just to the left there must have been a pit to guide the rope underneath the rails and on to the rollers which would guide it down the incline, between the rails. The retaining wall for the siding can be seen on the right. (Author)

On reaching the mine the siding levelled out and ran southwards along the contour of the hillside for some 250 yards. The total length of track was 2286 yards or around 1.3 miles. The incline rose a vertical height of about 165 feet at a gradient of about 1 in 6.

It was normal practice on inclines such as this for loaded wagons to descend balanced by empty wagons being brought up. The two would be connected by a rope passing around the winding drums above the top of the siding. Wagons would pass at the halfway point and this is the reason for the passing loop. To enable the ropes to run along the incline alongside each other on the upper section it was conventional to lay three rails, the centre rail being used in common by both ascending and descending wagons. This was the case here. *(Fig 10.2)*. Furthermore, to avoid wagons running over and damaging the rope it would be guided between the rails on the incline by a series of rollers. This was not unusual for the date. Such inclines were common serving mines and quarries all over the UK. The principle is still used today on funicular railways worldwide.

The length of the passing loop determined the maximum number of wagons which could use the incline at any one time. Here the loop gave clear separation of the tracks for about 60 feet, space for a maximum of three wagons to pass on either side.

Balancing the traffic on the incline required the descending load to be heavier than that on the way

*Fig 10.7.
The pinch bar found on the mine site, held by Mr John Brant. This is eight feet long. The chamfered end would be positioned under the wheel of a railway wagon, and the bar pushed down to get the wagon moving. It could have been used to move both standard gauge and narrow gauge wagons. The purpose of the pair of lugs on the underside, one by his hand and one that can be seen a little way in front, is not known. They may have been used to secure a shoulder pad to maximise an upward push, although if this were the case the leverage would have to be against a wagon body rather than a wheel. (Author)*

up. The rate of descent was controlled by a brake on the winding drum at the head of the incline. *(Fig 9.2 for its location on the site and see also Fig 10.3)*. The incline cable passed around the drum several times to ensure there was sufficient friction for the brake to slow the drum, and therefore, the wagons, without the cable slipping.

The photograph at Fig 10.3 shows that at Claxby there were two drums around 12 feet in diameter. These would be fixed on one axle and rotate the same way, one rope coming off the top of one and one off the bottom of the other so that as one wound out (downhill), the other wound in (uphill). Each half of the drum has a rim brake. The structure would have a roof over it to keep the rain off the brakes. The timber across the top *(Fig 10.3)* is likely to be the remains of the roof. The links attached to it are likely to be supports to keep the top of the brake band away from the liner when the brake was off. Shelter was probably provided by a timber structure as the First Edition of the Ordnance Survey map indicates that it was of timber or iron construction. The brake band would have been linked to a long brake lever positioned so that the brakeman had a clear view of the incline and the wagons on it. The photograph is believed to have been taken in 1927 when the structure was said to weigh over 50 tons.[1] Fig 10.4 is a conjectured appearance of the building when in operation. A short section of wire cable was discovered on the route of the incline in 1991.[2] *(Fig 10.5)*. This is about three inches in diameter.

The winding drum is located above the site and buildings of the mine, directly in line with the incline to give the brakeman an uninterrupted view of it. A stone wall on the route, almost where the rope met the railway, is built on an incline which must have matched that of the rope. *(Fig 10.6)*. Here it would have been guided into a pit below the rails and on to the rollers taking it up and down the hill.

Beyond the foot of the incline, adjacent to the sidings, a signal post is shown on the OS map. *(Fig 10.2)*. This can have no function to control any exit from the sidings by trains as it is not in the correct place for this. It is, however, in line with the incline and the winding drum. It is likely, therefore that this was a visual signal for communication between the brakeman on the winding drum and operatives at the foot to let the former know when to release and activate the brake.

A small building alongside the sidings, to the north west of the signal post, was probably a mess hut and shelter for the men working at the foot of the incline.

How the wagons were attached to the rope is not known. Practice on similar inclines in Britain suggests that chains may have been used, wrapped around the rope and secured with leather straps. As the weight of the wagons pulled against the chain the latter would tighten, holding the wagon securely to the rope. Alternatively, a shackle at the ends of the rope could have been secured to the chain on the end of the wagon.

The two loop sidings at the incline foot would provide for empty wagons and wagons with materials such as coal, waiting to ascend on one side with the other receiving full wagons from the top. The clear parallel length is about 500 feet, so their capacity would be about 25 wagons.

The 1881 working timetable for the Manchester, Sheffield and Lincolnshire Railway gives details of trains running between Holton le Moor and Ardsley.[3] This makes provision for three trains a week, one each on a Monday, Wednesday and Friday only. The trains reversed direction at Barnetby, running via Crowle and bypassing Doncaster by travelling between Adwick and Haggswood Junctions. They went on to Ardsley, via Wakefield. The ironworks of the West Yorkshire Iron and Coal Company were located at Ardsley. Trains left Ardsley at 11.00 am, arriving at Holton at 3.00 pm. Departure back to Ardsley was at 3.40 pm, arriving at 8.36 pm.

The incoming train would bring empty wagons and full wagons, the latter of coal for the calcining process. On arrival at the junction on the main line the train would have to wait while the engine crossed to the adjacent line, ran to Holton le Moor station to cross back and return to its train, but now to the rear. The wagons were then propelled across the fields for placing in an empty siding. The loaded wagons would be drawn out of the other siding, and taken back to the main line and on to Ardsley, via Barnetby. A set of crossover points was provided on the main line to facilitate the engine movements and is shown on the First Edition OS map.[4]

In 1890 the Great Northern Railway weighed 278 wagons taking ironstone from the quarries at Caythorpe, Lincolnshire, to Ardsley, for the West Yorkshire Iron and Coal Co. Their average net load was found to be 8.6 tons.[5] Taking 25 wagons as a typical maximum trainload dispatched by rail from the Claxby mine, that gives an average tonnage per train of about 215 tons. In the year of maximum production at Claxby, 1873, 69,445 tons equates to 323 train loads or around six trains a week. In 1880, with production of 17,854 tons, only two trains a week would be needed. *(See Table 4 in Section 16. Production)*.

Although the working timetable for 1881 makes provision for three trains a week these would not necessarily run. They would only run if required. This coped with fluctuations in demand. In the same way the working timetable could be revised from time to time to make provision for increased numbers of trains and this is the likely case in the mine's early years.

On the hillside all wagon movements would have been made with horses. What is believed to have been a pinch bar was discovered on site some years ago. This would have been used as a lever acting on the wheel for a man to give a push to a railway wagon to move it a short distance. *(Fig 10.7)*.

In February 1870[6] the death was reported of Thomas Beales of Osgodby. *(See Table 2)*.

> [He] tried to stop a wagon running away down an incline on the tramway by putting a sleeper between the wheels, when the sleeper struck him over the knee, producing a compound fracture of the left thigh. On Tuesday, he was conveyed to Lincoln and admitted into the County Hospital, where the limb was amputated but the poor fellow succumbed and died that evening.

It may be that this was caused by a wagon running away down the incline. We do not know the gradients of other slopes, especially on the narrow gauge tracks, although there were slopes on the narrow gauge siding running south past the winding house and there would have been a falling gradient down to the tipping stage.

11. Calcining

Calcining is a process that was often used in mines and quarries producing a relatively low grade ore. The process removed carbon dioxide and water from the iron ore by burning. The end result is that the percentage of iron in the iron ore was raised, it was in a state better for use in a blast furnace, and the lumps of stone were considerably broken down. Because of the loss of weight freight charges for the cost of transport were also reduced.

Calcining was normally carried out very close to the mine or quarry from which it was produced. A layer of coal around one foot thick was laid as a base. The iron ore was then mixed with coal slack in the proportion of about forty ore to one slack and tipped on top to form a heap. It was then set alight and burnt, a process that could continue for several weeks.

This did happen at Claxby. In November 1867 the press reported that 'the ore would be calcined before removal'.[1] In 1871 John Foster was injured by falling into a calcine clamp.[2] He was a miner who, 'whilst engaged throwing water to slake the calcined iron clamp outside the Claxby mine, accidentally fell into the midst of the burning mass, and was shockingly burnt.' Ashes could still be seen in 1927.[3] Ash and burnt ironstone can still be found to the north of the incline, on the slope to the west of Drift No 1 and the bank to the west of the siding south of the incline, exposed by the activities of rabbits.

The issue of the movement of iron ore to the calcine clamps has not been determined. However, if the tipping dock(s) were used this would be likely to lead to conflict on the movement of railway wagons around the site and conflict with the arrival and departure of wagons using the incline. There is no documentary evidence for any alternative but an assessment of the earthworks at the site does provide an alternative suggestion.

The movement of minerals between different levels in the latter half of the nineteenth century was often achieved with the use of metal or wooden chutes. So, for example, the transfer of coal between railway wagons and ships in dock or canal barges on rivers and canals was often by the use of a fixed or hinged chute. Their use in the ironstone extraction industry is much less common. There was an example at the East Rosedale Mine on the North Yorkshire Moors. Here, after the calcining kilns were closed, ironstone was loaded into railway wagons directly below with a lengthy chute.[4] This was happening by 1912, so is likely to post date any use at Claxby.

The Ordnance Survey First Edition 1:2500 map *(Fig 9.2)* shows a tramway leaving the mine entrances and running uphill to terminate by the winding drum. This is a little odd as it is not clear why the drum would need a rail access. However, a little further south and at a higher level is a small set of unusual earthworks which are of a size to take a narrow gauge line of rails. From this terminus sufficient height has been achieved above the railway siding below for a chute erected here to discharge stone direct to the calcine bank without disrupting rail traffic. A similar and shorter chute could have served the calcine bank to the north of the incline.

It must have been a problem to keep up constant production of calcined ore from Claxby. The process was very labour intensive, all loading and unloading having to be done by men with shovels. The restricted space on the steep hillside for clamps as well as the limited siding space must have created problems. Indeed, it may be that on occasion they had to despatch un-calcined ore to the iron works.

Calcining did not take place at all mines and quarries. It did not happen at the later Nettleton mines or the contemporary Monks Abbey mine in Lincoln. Neither is it known if it always happened at Claxby or if the process here was short lived. The strike of 1872 does provide a clue. *(See Section 14. The Strike of 1872)*. The *Stamford Mercury* reported that 'hitherto it has been their practice to first clamp and burn the loose or earthy metal upon the spot.'[5] This indicates that calcining ceased in 1872 and that the dispute was about a need for miners to remove material by hand that up to then would be removed by the calcining process.

As has been shown, the calcining process required coal, so loaded wagons of coal must have been delivered to the site as well. This is likely to have come from one of the the West Yorkshire coal mines in the Wakefield area. It could then be delivered as part of a train of empty wagons from Ardsley.

12. The Miners

Lincolnshire was not a mining county until 1868. As we have already seen Claxby was the first underground mine in Lincolnshire. No doubt the hard physical labour suited Lincolnshire men, but the skills and expertise had to be brought in from elsewhere. When the existence of workable quantities of ore was proved, there were high and unrealistic hopes that the discoveries would result in industrialisation and the local production of much greater wealth. The population figures from the national census do give an indication of the effect.

PARISH	1861	1871	1881
Normanby	149	138	162
Claxby	262	237	357
Nettleton	524	536	545
TOTALS	935	911	1064

Table 1
National Census of Population, Normanby, Claxby and Nettleton.

It is likely that miners travelled to work from other parishes, so these figures will not record the total effects. The figures do show that Normanby's population increased a little as did that of Nettleton, but in this locality only Claxby showed a significant increase, and the Census details reveal that this was due to an influx of ironstone miners. The *Stamford Mercury* revealed in 1870:

> Claxby a mining village! What! Ultra rural and lethargic Claxby! Yes, strange as it would have sounded ten years ago, and will yet sound to many ... formerly well acquainted with the place and its sturdy opposition to all innovation ... but ignorant of the social revolution in progress therat – it now has a mining population. Its green lane has been invaded by the builders, and its ancient hedgerows demolished to make way for rows of dwelling houses. Ten roomy and substantial cottages are already built and occupied by miners, a detached villa residence is in course of erection for the mining company's manager, and it is stated that the building of another ... ten cottages will be immediately proceeded with. They are urgently needed. Both lessor and lessees of the iron mine have reason to be satisfied with their profits; it is rich and inexhaustible in metal of a superior quality, but a continuance of successful working must ... depend upon skilful and experienced hands, to retain the services of which their domiciliary comfort and convenience must be cared for within reasonable distance of their work.[1]

The report went on to inform readers of other changes in the village and to speculate on the future:

> Claxby ... now lives, having received an impetus from another cause than that of mining. Some eighteen years ago the late patron and incumbent of the united Rectory of Claxby and Normanby, being then in delicate health and medically certified to die within the year, sold the living to the present Rector, who became Curate, and whilst waiting in patience the event up to a year since, has held an anomalous position in the parish. Since coming into his own, to the joy of most of the parishioners, he has set about the much needed restoration of St Mary's Church ... and is also making considerable additions and improvements to the rectorial mansion. In all probability the new population will shortly furnish such an increase of Dissenters and of juveniles, that more chapel and school accommodation will be required. Trade in general will look after its own wants. ... but great inconvenience to the transaction of business and proper entertainment of strangers already arises from the want of a public house in the village, and for this the lord of the soil should be petitioned to grant the remedy.

In addition to bringing trade and a demand for other local services into the area, there was also a need for houses to serve the needs of the miners. The building of a row of ten miners' cottages has already been referred to above, and they were occupied by 1870. *(Figs 12.1 and 12.2)*. In 1871 these were about to be extended by the building of five more. The Caistor builder, James Button, was engaged for the work.[2] Mr Button had already built the first block of ten, beginning work in March 1870:

> ...intended for occupation by the miners, to whom hitherto house accommodation within a reasonable distance has been a serious want, and in all probability a considerable village will soon grow up at this spot.

This spot was not within the village, but on the road northwards from Claxby towards Holton le Moor. Here, about 400 yards from the village, on the east side of the road, two terraces of ten cottages were

IRONSTONE MINING IN THE LINCOLNSHIRE WOLDS

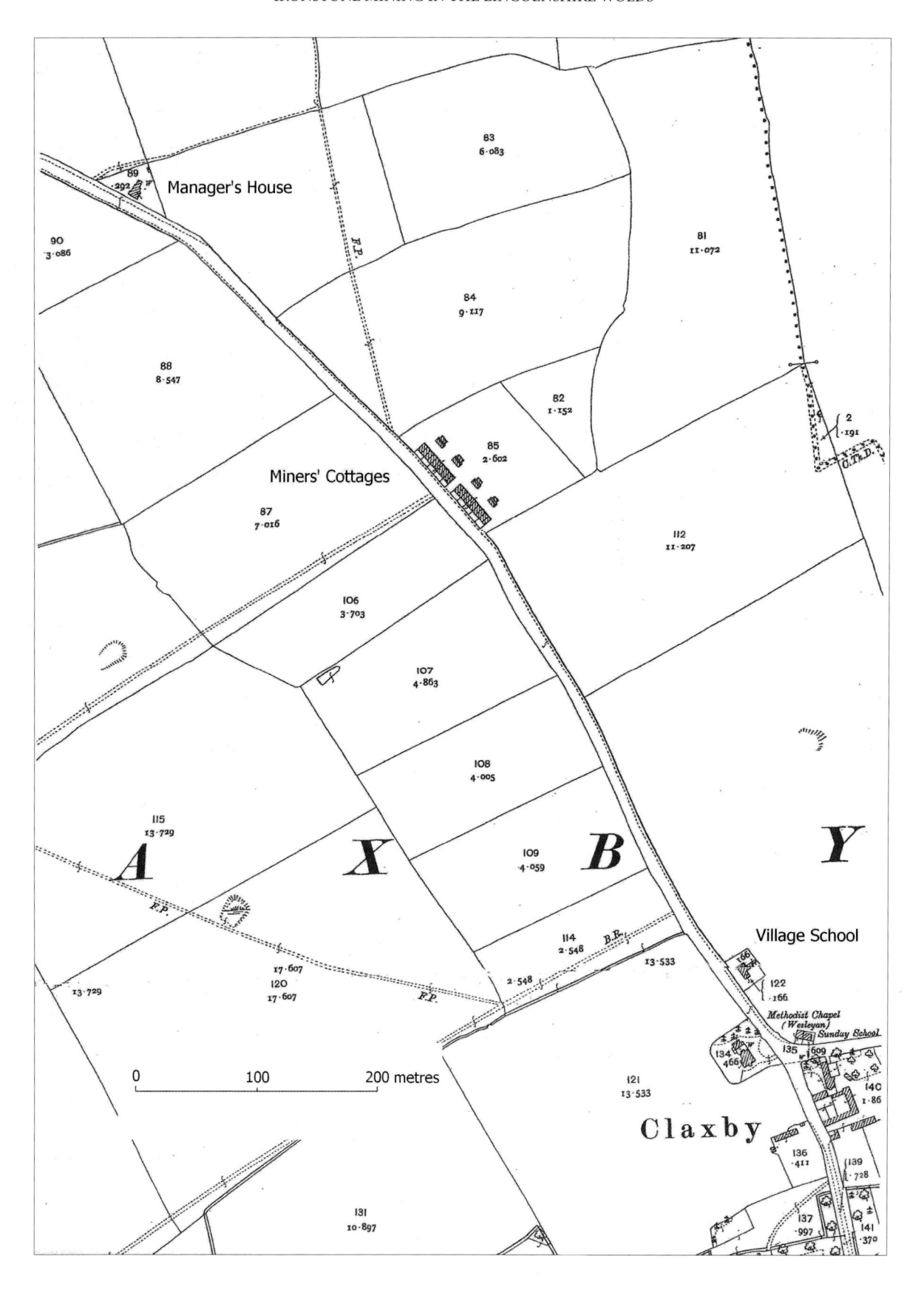

*Fig 12.1 (opposite page)
The miners' houses, the village school and their location in relation to the village. Extract from the 1906, Second Edition, County Series 1:2500 OS maps, XXXVII.12 and XXXVII.16 (Ordnance Survey, with annotations by Ken Redmore)*

*Fig 12.2 (Right)
Claxby Terrace, a pre World War One postcard. Note that four cottages in the far block and seven in the near are unoccupied with their windows boarded. (Author's collection)*

eventually built, at the point on the road nearest to the mine, but perhaps convenient for neither mine nor village. They were recorded in 1968, prior to their demolition:[3]

> Each block contains ten dwellings and is of brick and slate construction. At the rear of each are coalhouses and earth closets in rows of 5; these are of brick with pantile roofs. A standtap and ground sink is provided for every two houses. There is a small garden in front of each house which contrasts strongly with the very large rear gardens. The first 2 and last 2 houses in each block slightly protrude beyond their neighbours. There is a 22 foot gap between the 2 blocks. At one stage No.10 had its front room converted into a shop; the last shopkeeper was a Mr Sharp.
>
> The layout of each dwelling was similar to that of No.7, two up and two down. Downstairs the floors are of red quarry tiles; upstairs there are close wood boards, not tongue and groove. The cupboard in the front room consisted of a set of shelves from floor to ceiling with the lower three being enclosed in a cabinet. The pantry must be a later addition, formed by boarding in a recess between the chimney breast and the rear outside wall; not a very cool place! All the grates are of cast iron, the front room having one containing a boiler and oven — a typical mid Victorian piece.
>
> Now only five of the twenty dwellings are occupied and it appears that modern building regulations will soon require complete demolition. *(Fig 12.3)*.

Also, as has been referred to above, a house for the mine manager was built, 350 yards away further north along the road. (See Figs 12.1 and 12.4). This ensured a suitable separation between master and men! The optimism with which these dwellings were built was soon to be dashed. In 1875 production at the mine fell dramatically, culminating in closure in 1885. The terraces and the manager's house would not have been long occupied by miners at the Claxby mine. They did, however, continue to house village residents, including men who worked at the Nettleton mines after they opened in 1928.

After the closure of the Claxby mine they were not always fully occupied. In the 1891 Census there were only five with residents recorded. The photograph at Fig 12.2 shows eleven of them boarded up at an unknown date. The Yarborough Estate sold them in 1919 for £500 to a private landlord who lived in Scunthorpe. By 1972 only three were occupied[4] and demolition followed in 1972 and 1973.[5] The manager's house survives, and is still lived in today.

The miners were alleged to be hard drinking, certainly in local folk lore. It was said that more beer was spilt in the terraces in six months than is drunk now (1927) in all Claxby in twelve.[6]

The names of two of the managers are known. Jonathan Robinson, the mine agent, or manager included in

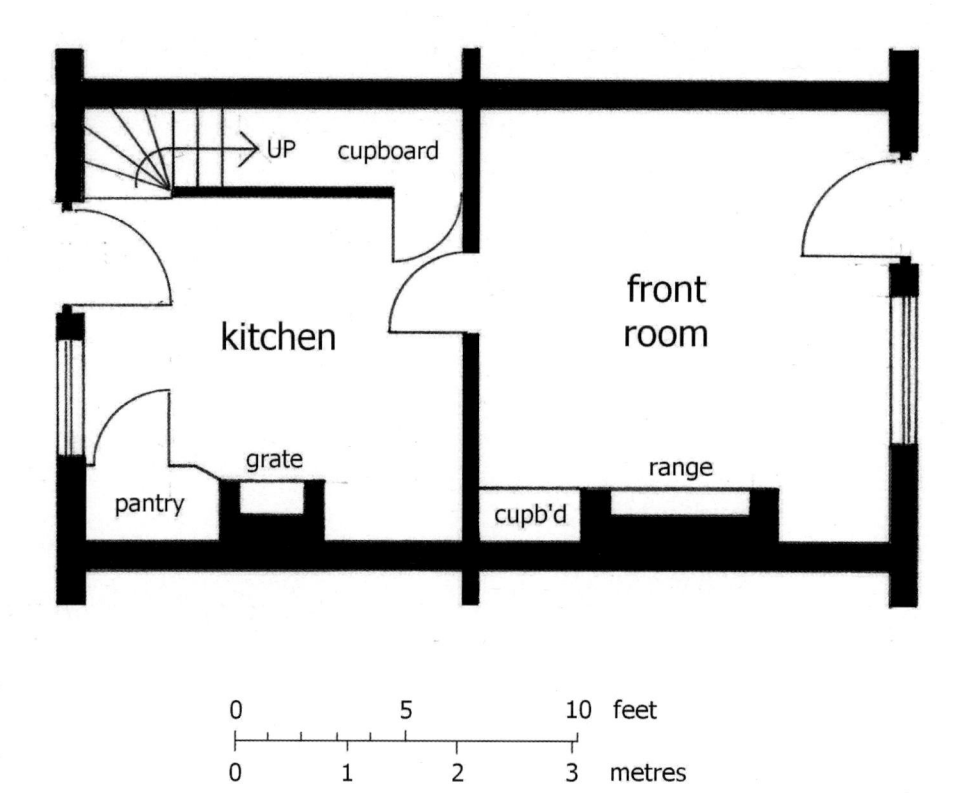

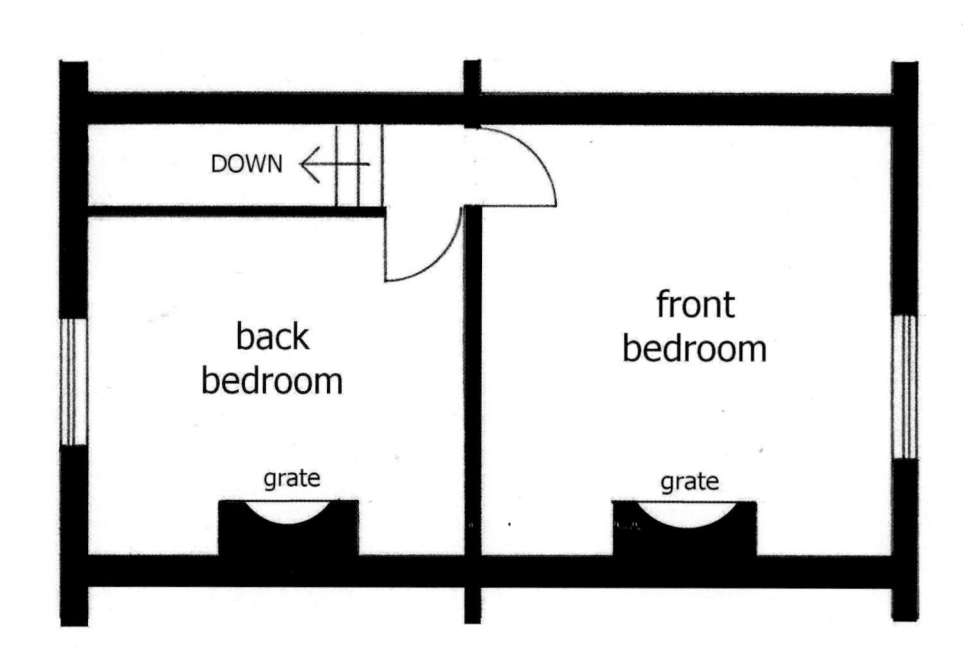

Fig 12.3
*Internal layout of 7 The Terrace, Claxby. Survey by J. Leverington and N.C. Birch, 1968.
Redrawn by Ken Redmore.*

the 1871 Census, was born in Weardale. He was also referred to in the correspondence in the pages of the Stamford Mercury at the time of concern about the 'gloomy cave of disaster', having been appointed 'more than a year ago', probably in 1870.

Later, John George Carr was appointed the mine manager. A coal miner's son from Little Hetton, Durham, he followed his father into the pit. He became a mine agent in Yorkshire but by 1881, at the age of about 41, he was manager at Claxby. A widower, he married Emma Turner, from Caistor, in 1884. After closure of the mine he moved to become manager of the West Yorkshire quarries at Caythorpe in Lincolnshire, 1882 to 1905. A prominent figure here, he was elected to the parish council in 1896,[7] and died in 1912.

In addition to the housing, the village school was also enlarged, in 1873/4. *(Fig 12.1)*[8] The peak year for numbers attending the school was 1871, with 91 children on the roll. By 1881 there were 82, falling to 57 in 1891. These figures reflect the changing fortunes of the mine and the numbers employed there.[9]

13. Accidents

The life of a nineteenth-century miner was hard. Illumination in the mine would be limited, and there were a number of injuries and fatalities, several of which have been recorded. These led to what is probably the best known quotation about the mine: 'that gloomy cave of disaster'. Table 2 *(below)* is a summary of accidents extracted from a variety of sources, from December 1869 to March 1880.[1] It does not claim to be a record of all accidents.

In December 1869 the *Stamford Mercury* reported:

> An inquest was held at the Hope Tavern, Holton Station, on the 22nd inst., on the body of a miner named John Buxton, who was accidently crushed in the mine whilst running before a truck laden with ore. The truck travelling too fast for him, he stumbled and got jammed between it and a post, and received an injury to the spine, which proved fatal the day after the accident.. .Dr Chalmers, the company's surgeon, attended the sufferer promptly, but the case was a hopeless one...Deceased has left a widow and several children, and was much respected among his fellow workmen, who raised a subscription for the widow and family.[2]

Osgodby School Log Book on 4 February 1870 recorded: Many of the children absent on account of

Fig 12.4
The mine manager's house in 2016. (Dr John Esser)

the funeral of a young man having met his death by an accident at the iron mine. Believed to be Thomas Beales. See Table 2.

Further accidents were reported in April and in May 1870:

> ...Benj. Hunt and John Coulson were seriously injured by the falling in of a large mass just as they were about to remove their waggon full of ironstone. Both were crushed down and shockingly bruised from head to foot, one of them having a boot sole torn off and the foot severely lacerated. Miner-like in foolhardiness, we understand they had worked beyond the regulation distance before shoring up.[3]

The comment in the final sentence indicates that at least this journalist had a poor opinion of the miners, but the fact that he dared to express it in print may indicate a general opinion held by people at large. A week later another accident occurred:

> On Monday another accident occurred....similar to the one reported last week a mass of about two tons weight fell in upon a miner named Geo. Belfield, who was immediately got out and carried to the village...the Doctor reports him to be in a very precarious state through internal injuries.[4]

Again, the next month, on Wednesday 18 May:

> a miner named John Southwell was at work, when upwards of a ton weight of ironstone and clay fell upon him, causing severe internal injuries, as well as breaking a thigh bone. The broken limb was

Date	Name	Result	Notes
22.12.1869	John Buxton	Died	Crushed underground by a truck laden with ore. Left a widow and several children.
01.02.1870	Thomas Beales	Died	Died from injuries received trying to stop a wagon running away down an incline.
21.03.1870	Benj. Hunt / John Coulson	Serious injury	Crushed by roof fall, caused by working beyond regulation distance before shoring up.
04.04.1870	George Belfield	Serious injury	Crushed by roof fall
18.05.1870	John Southwell	Serious injury	Crushed by roof fall, internal injuries and broken thigh.
05.08.1870	Two men, names not recorded	One broken leg, one severe bruising	Fall of stone
16.09.1870	? Baker	Fractured leg	Fall of stone
24.02.1871	Christopher Walls	Back injury and lacerations of arms	Roof fall
03.05.1871	George Ellick	Crushed spine	Roof fall. He was a 'timber shifter' living at Middle Rasen.
03.07.1871	John Dewhirst	Serious injury	Died in the County Hospital, Lincoln, 30.11.1871.
13.07.1871	John Foster	Serious injury	Fell into a calcine clamp, 'lingered in a hopeless state'.
21.07.1871	William Keal	'dropped down dead while at work' from 'a fit of apoplexy'	Lived at Binbrook, has headstone in Claxby churchyard.
21.07.1871	Unknown	Leg crushed	No reason given
10.08.1871	Richard Griffin	Died	'Died suddenly' after having been employed for a day or two. His name unknown at time of death and not identified until about two weeks later. Interred in Claxby churchyard. As a result all workmen were required to write their name, age and belongings in a register before starting work.
??.02.1872	George Walker	Injured	'by a mass of earth falling on him'. Dislocated knee and fracture of bone above. He lived in Caistor.
??.04.1872	Richard Maddison	Injured	Crushed by a fall of earth
25.04.1872	Thos. Baldock	Injured and died	Roof fall
07.05.1872			Letter by Revd Sumner calling the mine 'that gloomy cave of disaster'
07.01.1873	Unknown	Broken leg	Fall of stone
10.01.1873	Unknown	Broken leg	Fall of stone
23.03.1880	Jas. Wilkinson	Crushed	'Only a slight chance of his survival'.

Table 2
Claxby ironstone – accidents, mainly recorded in newspapers.

set by Dr Chalmers, the Mining Co's surgeon, under whose care the poor fellow is progressing favourably.[5]

John Southwell may have recovered from his injuries and returned to work. The 1871 Census records a mine employee of that name living in Market Rasen. At that time he was thirty-six, and married, having been born in Northamptonshire.

On 21 July 1871 William Keal, of Binbrook, died. His headstone is in Claxby churchyard, to the right of the gate from the road. *(Fig 13.1)*. The stone records:

In
affectionate remembrance of
William Keal
of Binbrook
who died at the Claxby Ironworks
July 21st 1871
aged 29 years
In the midst of life we are in death

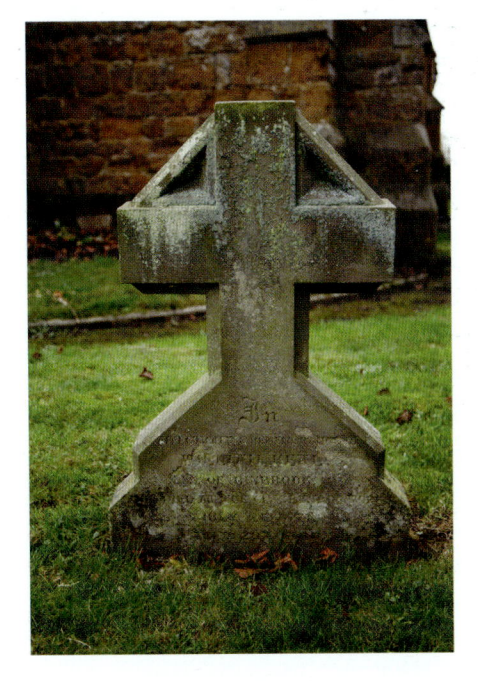

Fig 13.1 The gravestone of William Keal in Claxby churchyard. The inscription is recorded within the text. (Dr John Esser)

A William Keale (sic) is recorded in the 1871 Census as an unmarried miner, aged thirty, born at Binbrook and resident in Claxby.

On the day that William Keal died, there were other accidents being reported in the press:

> ... John Foster, a miner, whilst engaged in throwing water to slake the calcined iron clamp outside the Claxby mine, accidentally fell into the midst of the burning mass and was shockingly burnt.., but though subjected to the most humane and judicious treatment lingered only in a hopeless state. John Dewhirst, whose accident on the 3rd at the same mine we reported, was on the 12th inst. removed to the County Hospital, where only, in the doctor's opinion, such necessary care can be had of his case as may tend to prolong life, complete recovery being impossible.[6]

John Foster is recorded in the 1871 Census as living in Claxby. He was, at that time, unmarried, twenty-eight years old, having been born in Fulbeck.

Public opinion was rightly shocked, and the *Stamford Mercury* made these comments:

> The recent frequency of accidents to life and limb at the Claxby iron mine has naturally drawn public attention to the question — Is the safety of the workmen sufficiently or reasonably well cared and provided for by the company? Many of these men have already acquired a 'settlement', and any great increase of these accidents must bring about bankruptcy to their provident societies, with greater demands upon local poor rates for relief. Formerly, whenever an accident occurred the sufferers were invariably blamed for their foolhardiness in having pushed their workings too far before placing the upright and transverse timbers in position to secure their own safety; and at length the company wisely employed a staff of workmen specially to attend to the timbering. After all we are told that the intentions of the former are sure to be frustrated whenever the latter are not sharply looked after, and hence a great responsibility devolves upon the manager. From the appointment of Mr Jont. Robinson, as resident manager, more than a year ago, no serious accident occurred for many months together, which seems to be fairly attributable to his sharp looking after the men's safety.[7]

On 10 August 1871 an inquest was held at the Pelham Arms Inn

> ... on the body of a man who died suddenly at the iron mine on the day previous. Deceased had been only a day or two employed at the mine; his name was unknown, and there was nothing upon his person to aid in establishing his identity, beyond two addresses, supposed to be of lodging houses — one at Lincoln, the other at Boston. The

body was interred in Claxby Churchyard. The Manager has made it a rule for the future that every workman engaged shall write his name, age and belongings in a register at the mine before he commences work.[8]

Two points of interest arise from this. Firstly, it is not clear whether the unfortunate workman died as a result of an accident or illness, although the record that he 'died suddenly' may indicate the former. Secondly, there was clearly no complete record of employees, certainly until their first payday, when presumably there would be a need for record. It was not long, however, before his identity was discovered as Richard Griffin, a native of Boothby Graffoe.[9]

Accidents continued in 1872. In February George Walker, a miner living in Caistor, was injured. In April Richard Maddison was severely bruised and crushed by a fall of a mass of earth in the mine. Local concern had grown so much that the Curate of Nettleton wrote to the editor of the *Stamford Mercury*:

> Sir ... Another of our parishoners has succumbed to the injuries he received in that gloomy cave of disaster, the Claxby iron ore mine. Thomas Baldock aged 23 died at Lincoln Hospital yesterday. Scarcely a month passes without a serious accident to one or another of the men working at this mine. What is the cause? Is the mine subject to Government inspection? If not — why? Would that some gentleman of position and influence in the neighbourhood would act the part of the poor miner's friend, by taking up this matter and initiating some means of preventing if possible a recurrence of these distressing, heartburning accidents.
> Yours Truly
> M. H. Sumner, Nettleton, May 7th 1872[10]

Sumner's letter resulted in a speedy reply from the West Yorkshire Iron and Coal Company.

> Our attention has been drawn to a letter signed 'M. H. Sumner', which, if left unanswered might give rise to very erroneous opinions about the iron stone mines at Claxby. These mines have now been worked for 5 years and during that time have ... been very free from accidents, and when an accident has occurred it has generally been from the carelessness of the miner in not using proper precautions as to timbering, etc. well after repeated precautions, this was the case with Thos. Baldock who was injured in the 25th ult; he had hollowed out too far under the stone, (technically called 'holed') and had not taken the precaution to support the stone with timber, of which there is always plenty at hand. The stone began to fall and he got practically out of its way or he would have been killed on the spot. On this day (25th ult.) I was at the mines along with Mr Mammoth, a well known mining engineer of this district and left the inside of the mine ... not long before the accident. Leaving Mr Mammoth and our steward inside they heard of the accident and went at once to the poor man's assistance. The mine is a very dry one and a good deal safer than most mines; indeed with ordinary caution on the part of the men, accidents would be of rare occurrence. It is the wish of the directors that no expense shall be spared to render the works as safe as possible and Mr Mammoth has expressed his great satisfaction of all he saw both in and out of the mine ... .
> I am for the company
> W. H. England

A reply was prompt, again printed in the pages of the *Stamford Mercury*:

> That 'gloomy cave of disaster' the Claxby iron mine promises soon to have a list of killed and wounded equal to a hard fought field of battle. For some time past accidents have been alarmingly frequent. It was time that some notice be taken in the very way recently suggested by the Rev. M. H. Sumner of Nettleton. Mr England's reply. ... was astounding to most people, for its cool denial of facts. The company cannot be so easily exonerated. It is not the sufferers who are to blame for their foolhardiness. The company should provide sufficient men for the timbering to be in all cases done properly, and so prevent loss of time to the miners. Also watchful deputies numerous enough to ensure reasonable chance of safety to them whilst at work. The non provision of stimulants and of bandages at or near the mine in case of accidents is also to say the least a strange oversight ... . Correspondent[11]

Whilst it appears that no 'gentlemen of position and influence' befriended the miners, the miners themselves took steps to look after their own welfare. Some joined friendly societies, which gave financial support in illness, accident and death, and provided brotherhood at such times. When one such society, the Snowdrop Lodge of the Free Gardeners, held their fourth annual festival on the 17 July 1872 at Caistor

> About one third of the members, who are principally ironstone miners, marched in procession through the town with a band of music, and dinner and the usual convivialities followed at the George Inn.[12]

When a collection of £5 13s.9d. was made in Claxby Wesleyan Chapel around Christmas 1872, for the Lincoln Hospital,

> ... of this sum £5 3s 11d was contributed solely by the ironstone miners[13]

Accidents in the mine appear to have reduced dramatically after the early 1870s, or at least very few references to accidents and inquests have been found in the pages of the contemporary newspapers. There are suggestions as to why this may have been the case, some factual and others conjectural.

The first of these may have been the result of management change. It was in 1873 that the ownership at Claxby was changed from Firth and Co to the West Yorkshire Iron and Coal Co Ltd.[14] There are instances of ironstone quarries nominally owned by proprietors or directors of ironworks and this may be an example of that, the principal company taking over in 1873. Whatever the reason, it does indicate a management change.

William Firth does seem to have been an irascible fellow, unlikely to take kindly to criticism in the press. One of the enterprises he was involved with was the Bradford, Leeds and Wakefield Railway. When this was taken over by the Great Northern Railway in 1866, the year, incidentally, when the West Yorkshire Iron and Coal Co. was formed, he took a seat on the board of the GNR. His record was one of continual argument with his fellow directors, complaining that his own company was getting too few orders for the supply of coal to the GNR and criticizing the operating department. He stopped attending GNR Board meetings after January 1882 but continued to bombard staff with letters of complaint. These continued even after his resignation from the board in February 1883 and finally the GNR Board instructed their Secretary to ignore his correspondence.[15]

The production of stone from the mine fell almost by half from 1873 to 1874, and by 1875 the numbers of men employed had fallen from 250 in 1873 to less than 100. *(See Section 16. Production)*. The phases of mining also changed *(Fig 7.2)*. The central section of the mine had been worked out by 1872. Mining began on the second phase, to the north, in 1873 and to the south in 1874. The Mine Abandonment Plan[16] clearly maps all of the roadways and working areas in the north and south phases up to closure. The area of the first phase, by contrast, is only partly mapped, the words 'OLD WORKINGS' annotating blank spaces between roadways. Thus after 1872 record keeping can be said to have improved considerably. This would suggest that a combination of improved management and reduced employment and production together played a part in reducing accidents to miners.

14. *The Strike of 1872*

In 1872 there were reports of discontent at the Claxby mine.

> A report has been widely circulated that the Claxby iron miners are out on strike. Such....is not yet the fact, although there is reason to fear it may soon become so. The managers of the West Yorkshire Mining Company, by whom this mine is worked, have at length insisted upon the men riddling the ironstone before sending it out of the mine, such extra work to be done without any advance of pay, and to this the men unanimously object. The iron is about equally distributed in a stratum of hard rock, and in loose clayey soil above and below it, which it is indispensable to remove. The Company prefer the rocky metal on account of its being easier of carriage and less trouble to smelt....at their distant furnaces; whilst hitherto it has been their practice to first clamp and burn the loose or earthy metal upon the spot. Old and experienced miners assert that to trample under foot and leave in the mine all that would pass through the riddle would be a sinful waste of the finest metal. It is hoped that this dispute may at once be amicably arranged, since, owing to the character of the workings, liable at any time to cave in, and still more so if disused for a few days only, it is hard to determine which side would suffer most through a cessation of work.

> ... we have been requested by the foreman of the ... mine at Claxby to say that the miners are

required to leave the fine dirt and clay only in the mine. The small stone, free from dirt is acceptable, and that no 'sinful waste' of metal could accrue from the Company's insisting upon its being riddled.

Pending some fresh arrangements the miners.... have ceased work for the present.[1]

There is no report of the outcome of this dispute. Clearly the men were, on the face of it, angry that they were required to dig out material for which the Company was not going to pay them. This is very relevant when the men were paid piecework rates per ton of ore leaving the mine. Waste material was not, presumably, paid for. From the Company's point of view, calcining could be seen as delaying delivery, and hence payment, as well as requiring the importation of coal, adding to their costs.

15. 1871 Census

An analysis of the 1871 Census returns provide a range of interesting statistics. *(See Table 3)*. Limited to a study of the returns from Normanby-le-Wold, Middle Rasen, Nettleton and Claxby, they do not record all the miners employed who lived in other nearby parishes. However, the figures do total eighty-five men. Two years later it was said:

> The West Yorkshire Iron and Coal Mine Company are steadily increasing the number of their hands at the Claxby ironstone mine. About 250 men are now there employed.[1]

Although this figure is likely to have been less at the Census date, it may be taken as a good representative sample for statistical purposes.

Of the eighty-five, forty-six, or 54%, were born in Lincolnshire. As this was the first underground mine in the county this demonstrates that local men were quick to seize the opportunity this new form of employment offered. No doubt men used to hard physical work in agriculture would soon adapt to this unfamiliar environment, although it must have made a sharp contrast to work out of the fresh air.

The other 46% were born in the other eighteen counties recorded in their Census return. Some of these were in areas where mining was common, although not always for iron ore. Such counties were Cornwall, Derbyshire, Devon, Durham, Gloucestershire, Nottinghamshire, Shropshire, Staffordshire and Yorkshire. Some had probably travelled great distances to work at Claxby. The effect of the influx of these strangers with, in some cases accents difficult to understand, can only be imagined in rural Lincolnshire. There was, no doubt, a wider choice of potential marriage partners for local people. Several were recorded as lodgers, and this would enable residents with spare rooms to enhance their income.

The age range of the miners was from twelve to sixty-seven, the average being 31.5 years. This, too, probably reflects the hard physical nature of the work. Eight of them, 9%, were boys aged between twelve and seventeen. Two of these, aged thirteen and sixteen, were employed as drivers. Their task would be less arduous physically, and may indicate that such young people worked with pit ponies to bring ore out and return empty wagons to the working faces.

Of the forty-four whose occupations were noted, thirty-five, 79%, were miners and four were labourers. These figures are not surprising. Levels of management are represented by one deputy, and the mine agent. One other skilled man was an engine fitter. One is recorded as a miner and Primitive local preacher. This perhaps demonstrates that not all miners were hard drinking, as had been alleged in 1927.[2] Indeed, the working classes nationwide had embraced Methodism, and miners were no exception.

The table also gives an indication of the skills that were brought into what was an area with formerly no local mining skills. As already noted, there are men from mining counties such as Cornwall, Derbyshire, Durham, Nottinghamshire, Staffordshire and Yorkshire. Jonathan Robinson, the mine agent, or manager, was born in Weardale, County Durham.

Table 3
Mine employees – 1871 Census
*indicates that the person was a lodger

Name	Married/Unmarried	Age	Place of Birth
A. Normanby le Wold			
Thomas Tole*	U	25	Dunton, Beds
John Hill*	U	32	Tavistock, Devon
William Houghton*	U	20	Steeping, Lincs
George Bellhouse	M	39	Sudbrooke, Lincs
Richard Hill	U	24	South Kelsey, Lincs
B. Middle Rasen			
John Southwell	M	36	Northamptonshire
Charles Bellamy	M	29	Middle Rasen, Lincs
C. Nettleton			
George Evratt	U	29	Middle Rasen, Lincs
John Lincoln*	U	25	Tibits Hall, Norfolk
John Robinson	M	57	Rothwell, Lincs
Francis Lacey*	M	31	Grasby, Lincs
Charles Musk*	U	26	Edall, Derbys
John Smith*	U	26	Staveley, Derbys
David Skelton*	U	40	Caistor, Lincs
George Parker	M	23	Nettleton
Samuel Frow	M	36	Nettleton
William Smith	M	25	On board ship
George Padley	M	27	Mareham le Fen, Lincs
George Bilton	U	14	Caistor, Lincs
Jesse Wellebourne	M	35	Legbourne, Lincs
John Balderson	M	50	Caistor, Lincs
Joseph Balderson	U	12	Nettleton
James Temple*	U	27	Coningsby, Lincs
Samuel Temple*	U	17	Coningsby, Lincs
James Lilley*	U	22	Coningsby, Lincs
William Jackling	U	26	Nettleton
William Sturdy*	?	30	Pickering, Yorks
William Fox	U	15	Nettleton
Charles Kidd	M	31	Thornag(?), Norfolk
William Appleyard	M	42	Tattershall, Lincs
David Faith	M	25	Whorlton, Yorks

Robert E. Osgerby	U	13	North Kelsey, Lincs
George Stordy*	U	26	Pickering, Yorks
Edward Hand	M	28	Nettleton
John Baldock	M	26	Nettleton
William Green*	U	36	Seatonthorpe(?), Yorks
Thomas Clark*	M	37	Ryehill, Yorks
George Cowley	M	31	Bothamsall, Notts
Charles Hand	M	30	Nettleton
Jeffery Dinsdale	M	27	Hose(?), Yorks
Charles Pinder	M	32	Kirton, Lincs

Name	Married/Unmarried	Age	Place of Birth	Occupation
D. Claxby				
John Baxter	U	13	Kirton	Driver in mines
Edward Baxter	M	34	Kirton	Miner
David Hubbart	U	35	Hagworthingham	Miner
Philip Markham	U	24	Grasby	Miner
John Markham	U	34	Grasby	Miner
William Keale	U	30	Binbrook	Miner
Thomas Saunby	M	30	Claxby	Butcher and miner
Joseph Paynel	W	50	Gloucestershire	Deputy in mines
Job Lowe	M	51	S. Staffs	Miner
George Baker	U	38	Sausthorpe	Ironstone labourer
Charles Mower	U	28	Utterby	Ironstone labourer
John Robinson	M	33	Claxby	Labourer in iron works
William Jackson	U	35	Langtoft	Labourer in iron mines
Richard Bowman	M	42	Leeds, Yorks	Engine fitter
John Bowman	U	20	Hull, Yorks	Miner
George Marshall	U	24	Claxby	Miner
Benjamin Booth	U	30	Boston	Miner
William Godbold	U	27	Littleport, Cambs	Ironstone miner
George Breckley	U	27	Edinburgh	Ironstone miner
Thomas Basson	U	30	Lynn, Norfolk	Ironstone miner
Tom Lincoln	U	25	Lynn, Norfolk	Ironstone miner
Jonathan Robinson	M	49	Weardale, Durham	Mine agent
Thomas Hitchcock	M	50	Bromsgrove	Miner
Henry Bellamy	M	29	Middle Rasen	Miner

John Saley	M	38	Wedsbro(?), Staffs	Miner
Ted Hanson	U	17	Leicester	Miner
William Jenkinson	M	36	Bradford, Yorks	Miner
James Watson	M	36	Wisbech	Miner
John Foxley	M	66	Warwicks	Ironstone miner
William Lacey	U	67	Walesby, Lincs	Miner
Joseph Selby	M	43	South Kelsey	Ironstone miner
William Peniston	M	29	Lincs	Miner
John Stephenson	U	16	Burringham, Lincs	Driver in mines
Thomas Blewitt	U	22	Cornwall	Miner
John Foster	U	28	Fulbeck, Lincs	Miner
John Coulbeck	U	37	Cambridge	Miner
William Whiting	M	44	Gloucester	Miner
James Baldock	M	49	Barkwith, Lincs	Miner
Ezekial Hayward	M	32	Staffs	Ironstone miner
Edward Palmer	M	30	Shropshire	Miner
William Birchnall	M	35	Yorkshire	Miner
John Rimington	W	27	Durham	Miner
William Hart	M	26	York	Miner
Nathan Palmer	M	32	Kelby(?), Yorks	Miner and Primitive local preacher

16. Production

The expected level of production stated at the time the mine opened was twenty wagonloads a day.[1] Using the figures for converting wagon loads to tonnage set out above *(Section 10, Railway Siding and Incline)*, this equates to around 172 tons a day or *c.*50,000 tons per year. Figures in Table 4 below show that this figure was reached or exceeded only in the years 1871 to 1873.

Production figures from the mine throughout its life are set out in Table 4 and Fig 16.1 below.[2] This shows that almost 500,000 tons of ironstone were taken, along with almost 20,000 tons of sand and ten tons of limestone. The peak years were from 1868 to mid 1877, after which ironstone production fell dramatically. In 1879 and in 1881 there was no ironstone mined at all for at least half the year. Between 1876 and 1885 there were repeated requests to Lord Yarborough for a reduction in royalties and rent because of a bad state of trade.[3] In 1875 it was reported that:

> The greater facility with which the West Yorkshire Iron and Coal Company are able to procure the Greetwell Ironstone has (for a time it would seem) caused a very extended diminution of their operations at the Claxby iron mine, wherat little has been doing for some months past.[4]

The Greetwell Ironstone Mines were owned by the Mid Lincolnshire Ironstone Company.[5] If the West Yorkshire Iron and Coal Co were 'procuring' ironstone from the former they must have been buying it and at a cost less than they were able to produce it at their own Claxby Mine.

Two years later, in 1877, there was a report of a depression which included a cessation of work in the mine.[6] Production fell dramatically as Table 4 shows. In February 1882 a further report stated:

> Ironstone operations at Claxby have been almost nil for some time past, but now it is said that there will soon be a considerable increase in the number of men employed.[7]

Production did increase for a short period but in 1885 the mine closed.

Although the taking of limestone and chalk were specifically mentioned in the lease of 1866 *(see Section 6. In the Beginning)*, no mention was made of sand although the rights to work other unspecified minerals were retained by the Yarborough estate. However, sand was also a significant product, for which demand increased in the final years.

Table 4
Ironstone, sand and limestone taken, Claxby mine, 1868–1884

Year	Ironstone (tons)	Sand (tons)	Limestone (tons)	Notes
1868	13,372	171	0	a
1869	31,124	321	0	
1870	42,687	330	0	
1871	50,630	874	0	
1872	62,652	1,323	0	
1873	69,445	1,334	0	
1874	39,372	1,616	0	
1875	33,791	1,339	0	
1876	45,653	880	10	b
1877	15,951	995	0	c
1878	16,024	972	0	
1879	322	0	0	d
1880	17,824	1,690	0	
1881	6,416	1,100	0	e
1882	10,773	2,973	0	
1883	14,386	1,494	0	
1884	7,320	1,590	0	f
1885	0	377	0	g
TOTALS	477,742	19,379	10	

Notes
a Weighed production started from 1 June 1868. In addition to this figure was an allowance for 1100 tons from the outcrop previous to ironstone being weighed.
b 1876 was also the only year in which there is a record of limestone being produced.
c The first half year's production of ironstone was 14,190 tons. The second half saw a dramatic fall to only 1,761 tons.
d No ironstone was taken in the first half year.
e No ironstone was taken in the second half year.
f The last year that ironstone was taken
g Mine closes

In its most prosperous times the mine was worked night and day with three shifts of eight hours each.[8] In 1873, the year of peak production, 69,445 tons, about 250 men were employed.[9] Two years later, with almost 50% loss in production, numbers had fallen to under 100.[10]

17. Closure and After

After the mine closed there appeared to be little urgency to destroy all traces. The 1888 OS survey, *(Fig 9.1)*, showed that the rails both for the mine and the incline remained in place. By the time of the 1905 survey all rails had gone but earthworks and some buildings remained. From time to time since then buildings and structures have gone, but slowly. The stables were standing as a roofless structure in 1905; the winding drum was demolished in 1934; the ventilation shaft was infilled in 1955; and the powder house finally demolished in the early twenty-first century. However, the earthworks remain substantially as depicted on the early OS maps.

The reason for this is partly because the site is away from public roads with no public access. There is little opportunity for trespass and vandalism. Furthermore, the steep hillsides will have always been used for grazing animals. They are never likely to under threat from ploughing and conversion to arable land.

During the Second World War Lysaghts, who owned the Nettleton Top mine, purchased the mineral rights of 37 acres of land to the south. Their intention was to explore the possibilities for the exploitation of the ironstone bed to the east of the former Claxby Mine right up to Caistor High Street. Nine boreholes were proposed.[1] The area was given as approximately 478 acres, only slightly larger in area than the surviving lease for the Claxby Mine. *(See Section 6. In the Beginning)*. They were hoping to prove workable reserves of about 7 million tons.

The boring was carried out in November 1942. In the event only six holes were driven. The quality of the stone was very poor and large faults with throws of up

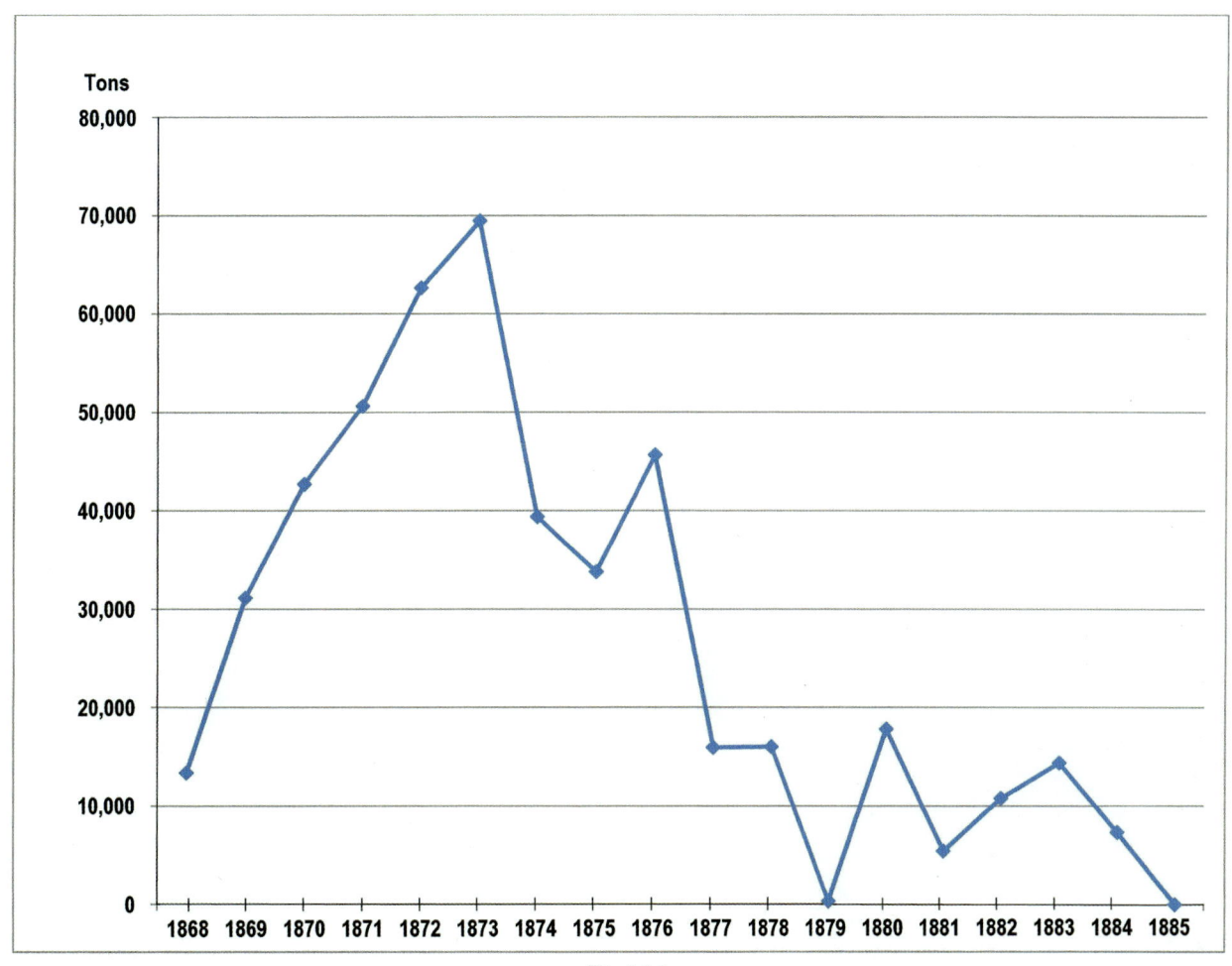

Fig 16.1
Claxby mine: Ironstone production, 1868–1885 (Ken Redmore)

to 20 feet would be encountered. Hence the decision was made not to proceed further.

Claxby mine was closed at a time when the demand for iron was fluctuating badly. However, the West Yorkshire Iron and Coal Co were working to the east of Normanby Road and if the quality of the stone was deteriorating here they would have known this. If so, this may have been a determining factor in abandoning mining here in 1885.

During the Second World War the Claxby hillsides, to the north and south of the village, were used for Army battlefield training. Live ammunition was used and trenches dug.[2] Despite this, little damage appears to have been done to the mine remains. The exception may be the wall below the tipping dock, supporting the end of the embankment. Other original walls survive undamaged but this one is largely demolished with some original blocks in situ but others scattered nearby. *(Fig 9.6).*

18. Claxby Parish Church

In 1870 and 1871 the parish church of St Mary in Claxby was substantially rebuilt. The previous building must have been in a poor state for some time as it was reported in 1871:[1]

> The dilapidated condition of the church here having become a reproach the Rev. S. W. Andrews (then Curate, and now the Rector) some years ago made an attempt to raise funds for its restoration. This, however, was frustrated chiefly through the late incumbent being opposed to the scheme, but almost immediately on his demise the good work was taken in hand, and brought to a successful issue.

The old church was closed in March 1870 and the new, to the design of the Louth architect James Fowler, opened in June 1871. The same report recorded the cost as being £1,600 and that the Earl of Yarborough, who owned most of the parish, had given all the new stone and sand required for the building. He also gave a donation of £350. *(Fig 3.8)*.

The church was built of ironstone *(see Section 3. Geology)*, but the source of that stone is not recorded. As with most local building of that period the materials would be found nearby and the source must have been somewhere along the ironstone outcrop on the hillside above the village. A comparison of weathered outcrops of stone from the hillside with the stone of the church shows that this was the case.

The Claxby ironstone mine was working at that time and, as referred to earlier, the land on and under the mine was leased from the Yarborough Estate. So, did the stone come from the mine or from another source? The latter is likely to have been the case. The OS maps of 1888 and 1906 show a quarry some 150m south of the southern boundary of the surface leased area of the mine.[2] On the former map this is annotated as 'Ironstone Pit'. *(Fig 18.1)*. Furthermore, a narrow terrace was created, visible on the ground as well as shown on the map, carrying a roadway from the mine site, to the north of the parish boundary. *(Fig 18.2)*.

If the stone was not from the mine but from another place on the Yarborough estate, then this is the likely source. The only road access to the stone outcrop in 1870 was via the mine with its road link to Normanby Road. The quarry, therefore, would have had this road access through the mine site.

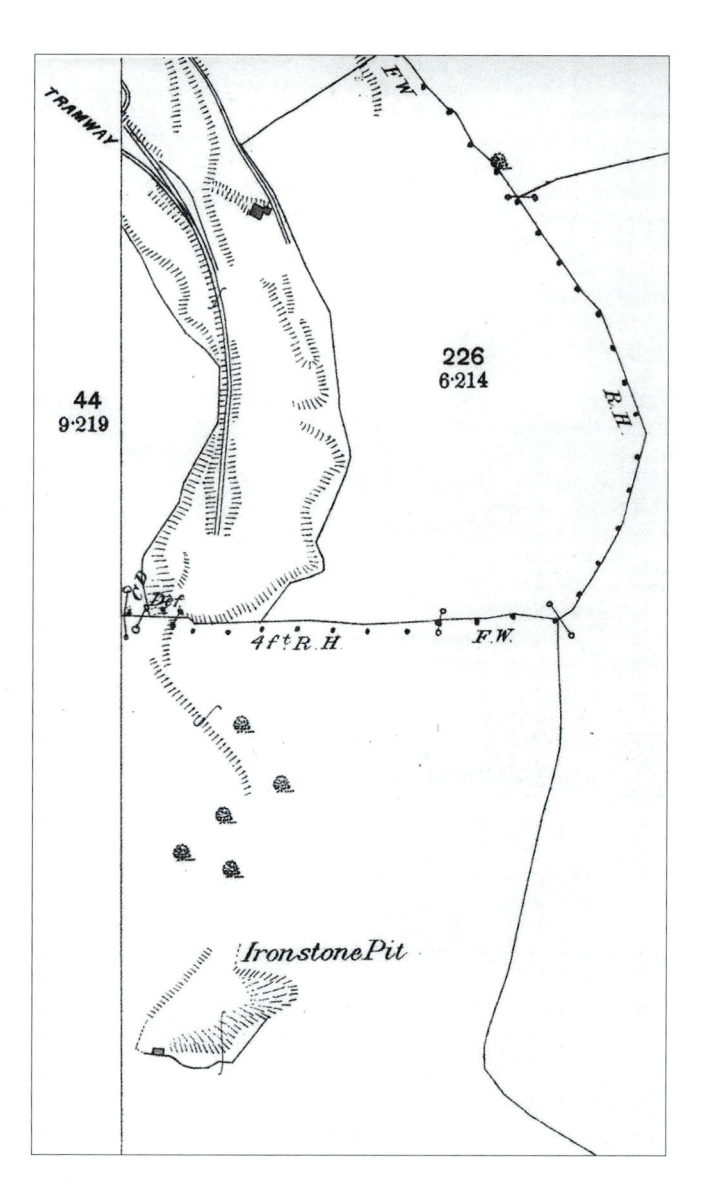

Fig 18.1. (Above)
The Ironstone Pit, shown on the 1888 OS map. Note the line of slope symbols between the south end of the mine at the parish boundary and the centre of the five bush symbols half way to the quarry site. This indicates the route of a former access roadway running on a hillside terrace to the quarry.
(Ordnance Survey)

Fig 18.2. (Left)
The location of the ironstone pit is identified by the trees in this view from the north. The terrace for the former access road runs left to right to the edge of the photograph where it turns towards the camera.
(Dr John Esser)

NETTLETON TOP MINE

19. Early Proposals

The terms Top and Bottom mines are used for clarity. However, until the Bottom Mine was first considered, Top Mine was known simply as Nettleton Mine.

There is evidence of a series of investigations into the opening of a mine at Nettleton Top from 1868 up to work finally beginning in 1928. In 1868 W. J. Roseby negotiated with Thos. John Dixon of Holton-le-Moor for a lease to mine ironstone[1]. Nothing came of this.

In March 1905 the *Hull Daily Mail* reported that the Lincoln Iron Firm [presumably the Mid Lincolnshire Ironstone Company Ltd] 'who were under negotiations for the purchase of certain land at Nettleton, have sent down some men to dig for samples of the iron ore, and to ascertain whether it is in a sufficiently

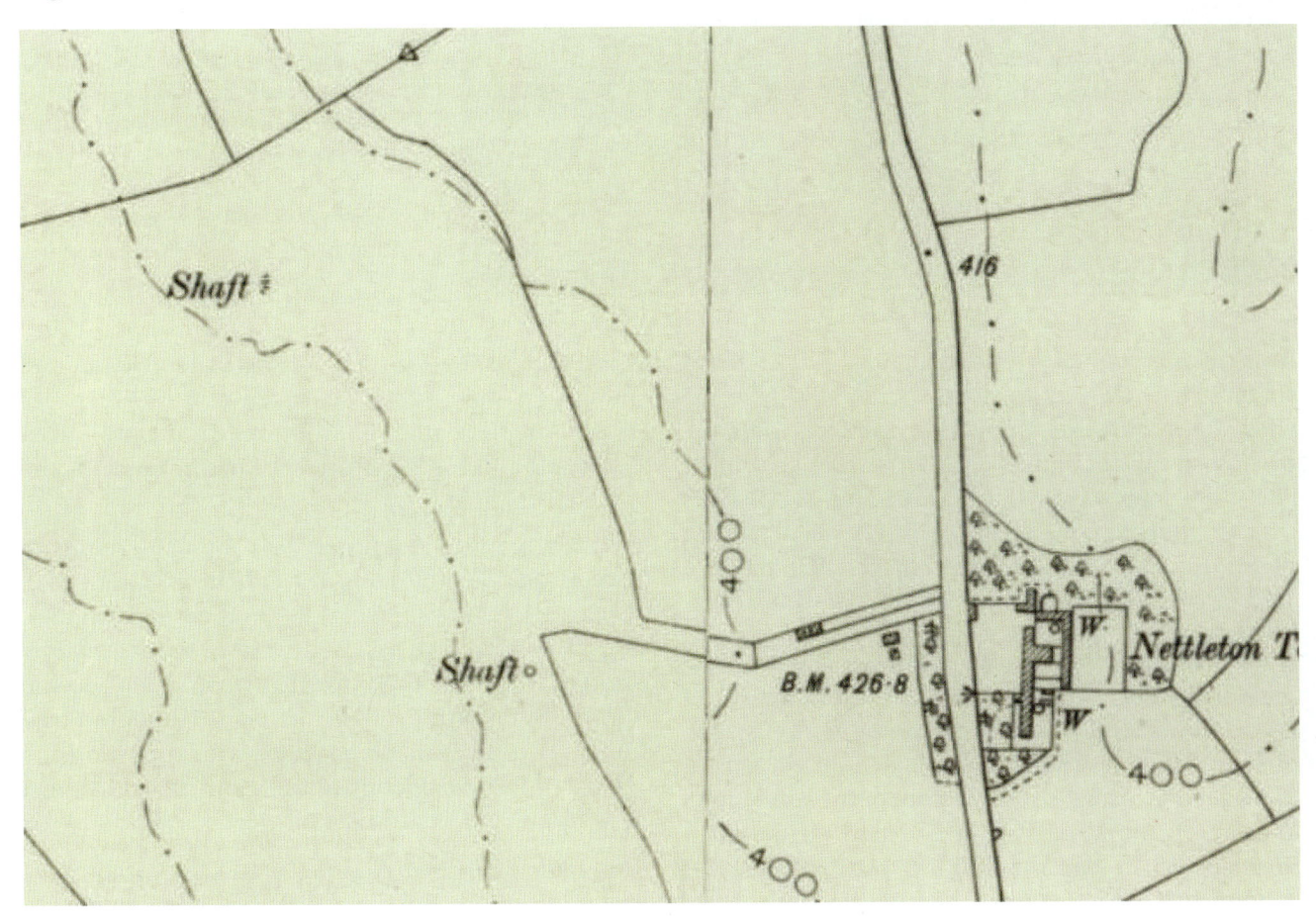

Fig 19.1.
The trial holes as shown on the 1907 OS map. Extract from the OS Six Inch to One Mile maps, XXXVII NE and XXXVIII NW. (Ordnance Survey)

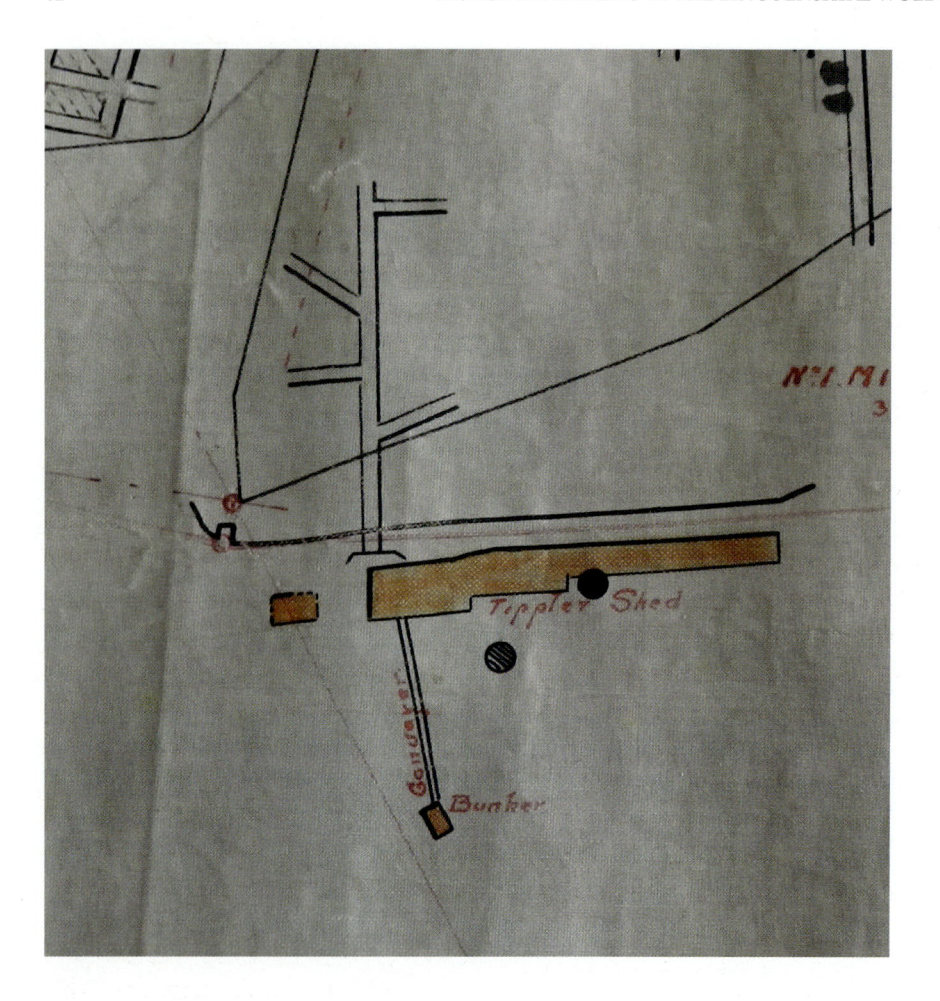

*Fig 19.2.
A drift entrance to a tunnel isolated from the rest of the mine, behind the Tippler Shed, the building in the centre. This may be the evidence for the trial hole of 1905, dug here on the outcrop line to prove the quality of the stone. The black dot is the location of the hole as plotted by the mine surveyor. The hatched dot is the location of a 1916 trial hole. (Extract from a plan of Nettleton Mine, Scunthorpe Steelworks archive, copy held by Author)*

large quantity to be worth digging for'.[2] The 1907 OS six inch map[3] shows two shafts on the hillside to the west of Nettleton Top, both at the ironstone outcrop. Because of this they are likely to have been horizontal drifts. The map was revised in 1905 and, as no shafts here are shown on the First Editions of the map, they may be the result of the digging referred to in the *Hull Daily Mail*. (Fig 19.1).

A plan of the area between Nettleton Top and the present day A46 at Holton le Moor, dated March 29 1906,[4] shows a railway siding running for a distance of some 1.5 miles from the south side of Holton-le-Moor level crossing east to the foot of the scarp slope and then turning north to end just below the most northerly of the two shafts shown on the OS maps. A tipping dock was shown near to the end of the siding so it was anticipated that stone from the mine would be brought out and tipped straight into railway wagons. This is very similar to the operation of the Mid Lincolnshire Company at their Greetwell mines. The plan is signed by B. Ramsden who was manager of the Mid Lincolnshire Ironstone Company Ltd at Greetwell and his signature appears on many of the mine plans there.[5]

British Geological Survey records show the results of six vertical trial holes dug at Nettleton in June 1906.[6] A plan also exists showing the location of trial holes dug in fields to the east and west of the Normanby Road at Nettleton Top into what would later become Nettleton Top Mine.[7] There are eight numbered trial holes, all vertical shafts, together with the two drifts referred to above, identified as 'A' and 'B', and shown as 'Mid Lincoln Trial Holes' of 1906.

This same plan then goes on to add the locations of an additional seven trial holes over the same area, attributed to John Lysaghts in 1916, with a further three dated 1929. With the exception of the latter, which were dug at the time that work on opening up the mine

Fig 20.1.
Work begins in 1929 to dig the Nettleton Top mine. The men are said to be, left to right, Harry Plaskitt, John Arthur Shaw, Jim Shacklock, Eddie Ryder. (Author's collection)

began, they do show that there was renewed interest in mining here for much of the early twentieth century.

Trial holes were commonly infilled after investigation, but the location of the two outcrop drifts is of interest. Neither survived to be used as main entrances to the mine. That to the north may have been used for ventilation and access as production moved northwards. An entrance here is shown on mine maps but this may be coincidence. The area around it formed part of the remoulding and restoration of the hillside following ironstone quarrying along the outcrop in the period 1957 to 1959, so no evidence survives.

The southern drift, Drift No 1, opened onto what became the platform created for the tipping stage, just north of the No 1 Main Entrance. A mine map of about 1949 shows a drift entrance here, behind the tippler shed, with side branches, isolated from the rest of the mine underground. *(Fig 19.2)*. This plan also shows the sites of two of the earlier investigations. One, shown as a black dot, is one of the Mid Lincolnshire trials identified as 'B' on the trial hole map. The second, hatched, is one for John Lysaght Ltd in 1916. The isolated drift may be evidence of the 1905 investigation that was carried out. Examination of the OS map shows that their survey plot of the trial hole was closer to the isolated drift entrance rather than the location of the dot as plotted by the Nettleton Mines surveyor. This entrance has also now been lost with the alterations to the mines yard required for the opening of the Nettleton Bottom Mine.

20. In the Beginning

It was the Mid-Lincolnshire Ironstone Co Ltd[1] who dug and worked the Nettleton Mine. At this time they had a close relationship with John Lysaght and Co at Scunthorpe. Lysaghts obtained control of the Mid-Lincolnshire Company in 1934, taking them over in 1944. In 1930 Mid-Lincolnshire were reporting on progress at Nettleton to Lysaghts at Scunthorpe, so there must have been a very close relationship at that time.

Lysaghts' head office was at Newport, South Wales. Their Scunthorpe steel works, on Normanby Road, were built in 1910. Even after changes of ownership the works were always known locally as Lysaghts. Closed in 1982, the site has since been redeveloped.

Fig 20.2. (Top)
A view from above the first adit with stone being tipped to form the pit bank, 1929.
(Author's collection)

Fig 20.3. (Bottom)
The pit bank almost complete. Ironstone is being removed from the outcrop on the hillside, probably because of problems with instability.
(Author's collection)

Work began on digging Nettleton Top Mine on 18 March 1929[2] and continued without interruption throughout the year. *(Figs 20.1 and 20.2)*. A suitable line was projected running due east, through the centre of the leased area, for the benefit of underground haulage. The entrance being dug became the No 1 Main Entrance. At this point the ironstone outcrop was bared, that is, exposed and dug into, not only to start mining operations but also to make a pit bank, the name given to the area immediately outside a mine where the stone comes to the surface and is processed. As at Claxby mine in 1868, a flat area had to be created on what was a steep hillside. Here the pit bank was large enough to provide for 'tub standage', that is, wagons full of stone coming out of the drift as well as empty ones waiting to go back in, for an output of 3,000 tons per week. It also provided space for the tubs to be emptied using a tippler. *(Fig 20.3)*.

The drift entrance as constructed at this time was seven feet high by eight feet wide, from an Ordnance level of 320 feet. Because of geological faults the ironstone seam was rising quickly from this point, so the entrance level of the drift was raised by a further five feet.

By 31 December 1929 the drift had been driven 651 feet into the hillside, all at a size of nine feet by nine feet, and some 2,900 tons of iron ore extracted. A large proportion of this stone had been tipped to form the pit bank but about 1,000 tons remained by the pit mouth. When in operation it was estimated that production would be 100 to 120 tons a day with a double shift. Samples proved that the iron content varied between 28.4% and 29.4%. The ironstone bed was about 14 feet thick, some 10 feet of which was good stone.

The method of working was to be 'bord and pillar', also known as 'pillar and stall', the same method as at Claxby mine beforehand. Stone was removed on a grid system ('stalls'), leaving 'pillars' of stone between to support the ground above. Some stone would also be left in the roof to protect the tunnels. This removed about 34% of the stone in any given area. The pillars would subsequently be removed leaving the ground above to settle into the void. This system ensured that up to around 85% of stone could be taken out of the mine. Opencast quarrying, by contrast, took away 100% of the stone.

The stone was soft, requiring little explosive to be used. Haulage out of the mine would be easy, as the gradient fell towards the drift in favour of the loaded wagons. The amount of timber being used was very high, however. This was because of the support needed for the roof as well as the difficulty they had in stabilising the hillside. The use of steel hoops for the haulage roads was recommended, supporting timber 'lagging', the horizontal roof supports between the hoops. Steel hoops were specified because timber would need regular replacement. This became the norm for both Nettleton Top and Bottom Mines. *(Figs 21.2 and 21.4)*.

Finally, the report set out the expenditure incurred for the year ending December 1929 as a total of £1,883.

A report dated 23 August 1930, again by the Mid-Lincolnshire Iron Co Ltd,[3] concerned the considerable amount of timber needed to keep the drift safe. This was due to the unstable nature of the ground, together with the need to raise the floor levels because of the rise of the seam. Additional use of steel arches was recommended, for a total of 240 feet, on the main haulage road.

Another report, dated 27 March 1931, was addressed to John Lysaght Ltd at Scunthorpe and initialled TS at the end. This indicates that the other reports on development may well have been made to Lysaghts by the same author. The initials TS will be those of Thomas Stephenson, who was the first mine manager.[4]

Work had continued underground until the middle of 1930 when all labour except safety men was stopped and no further work was done at the face. By that time the face was 550 feet from the drift mouth. Two hundred and thirty feet of the underground haulage road had been supported with 135 steel arches with a further 37 arches being installed. Three-foot wide refuge holes had been provided at 10 yard intervals. Refuge holes were for miners to use if a train of wagons was approaching. Limited clearance in tunnels was a regular cause of accidents in mines. *(Fig 24.3)*. Starting in the last week of October 1930 a retaining wall and drift mouth had been built. Expenditure for the year ending 31 December 1930 had been £2,467.

By 1931 the mine was ready to go into production, but it did not because of the national economic depression at that time. It was in October 1934 when mining started in earnest, at a time when economic recovery was underway. The local press reported in September that 'active production was to start within the next month'.[5]

The second entrance into the mine, North No 1 Main, was opened up in 1937.[6] The early production would be entirely from the excavation of the main and secondary access tunnels. Once this infrastructure was in place, districts within the mine could be selected for robbing. Mapped areas with dates for the robbing having taken place, and thus those areas mined out, give the earliest dates of 1936 inside the main entrance and 1938 just inside North No 1 Main.[7]

In 1944 *Mine & Quarry Engineering* reported:[8]

> At Claxby, near to Caistor, is a deposit of some importance. This ironstone is at the base of the Tealby Clay and immediately above the Spilsby Sandstone (Lower Cretaceous). There is a maximum thickness of 14 ft., but only the lower part, about 6 ft. 6 in., is worked. The ore is mainly siliceous. One mine is working the Claxby ironstone at Nettleton. At Nettleton, in 1938, there were 97 men underground. Two main haulage adits have been driven into the hillside, and there is a ventilation shaft on the hilltop. The method of working is pillar and stall and the last stages of the pillars are removed by slicing, giving 85 per cent. recovery. Pneumatic picks are used, and also some hand drilling is done. Loading is by hand. Horses are used for auxiliary haulage and a Ruston diesel locomotive for main haulage. Ore is carried by aerial ropeway to Holton le Moor station, a distance of 1¼ miles.

21. Underground

There were two main drift entrances into Top Mine. The first to be dug, known as Drift No 1, ran eastwards while the other, known as Drift No 2, ran to the north east.[1] From these it was worked on a 'pillar and stall' basis, the pillars subsequently robbed. From the main roadways a series of working areas, or districts, were created by working in a grid system with main roadways at intervals of around 700 to 800 feet. The measurement was also varied below this in places, limited by the exterior shape of the mine, determined by the ironstone outcrop on the adjacent hillsides, together with the need to leave pillars to support the buildings at Nettleton Top and the road between Nettleton and Normanby le Wold. *(Fig 21.1)*.

The main roadways were semi-circular in section, supported by steel hoops with timber backing between. The height in the centre was around nine feet, as was the width at floor level. The tramway, mostly single track underground, was laid off-centre, allowing men to stand or walk in safety and avoid passing trains. *(Fig 21.2)*. A plan of the mine of 1941 shows a separate drift entrance to the south of No 1, to the rear of the locomotive shed, *(Fig 22.3)*, which could be used by men walking in and out of the mine away from the double line of rails in Drift No 1. *(Fig 21.3)*.

Locomotives were used underground from the beginning to bring trains of loaded tubs out of the mine and empty tubs back in. Details of the locomotives and rolling stock used are in *Section 30. Locomotives and Rolling Stock*. Locomotives were used in the main haulage roads with tubs being transferred to and from the working faces with the use of horses. *(Fig 21.4)*. Horses were always used in Top Mine. The last two were retired in 1962.[2] *(Fig 31.2)*. In an emergency, especially if the lighting failed, men were instructed, if they could, to hold on to a horse's tail to escape, as the horses knew their way out in the dark.[3]

It was very dark underground. Lighting was mainly by carbide lamps, also known as acetylene lamps, carried by the miner, and a helmet lamp.[4] The lamp would be hung on a convenient post by the miner when working. *(Figs 21.4 and 21.5)*. Developed in the 1890s they were quickly adopted for use in mines, especially ironstone mines where there was little risk of explosion.[5] Easy to use and maintain, a miner would carry spare water and carbide pellets to refuel the lamp as needed.

The traditional mine safety lamp, often referred to as the Davy Lamp after its inventor, was not used at Nettleton as it was a gas free mine.[6] However, by law, mines deputies had to carry a safety lamp when carrying out their inspections. They would be the first men into the mine every day in their role of protecting the safety of the underground workers.

In the early years candles were also used, supplied by the management with the costs deducted from wages. In 1935 R. Stephenson had 4d (1.6p) deducted for candles.[7]

In 1954 miners used a pneumatic pick to get the ore down from where it was shovelled into a tub (a mine wagon), which held up to one ton in weight.[8] When full it would be pushed out of the way and replaced from a short shunt siding with an empty tub. The procedure was to cut a hole at the bottom of the face to a size of about six by eight feet. Temporary rails would be laid in the hole to enable a tub to be placed in it. The hole was then widened: the stone, as far as possible, being removed from over the tub so that it fell into it. This reduced the amount of stone that had to be shovelled from where it had fallen on the floor of the opening.

As the stone was being removed the roof would be tapped regularly with a pick handle. If it sounded solid it was safe to continue to work. A deputy responsible for that part of the mine would inspect the roof in the same way before the first shift went underground and then once or twice during the shift.

The hardness of the stone being worked determined how much stone could be got in a shift, but 12 to 15 tons a day was the norm. A horse driver, known as a 'trammer', would collect the loaded wagons and take them to a siding where a locomotive could collect them to take them out of the mine. When robbing old workings, that is, taking the pillars out from between the stalls, up to 20 tons a day was possible. The men would be sure to tell the trammer that extra tubs would be needed. The stone would be easier to work because the stalls had already been excavated.

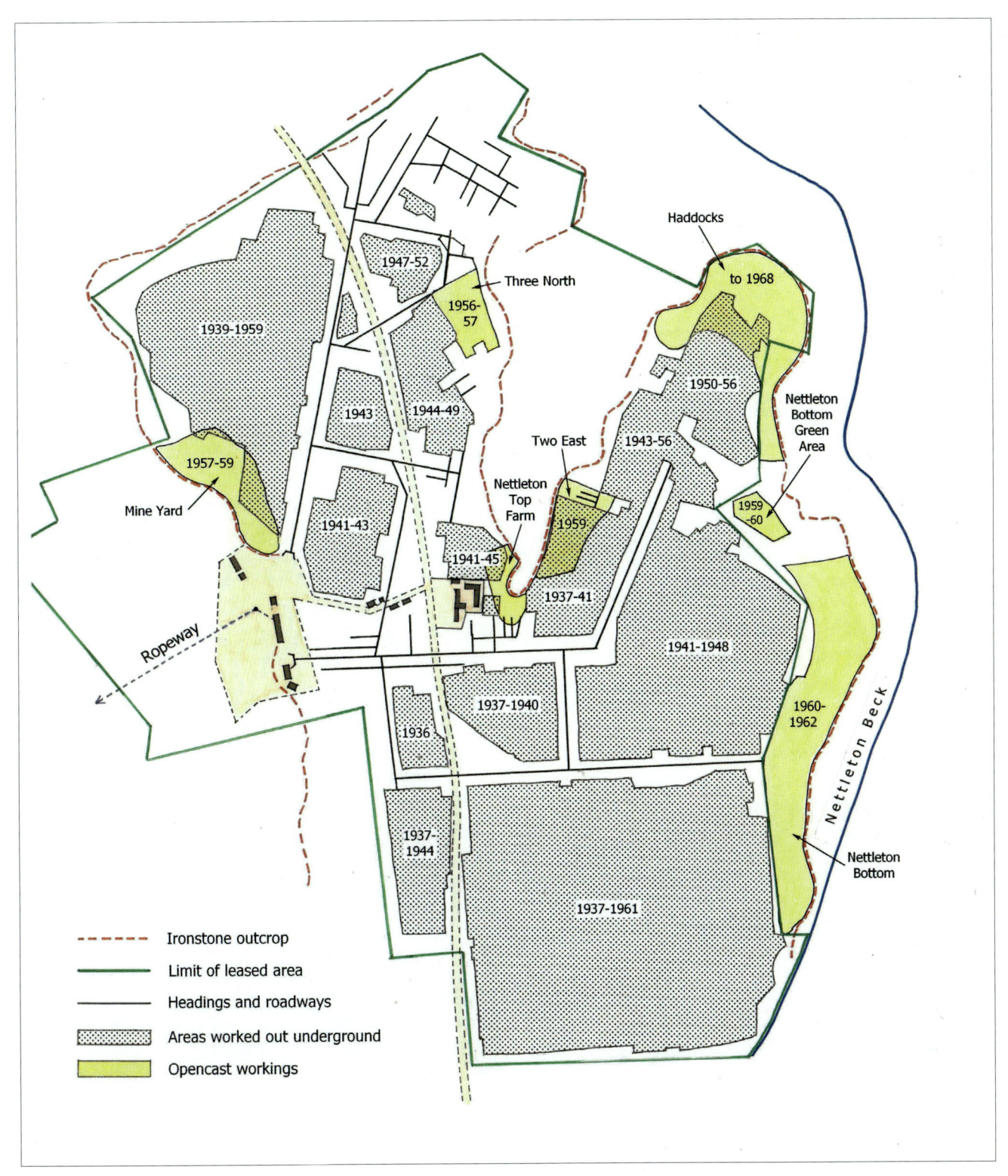

Fig 21.1.
Nettleton Top Mine, underground layout. Note that much of the open cast along the eastern edge of the mine took place after the new lease for the land of Bottom Mine had been agreed. (Drawn by Ken Redmore)

Fig 21.2. A loaded train being taken out of Top Mine, taken in the late 1930s. The train is turning on to the main roadway, along which a double line of rails is laid. In the side roadways the second line was not laid, allowing space for men to walk and stand away from passing trains. This is a posed photograph as the man behind the loaded tub is standing in a very restricted space. (Author's collection)

Working in this way the face, and the access tunnels, would be advanced. Supports, in the form of curved steel hoops, were required at intervals of four feet. The working face in advance of the last hoop could only be worked for a distance of three feet before being supported by a temporary timber frame. From there a further three feet could be worked.[9]

Then the face had to be left temporarily for an additional hoop with timber lagging behind to be built for support and the tub rails to be extended more permanently. For this reason several faces had to be available to be worked at any time to enable production to be maintained.[10]

Miners were paid piece work at so much per ton of stone dug. The wages were good and there was the opportunity to earn money quickly, despite an early, 6.00 am start.

Lunch breaks would be taken at locations where electric light was available. Men walked here, in pairs, walking along the rails rather than the sleepers. Here men would gather for a short break, for a snack, a drink of water and a smoke. Breaks were short to maximise working time and hence wages.[11] If working near to a drift or a daylight hole, the opportunity would be taken to sit and eat in the open air.

Ventilation in the mine was by a mix of vertical shafts and horizontal drifts to the open air. For much of the northern half horizontal drifts were easily provided, simply by extending existing roadways. These were known as daylight holes. They would be created, and closed, as different parts of the mine were exploited and abandoned. The aim was always to ensure a flow of fresh air to all areas being worked as well as to the communication roadways.

Vertical shafts were needed as they acted as chimneys and drew air in from the drift entrances by natural convection. One shaft, 58 feet deep, was dug near to No 1 entrance.[12] Three others ventilated the northern end of the mine, all to the east of the road to Nettleton. The depth of one is unknown, the others being 15 feet 5 inches and 14 feet deep. Rising ground around the south end of the mine meant that daylight holes were not a practical proposition. Here, again to the east of the road, south of Nettleton Top Farm buildings, a shaft 91 feet deep was provided.[13]

Explosives were rarely used in this mine as, generally, the stone could be broken using pneumatic picks and hand tools. Areas of hard stone were encountered from time to time that did require blasting. If explosive was needed this was supplied to the miners and the cost deducted from their wages. In July 1935 R. Stephenson had 6 shillings and eight pence (33p) deducted from his wages for explosives, supplied at 10d (4p) per pound weight.[14] In February 1938, at the Caistor Petty Sessions, an application was granted for the renewal of the licence to store explosives at the mine.[15]

Perhaps the only instance of subsidence damage to a surface building was at Nettleton Top Farm. Highfield House at Nettleton Top was built in 1950 as a replacement for the farmhouse on the opposite side of the road.[16] Mine plans show that the stone to the north and east of the earlier house was worked out in the period 1941 to 1945.

The final workings were in two locations: the first in the north-west of the mine, north of the mine yard, accessed by No 2 Drift. The other was at the south end. From 1957 to 1959 alterations within Top Mine were being made for the haulage tunnel to serve the new Bottom Mine. This came briefly into the open air at Back o' the Farm and from here, in 1960, a short new link was made with an existing underground haulage road running to the south. The final loads of stone from Top Mine were taken out through this and the mine closed in 1961. The abandonment plan for Top Mine is dated 4 August 1961.[17]

Fig 21.3. (Top)
The main entrance to Top Mine, shortly after going into production in 1934. A train load of wooden bodied mine tubs is being propelled towards the tippler for emptying. A separate drift entrance for the use of the men, avoiding conflict with trains running in and out, was provided at one time behind the buildings. (Author's collection)

Fig 21.4. (Above)
A horse hauling loaded tubs out of the mine. It is using one of the main haulage roads, lined with steel hoops with timber lagging in between them. Note also the acetylene lamp hanging on the right, acceptable for use in gas free mines such as this. (Author's collection)

Fig 21.5. (Left)
Carbide (acetylene) lamp and Safety lamp formerly owned by Edward (Ned) Mumby who retired from Nettleton Top mine in 1949 aged 70. (Dr John Esser)

22. Surface Works and Buildings

The surface works and buildings were in two separate but nearby locations. One group was at Nettleton Top, mixed in with the farm cottages that had been constructed earlier and remained in farm use.

Nettleton Top was a quiet and peaceful place before the mine. This is an exposed site, particularly from the west, 425 feet above sea level. Set within the protection of small groups of trees was a farm house and farm buildings on the east side of the road. To the west a short lane, later to become the main access to the mine, led to two pairs of semi detached cottages. *(Fig 22.1)*.

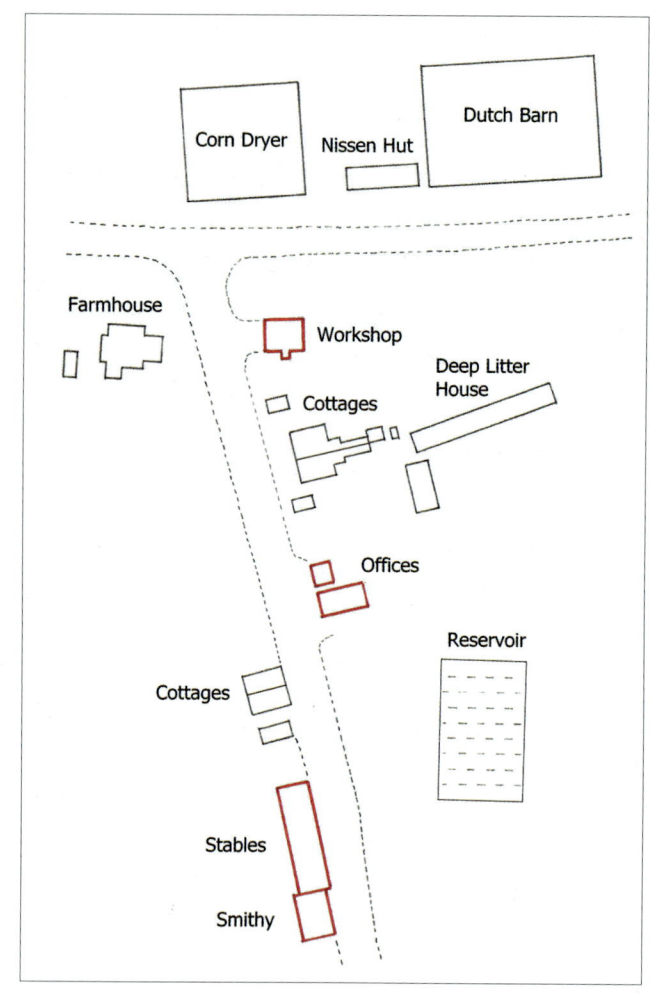

Fig 22.1.
The buildings at Nettleton Top in December 1964 with the original buildings for Nettleton Mine highlighted. North is to the left. (Redrawn from a plan in the Scunthorpe Steelworks archive, copy held by author, by Ken Redmore)

Within this small group, on the south side of the road, three mine buildings were located. Nearest to the road was a workshop, built about 1930 of corrugated iron. Then came a pair of farm cottages and beyond that the single storey mine offices, also of about 1930. Here the production records were kept and from here the miners collected their weekly pay. When the new buildings for Bottom Mine were built in 1960 both workshop and office were superceded by more modern replacement buildings down the hill. Both survived though, with the office block being converted into a bungalow for the blacksmith.

To the north of the road was a former pair of cottages, by 1964 converted to one dwelling. The front garden of this, certainly during the construction phase for Bottom Mine, was used as a car park. West of this house were the stables and smithy. The stables had accommodation for six horses and the names of the last six, Prince, Duke, Shorty, Jock, Laddie and Darkie, still remained above their stalls at the time of writing. A full-time horsekeeper was employed to look after their needs. *(Fig 31.1)*.

Immediately west of the smithy was a washdown area for the horses. They worked underground during the working day but came out of the mine every day. They were washed when they came out prior to feeding and bedding down in their stable. Rest days and the annual two week summer break were spent in the field to the south of the stable block.

The roadway was extended from here, extending at an angle down the hill to ease the gradient, into the mines yard. The yard, or pitbank, was limited in extent to north and south, limited to the south by Drift No 1 and its associated buildings and to the north by Drift No 2. *(Fig 22.2)*.

The mine railway was built to a gauge of 2 feet 6 inches, largely using 30 lb per yard rail and wagons, brought from the Mid Lincolnshire Company's previous mine at Greetwell, near Lincoln.[1] The railway layout is shown in Fig 22.2, forming the shape of a letter 'Y', the junction of the 'Y' being outside the No 1 Main entrance. Here, two lines of rails ran out from the mine, heading north on to the pitbank. On the pitbank a pair of sidings ran down towards the tippler,

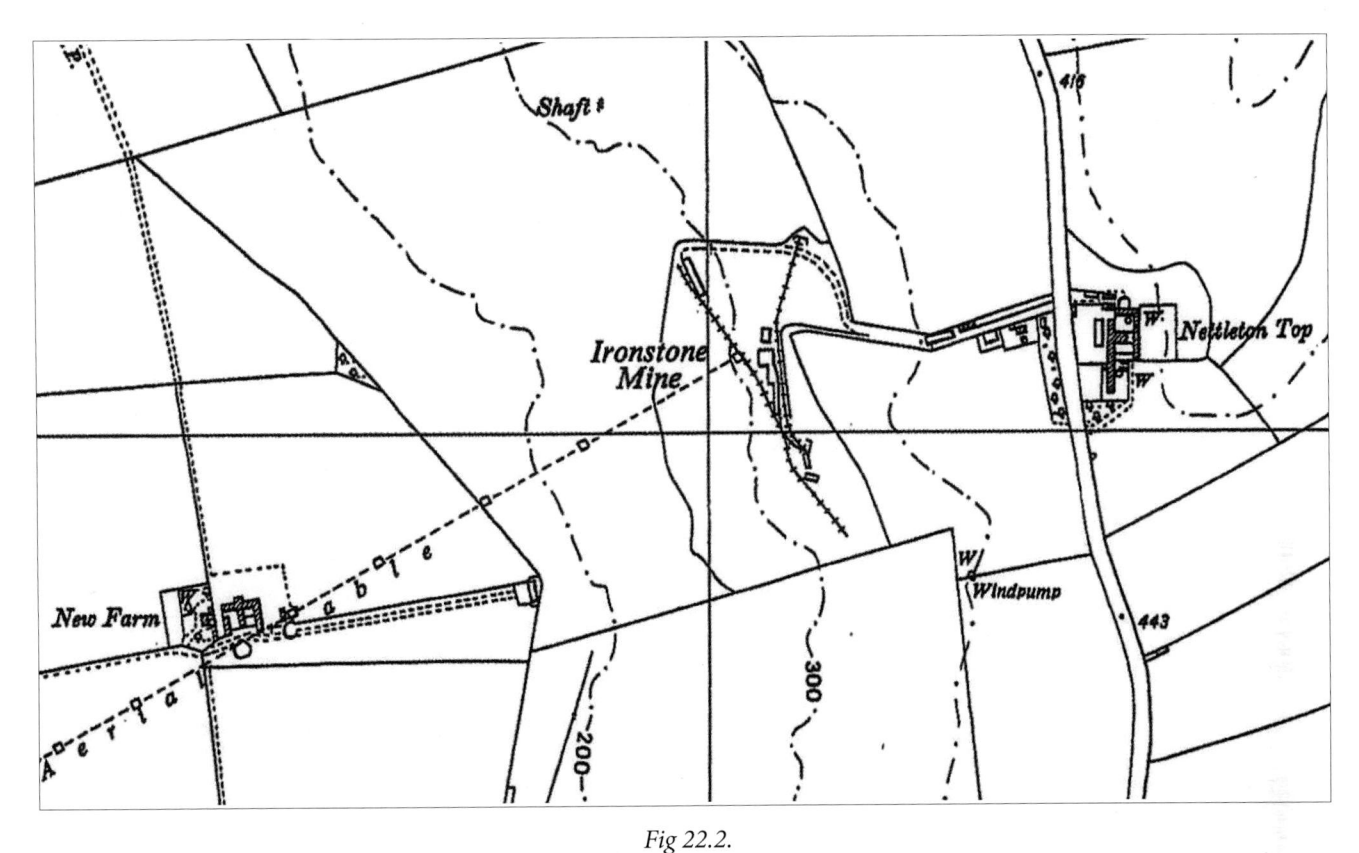

Fig 22.2.
The extent of the mines yard as shown on the six inch OS map, TF 19 NW, 1956 revision of 1951 survey. The mine railway enters Drift No 2 at the north end and Drift No 1 by the buildings towards the south end. The siding running to the power house and workshop is shown, running to the north west, as well as the eastern half of the aerial ropeway.
(Ordnance Survey)

while a single line carried on at a higher level to enter the mine again at the North No 1 Main entrance. On the way it passed the open yard where steel hoops and timber props were stored for use in the mine. The lower section of the 'Y' led first to the locomotive shed, from where it became a long headshunt which would also supply storage space for railway locomotives and tubs temporarily out of use.

The siding forming the north western arm of the 'Y' ran steeply downhill to the power house and workshop at the lower end of the site. Tubs using this would be braked with a 'sprag' through their wheels to avoid running away. *(Fig 30.1)*.

The individual buildings at the mine surface are shown on Fig 22.3. Immediately to the south side of the main entrance was a range of single storey buildings. *(Fig 22.4)*. These are identified on Fig 22.3, from the north to the south, as D, A, BS and OH with no explanation as to what the initials mean. BS has a stable door and a chimney and is probably the blacksmith's. D may be an office for the deputies responsible for mine safety and, therefore, in and out of the mine frequently every day. A may stand for accounting, keeping a record of who comes in and out of the mine through the day. OH is very small and may be the outside hovel, a coal store or a toilet. Hovel is a word once often used in Lincolnshire to describe a subsidiary building or outhouse accessed from outside the home for these uses.

Just south of these buildings was the loco shed. No contemporary photograph of this has been discovered.

To the north of Main No 1, on the pit bank, was the tippler shed. It was of timber or corrugated iron construction. Although this appears in photographs at

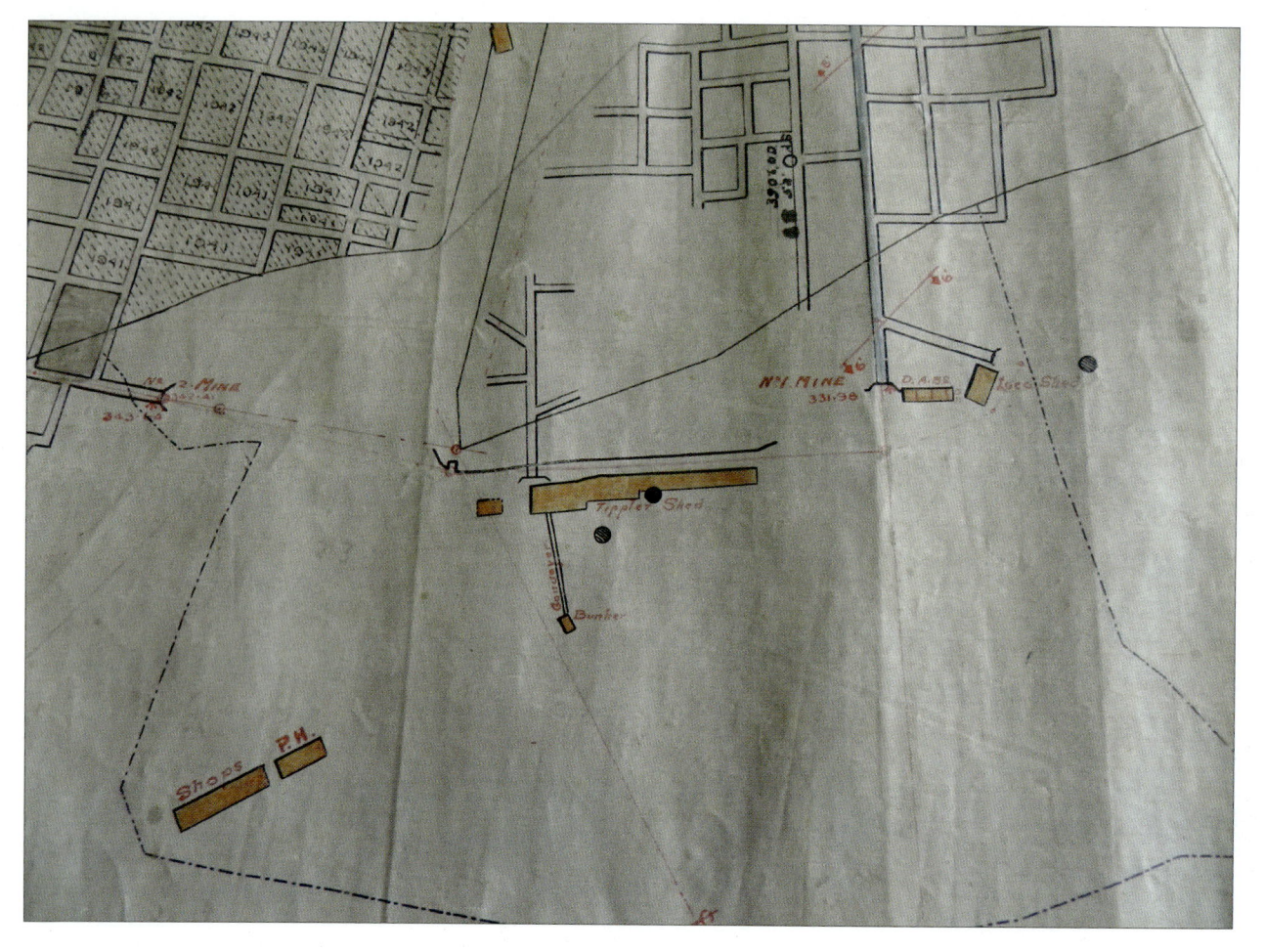

Fig 22.3.
Undated map of 'Nettleton Mine' showing the surface buildings. On this the latest date shown for mined areas is 1949. North is to the left. Note also the separate drift entrance to the rear of the locomotive shed. This is the only plan on which this is shown; a separate entrance for men to avoid the activity of trains entering and leaving the mine at a point where their eyesight would need to adjust. (Extract from a plan in Scunthorpe Steelworks archive, in author's collection)

a distance, the materials are not clear. This enclosed the sidings running down to the tippler together with the entry and exit from the latter. At first the operations here were undertaken in the open air and contemporary photographs clearly illustrate the procedures. *(Fig 22.5)*. The tippler was a circular revolving frame which held one mine tub. Full tubs would be placed on the siding leading down to it. This siding had a falling gradient. Tubs would be braked or 'spragged' with a pole through their wheels to hold them. Each would be uncoupled in its turn, run on to the tippler, which was revolved, emptying the ironstone into a bunker underneath. The tub, when upright again, was pushed out but was now at a lower level than the rest of the sidings. It ran forward to connect with an endless chain which hauled it up a steep slope to 'ground' level, where it would be reconnected to the others in its train, ready to be taken back underground to be refilled. *(Fig 22.6)*.

The small building immediately north of the tippler building was a small office or mess room, again with materials indistinct in photographs but probably of timber or corrugated iron. The last buildings on the site were at the bottom of the slope below the mine. Here, to the south, was the power house with the workshop beyond. *(Fig 22.7)*. The workshop provided space for the sawmill, welders, electricians and the blacksmith. The power house was equipped with a Ruston 10 HRE diesel engine with an electric flywheel driving a BTH generator. *(Fig 22.8)*.

Fig 22.4. (Top)
The range of buildings immediately outside the main entrance to Nettleton Mine. From left to right these are identified on Fig 22.3 as D (deputies), A (accounting), BS, (blacksmith) and OH (outside hovel). The siding to the right led to the loco shed and the headshunt. (Author's collection)

Fig 22.5. (Middle)
The tipping operation to empty loaded tubs, taken shortly after the mine opened and before the area was enclosed inside a building. In the background loaded mine tubs wait on a siding with a falling gradient. One by one they ran forward to the tippler where they were inverted to empty their load into a bunker beneath. (Author's Collection)

Fig 22.6. (Bottom)
An empty tub being hauled by the endless chain back up from the tippler to 'ground' level. (Caistor Heritage Trust)

Fig 22.7. (Top)
The power house, front, with the workshop beyond. The latter has a pile of sawn timber for use in the mine immediately to its rear. In addition to the sawmill it also housed the welders, electricians and blacksmith.
(Roy Thomas collection)

Fig 22.8. (Bottom)
The interior of the power house with a Ruston 10 HRE engine with electric flywheel driving a BTH generator.
(Author's collection)

23. The Aerial Ropeway

Mined ironstone was tipped from the tippler into a bunker below. From here it had to be taken down to new sidings alongside the Lincoln to Barnetby railway line, immediately south of Holton le Moor station level crossing. That link was provided by an aerial ropeway. This was unusual for Lincolnshire but common within Britain, especially where mines on high hillsides needed to get their product down to railway sidings in the valleys below. *(Fig 23.1)*.

Despite being well understood technology, the ropeway at Nettleton was of enough interest in its design to be described in detail in *The Iron and Coal Trades Review* of Friday 1 March, 1935. This is reprinted below, together with some of its illustrations.

Fig 23.1.
The aerial ropeway seen from the mine. This was taken just before its demolition, as the road that replaced it can be seen running alongside the trestles supporting the ropeway.
(Barry Graham-Rack)

AN INTERESTING aerial ropeway has recently started to work transporting ironstone from the Nettleton Top mine of the Mid-Lincolnshire Iron Company Limited, a subsidiary company of John Lysaght Limited, down to the London & North Eastern Railway at Holton le Moor station between Lincoln and Grimsby. The ropeway is of the monocable system, in which one endless steel wire rope supports and hauls the loads. The distance from the loading station is approximately 6,060 ft. with a difference in level, in favour of the loaded buckets, of 205 ft. The plant is designed to carry a final capacity of 75 tons per hr. but only sufficient buckets and hangers to deal with 25 tons per hr. have been supplied in the first instance. The additional buckets and hangers will be added from time to time as a larger capacity is required.

The rope travels at 130 yds. per min. or roughly 4½ miles per hr. The buckets hold 12 cwt of ironstone, so that when dealing with 75 tons per hour there will be 125 loads per hr., at intervals of 28.8 secs. and a spacing of 16 yds between each bucket. When carrying 25 tons per hr. there will be 41.6 loads per hr. with intervals of 86.5 secs. and a spacing of 48 yds between each bucket.

Fig 1 shows a view of one of the trestles with four supporting sheaves on the full side and two on the empty or return side. The sheaves are mounted in pairs and are free to circulate on a central spindle while on the full side two pair beams are mounted in a quadruple beam so that all four sheaves are free to circulate round one central spindle. This system of mounting (originally used and patented by Mr J. Pearce Roe) ensures uniformity of pressure between the rope and the sheave, which results in the uniformity of wear on the sheaves and on the rope. There are 13 of these trestles, the tallest of which measures 40 ft. from ground to rope. The

Fig 1.
View of one of the trestles. (Author's collection)

Fig 2.
General view of belt conveyor, storage bunker, ropeway station, etc. NB: Though not the view included in the article it illustrates the same features. (Author's collection)

ground over which the ropeway passes is agricultural and fairly level with the exception of the first 1,000ft. from the loading station, which is rough and steep. Wherever possible the trestles have been located in the hedges so as to reduce as far as possible the inconveniences to farming. The rope is constructed of six strands of seven wires each around a hemp core, and is made up on Lang's lay in which the wires in each strand are wound in the same direction as the strands in the rope, this construction resulting in better wearing surfaces and a longer life than the ordinary lay in which wire and strand are wound in opposite directions. The buckets and hangers are supported from the rope by inverted V or saddle clips fitted with a small projection that engages with the lay of the rope (originally used and patented by the late Mr J Pearce Roe), allowing steep grades to be used with safety. These clips are still the simplest, cheapest and, if correctly designed, the most satisfactory clips for monocable ropeway work.

The ironstone from the adit is brought in mine tubs to a tippler which delivers the mineral to a picking belt, which in turn delivers it to a belt conveyor delivering to a storage bunker of 100 tons capacity, fitted with two shuts for filling the ropeway buckets. The ground immediately in front of the adit is clay lying on rock, and is of a very treacherous nature, frequently slipping or rolling, and for this reason it was not practicable to place the loading station nearer the adit and the belt conveyor was rendered necessary. Fig 2 gives a general view of the belt conveyor, the storage bunker, the ropeway station and the first trestle.

Fig 3 shows a view of the terminal gear and steel frame of the loading station, together with the bucket and hanger. The driving gear consists of a built up terminal sheave 9 ft diameter on tread, to which is attached a double-helical spur ring, the sheave being carried on a mild steel shaft running in roller bearings. The spur ring gears with a spur pinion carried on a vertical countershaft, fitted at its lower end with bevel gear, driving the horizontal countershaft coupled by belt to the driving motor. The shunt rails on which the buckets travel are graded so as to reduce to a minimum the work entailed in pushing the empty buckets round to the loading shuts and the full buckets to where they join the moving rope. The main driving frame is bolted

Fig 3.
View of the terminal gear and steel frame of the loading station. (Author's collection)

to an inclined block of concrete in the base of which, below ground level, are incorporated substantial anchor bars, so that if at a later date the ground shows any signs of instability, the bar can be coupled up to long ties carried well back into the solid rock.

At the unloading station, shown on Fig 4, the loaded buckets pass over a storage bunker of some 20 tons capacity, from which the railway wagons, on the siding below, are filled. The buckets unload their contents automatically, passing in an inverted position down to the tension or return station at ground level. The ropes pass below the station frame under the bucket path to the tension trolley.

The tension trolley consists of a plain 9ft. dia. terminal wheel fitted with mild steel shaft running in roller bearings, the whole being mounted on a mild steel trolley travelling on steel track rails. The back of the trolley is fitted with a tail sheave round which the tension rope passes, one end being coupled up to the blocks and special worm winch, and the other passing round an inclined jib fitted with head sheave down to the suspended concrete deadweight, which gives the necessary tension to the rope.

Fig 5 shows the return station frame with the inclined tension jib in the foreground and the top of the hanging weight just appearing above ground level. [*In the background in the photograph used here with the weight out of sight.*] The tension trolley travels just below the level of the ground and does not appear in this illustration. The loaded railway wagons pass over a weighbridge and the sidings have been specially constructed for dealing with this traffic. The labour charges for operating the ropeway are very low, one man looking after the filling and despatch of the buckets at the loading station, and one man righting and sending off the empty buckets at the return station.

The ground adjacent to the return station will be used as a storage depot for mine stores such as pit props, timber, rails etc., and material that cannot be conveyed back to the mine in the ordinary mineral buckets will be transported on special carriers for that purpose. The ropeway is now using about 10 b.h.p. for 25 tons per hour capacity, and this power will be reduced to about 7 b.h.p. when the output increases to 75 tons per hour. Electric power is generated by a crude oil engine, and in addition to driving the ropeway, is used for the other machinery and for lighting the workings.

The plant was supplied by Messrs. John Lysaght Limited, Normanby Park Steel Works, Scunthorpe, Lincolnshire, in accordance with the designs of Mr Reginald H. Pearson, consulting engineer, of 267, High Holborn, London, WC1.

Fig 4.
View at unloading station. (Author's collection)

Fig 5.
Return station frame with inclined tension jib.
NB: This is not the view included in the article but illustrates the same features. (Author's collection)

The article shows that the ropeway was also designed to carry materials up to the mine as well as ironstone down from it. In the winter of 1947 when deep snow closed roads all over the county the ropeway became a lifeline. Nettleton Top was cut off and it was reported in January that five isolated families received their bread via the ropeway.[1] In February it was reported that the ropeway was used three times a week to take bread, meat and groceries up to Nettleton Top.[2]

The intensive daily use of the ropeway meant that it required maintenance. The annual maintenance period was timed for the two week shutdown for the summer holiday, always two weeks in August. Major work such as the replacement of the rope would be carried out at this time.

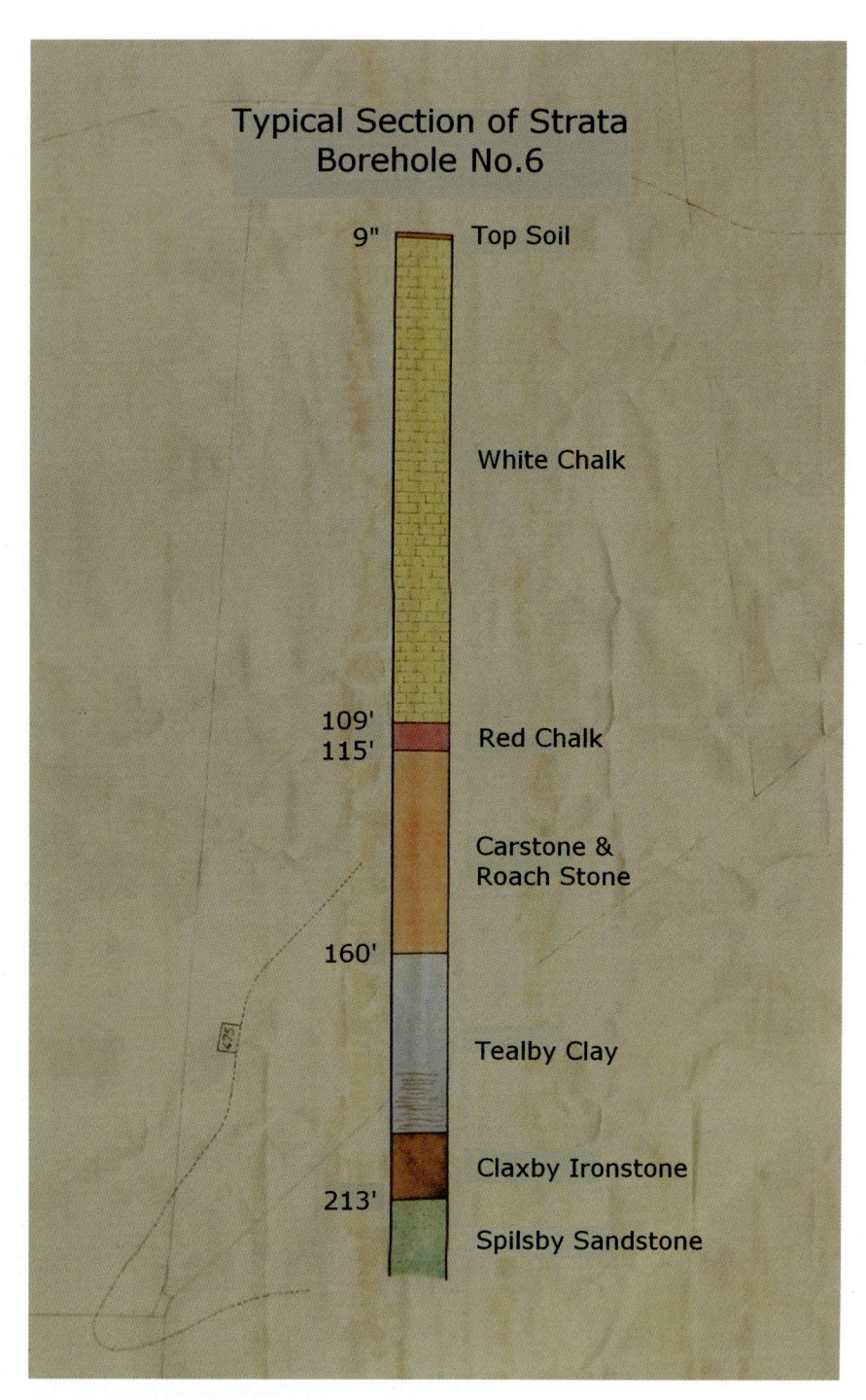

Fig 24.1.
Borehole No.6 was one of the fourteen boreholes driven in 1954. It was located almost at the centre of the proposed mine, close to the junction of the East Main and South Main. (Fig 25.1). This shows that the ironstone bed was 14 feet 6 inches in depth, with its base 213 feet 6 inches below ground level at this point. (Taken from a plan; Nettleton Bottom Mine; Claxby Ironstone Bed, dated July 1965, copy held by author, amended by Ken Redmore)

NETTLETON BOTTOM MINE

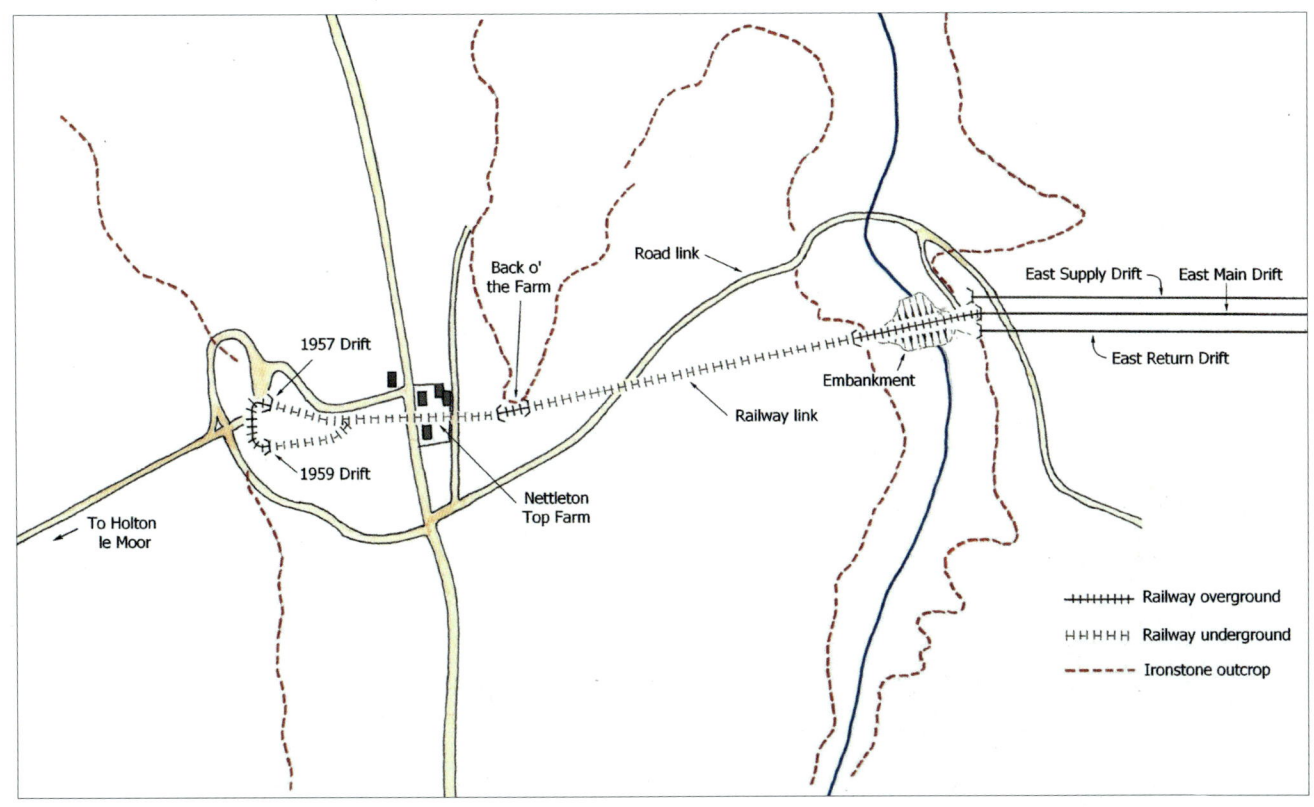

Fig 24.2.
Nettleton Bottom Mine, entrance drifts and new railway and road. (Drawn by Ken Redmore)

24. Development

A series of 14 boreholes were driven in September 1954 to investigate the geology of the land to the east of Nettleton Beck, up to Caistor High Street. These were to investigate the ironstone bed and determine if it was worthy of exploitation. *(Fig 24.1)* This proved that the bed was up to 14 feet thick, similar to that at Top Mine.[1]

A preliminary report on the extension of the mining area was submitted to Lysaghts in April 1955.[2] This concluded that under an area of 407 acres up to the Caistor High Street, there were workable reserves averaging eight feet six inches with 8.6 million tons of stone. 65% of this could be extracted, so for a mine planned to produce up to 4,000 tons a week or 200,000 tons a year there was enough stone for 30 years' production. Furthermore, there was enough to the

Fig 24.3.
Building the 1959 entrance. Note that the face has been bared, the tunnel mouth created and the retaining wall is being built in reinforced concrete. (Author's collection)

Fig 24.4.
The interior of the 1957 Drift looking out into the yard. Note the double line of rails. The dark shape on the left hand side is a refuge hole or manhole, a recess in which a man could step to keep him safe as a train went by.
(Author's collection)

east of Caistor High Street for a further 30 year period provided that there was no deterioration in quality.

The report recommended that the mine should use fully mechanised power loading together with the use of locomotive haulage for all transport, hauling larger tubs of a capacity of at least two tons.

The proposed entrance was at the northern end. Two alternative suggestions were made as to how the stone should be taken away. One was to build a new aerial ropeway all the way from Holton le Moor to the new mine entrance. The second was to link the existing main drift within Top Mine with the new mine, crossing the Nettleton Beck valley on an embankment with trains using an alternative entrance on the western flank of the new mine. This would enable continued use to be made of the existing ropeway. All new buildings would be built as a redevelopment and extension of the existing yard and 109 men would be required in total. They also suggested that development of the new mine should run alongside the working of the existing one so that production would be maintained seamlessly.

The recommendations of this report were largely accepted. The main entrances were moved to the west side of the Nettleton Bottom valley with diesel loco haulage of much larger tubs to a new tippler in an extended mines yard. The aerial ropeway, however, was to be replaced with a roadway along which dumper trucks ran to the railway sidings. *(See Section 29. Holton le Moor Sidings).* And, instead of using an existing roadway through Top Mine a completely new tunnel was driven, with two new drifts in the yard. The new drifts were dated, that to the north 1957 and to the south, 1959. *(Figs 24.2, 24.3 and 24.4).*

Eurig Thomas was appointed as the manager of Nettleton Mine in 1956. His was the responsibility for managing the change that was to come.[3] The planning application for the mine was made in 1959.[4]

It took 18 months to get the new tunnels through to, and over, the Nettleton Beck valley.[5] *(Figs 24.5 and 24.6).* The first section, from the yard to Back o' the Farm, was the most problematical. Part had to be driven through a very unstable clay fault. The miners worked day and night, using quick setting cement. At first cement was mixed outside and brought in by lorry. The lorry exhaust created problems for the men and, if they did not act quickly enough, the cement set before it could be used.[6]

Three drift entrances were driven for the new mine, the East Supply Drift to the north, the East Main Drift in the centre with the East Return Drift to the south. The latter was at a lower level than the other two. *(Fig 24.6).* East Main and East Return were

Fig 24.5.
Nettleton Bottom Valley looking eastwards immediately before mining began. Routes for the new roadways are being constructed, with a bulldozer in the lower right. In the bottom left hand corner work is underway for the construction of the embankment. On the hilltop, to the right of the tree, is the site of what became the chalk quarry.
(Roy Thomas collection)

started in 1959 and East Supply in 1960.[7] Because of a fault along the valley side, the East Supply and East Main Drifts were driven along the top of the outcrop, on the fault, to reach the ironstone bed inside the hill. The East Return Drift, at the lower level, was driven into the faulted stone bed. This drift was for air circulation and to provide emergency access if needed. *(Fig 24.7)*.

A new mine railway was built for the new mine. Under Nettleton Top it was mostly double track. It became single in the middle of the second tunnel but was again double over the embankment and into the mine. Right hand running was in force.[8] Larger, heavier, wagons needed bigger locomotives to haul the trains. The first of the Ruston and Hornsby LHU 75hp locomotives was delivered in 1958 *(see Section 30. Locomotives and Rolling Stock)*, together with some new steel wagons, and used for the development stage. New, heavier, rail was also laid, suitable for carrying the heavier loads.[9]

A new road was also built to link the new mine with the new mines yard and the road to Holton le Moor sidings. The route had to take account of the steep gradients on the way and hence it took the form of a long recumbent 'S'. *(Fig 24.2)*.

Fig 24.6.
Nettleton Bottom Mine Drift entrances about 1960. From left to right these are the East Supply Drift; the East Main Drift; and the East Return Drift. Note also the chalk quarry at top right. (Grimsby Evening Telegraph)

Work on the new buildings in the mines yard was also underway. Ground was 'now being levelled for workshops' in June 1957.[10] By the summer of 1960 work was complete and production began in August 1960.

In 1968 ownership of the mine was vested in the British Steel Corporation. The BSC was formed in 1967 through the nationalisation of the UK steel industry.

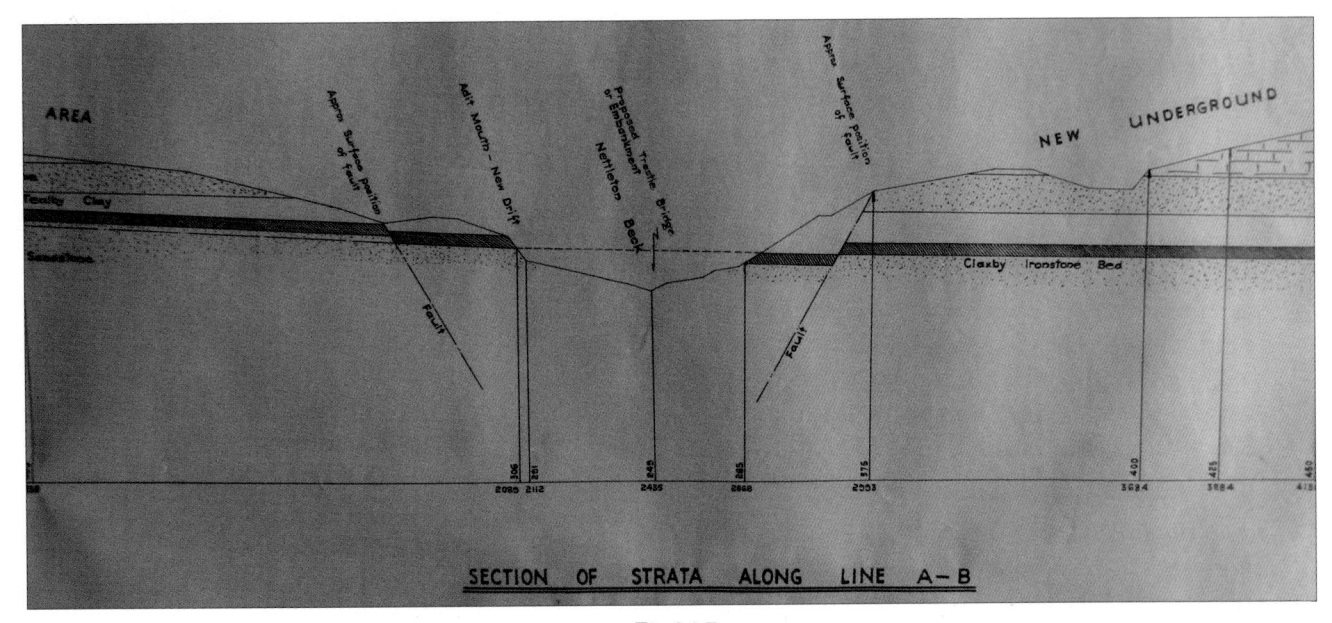

Fig 24.7.
The geological fault on both sides of the valley of the Nettleton Beck. (Extract from plan held in Scunthorpe Steelworks archive, copy in author's collection

Fig 25.4.
The form of sublevel caving mining adopted at Bottom Mine. An increasing number of cross cut parallel tunnels are driven to the maximum as seen here on the left, near to Caistor High Street. The retreat process sees the area progressively worked out from the extremities. From a mine plan updated to March 1968.
(Extract from a plan in Scunthorpe Steelworks archive, copy held by author)

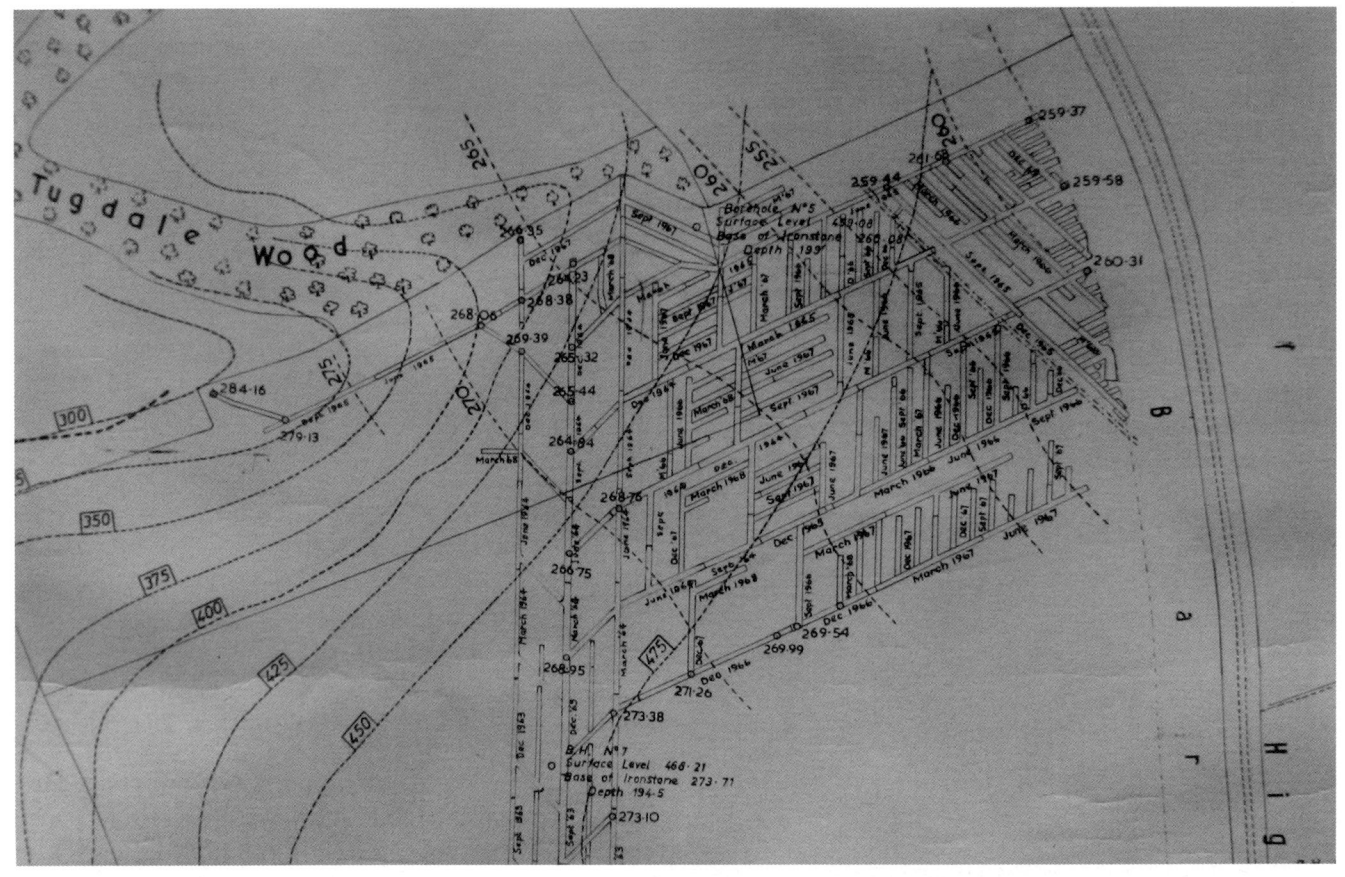

Fig 25.5. (Left)
An Eimco Rocker Shovel. Eric Farmery, the Under Manager, is showing the shovel to pupils from De Aston School, Market Rasen, in June 1961.
(Grimsby Evening Telegraph)

Fig 25.6. (Opposite page, top)
Two of the main haulage tunnels inside Bottom Mine. North Main is turning off to the left and East Main to the right. The space is electrically lit with white painted concrete walls as part of the permanent infrastructure. Note safety posters on the walls and the train approaching from East Main, 1968.
(Author's collection)

Lighting was by electricity in the main haulage tunnels, which were also concrete lined and painted white. *(Fig 25.6)*. Individual miners had battery powered electric helmet lamps. The main tunnels were 12 feet wide by 10 feet high.

Ventilation was by the three main drifts together with two additional openings in the hillside. One was at the north end, a drift to the open air; the other to the south, a vertical shaft with an electrically driven fan at the bottom to ventilate the district immediately north of the East Main. *(Fig 25.1)*. But, only a very small area of the mine was ever worked and underground mining ceased in March 1968, after only seven years and five months.

Fig 26.1.
Two of the large 75 hp LHU Class locomotives, one at each end of this heavy train of 15 loaded wagons, coming out of Bottom Mine and across the embankment in 1967. Interestingly, although the line is laid for double track, the train is running along the space between them. The wagons are the larger, steel sided variety, introduced for the opening of Bottom Mine. Bill Johnson is the driver. (Author's collection)

*Fig 26.2.
The surface buildings to serve the new Bottom Mine.
A photograph taken in the summer of 1961. (Author's
collection, annotated by Ken Redmore)*

26. Surface Works and Buildings

The new mine had no dedicated buildings at its drift entrances. The route for the new railway link required a new embankment over the Nettleton Beck. *(Fig 26.1)*. This was 57 feet high in the centre and 600 feet long. It was pierced by a culvert carrying the Beck and a pedestrian tunnel on the route of a public footpath. The latter was long enough at 80 feet to give a flavour of what the interior of the mine was like, supported by 40 of the same steel hoops used in the mine but lined here with corrugated iron sheeting.

Nettleton Bottom was a modern mine for which extended and updated support facilities were required. As a result a drastic change was made to the yard below Nettleton Top with more space and modern buildings. The newly completed yard is shown in Fig 26.2, which also identifies the main elements. These include offices and welfare block, workshops and stores, stone handling, haulage roads, and water supply.

The ironstone was brought out of the 1957 drift into a tippler shed. This shed was linked to both the 1957 and 1959 drifts by a shelter shed, to protect the workers on this exposed, west facing hillside.

The locomotive would bring its train to the drift, then detach, run behind, and push the tubs towards the tippler. Tubs would be detached individually, the older ones with a metal sprag through their wheels to make them slide down into the tippler shed, newer ones by applying their handbrake. They were further slowed at the tippler by a spring loaded buffer operating onto rubbing strips on the tub sides. Each tub was pushed in and out of the tippler by a pneumatic ram. The tippler was electrically driven, and inverted the tub allowing the stone to fall into a bunker below. *(Fig 26.3)*.[1] As it left the tippler the automatic coupling reattached it to the tub in front.[2] In the meantime the locomotive reversed up the tunnel, running round to exit the 1959 drift to collect a train of, now empty, tubs to take back to the mine.

Stone was then fed from the bunker into a lorry waiting below and taken along the new haulage road to Holton le Moor sidings. *(See Section 29. Holton le Moor Sidings, for operations at this point)*.

Fig 26.3. Tub in tippler with another waiting its turn. The number 3 is the permanent tub number. The number 28 chalked on the side told the weighbridge operator which miner or pair of miners had filled the tub. (Roy Thomas collection)

To the north of the 1957 drift was the workshop with a connection to a smaller welding shop alongside. The largest building on the site, the workshop provided space for stores, electrician's shop, machine shop, blacksmiths shop and a fitter's and erecting shop. A railway siding ran into the shop with a short and long siding inside, accessed by a turntable in the floor, for maintenance on locomotives and rolling stock.[3]

In the yard outside the workshop was the filter house, a small brick building housing water filtration equipment. Water for both the yard buildings and the houses and farm at Nettleton Top was pumped up from a spring on the hillside just south of the east end of the haulage road to Holton le Moor. Filtered here, it was pumped up to an enclosed tank near the road at Nettleton Top from where water was circulated around the area.[4]

The open reservoir at Nettleton Top, also built at this time, provided water for washing ironstone. This was not required very often, mainly to wash contaminated ironstone before it left the site. It was also used to provide a supply for the sand washer.[5]

Surface water drainage from the hillside and buildings in the yard was collected in a new reservoir at the foot of the hill, adjacent to the road to Holton le Moor sidings. Water was retained here to avoid any potential contamination of water courses.

The other large building was the offices and welfare block. On the ground floor was the canteen, locker room, showers, toilets, pay and time office, lamp room, boiler room, ambulance room, and offices for attendant, yard and quarry foremen, overmen and deputies, all entered through a footwear cleaning porch. On the first floor were offices for the manager, assistant manager and surveyor, and the drawing office, strongroom, wages office and reception.[6] The mine passenger train would leave from the rear of this building to take men to their working places in Bottom Mine. *(Fig 30.4)*

To the north and east of the office block were a variety of specialist and general storage buildings together with the joiners' workshop and sawmill. Here also was a weighbridge for materials carried by lorries and space for the open storage of steel hoops and timber props for use underground.[7] A sand washing plant was built here in 1963 to deal with the sand being quarried from the hillside. *(Fig 26.4. See also Section 27. Opencast Working).* Around the site were roads linking the various buildings with each other together with roads over to Bottom Mine and the chalk quarry, and to Holton le Moor sidings.

The mine tramway of 2 foot 6 inch gauge was retained but modified and extended with 40lb and 60lb rail to suit the heavier locomotives and the larger weights they hauled.[8]

NETTLETON MINES AND MINERS

27. Opencast working

The names and locations of the opencast quarries around Nettleton Top Mine are shown in Fig 21.1. In surviving correspondence and reports names are not always consistent and maps are usually missing. The names used in this chapter have, therefore, been derived from a variety of sources but are believed to be accurate. This quarrying took place between 1956 and 1968.

Opencast working at Nettleton Top was considered in a report by Lysaghts in 1957.[1] This concluded that:

- The ironstone seam varied from 14 to 20 feet in thickness and the majority of the overburden was under 50 feet
- The effective acreage of the mine area within the outcrop lines was 385 acres
- The original mine was estimated to contain some 19.5 million tons of ironstone, of which 2.8 million tons had been extracted. Around 16 million tons remained

Fig 26.4
Top Yard sand washer. The joiners' shop is in the left background. Those in the centre and right backgrounds include storage buildings and the weighbridge. (Roy Thomas collection)

Fig 27.1
Nettleton Bottom opencast quarry, June 1961. In the centre the ironstone has been exposed and is being removed. Above this a number of crawler tractors, scrapers and bulldozers can be seen, while below the face a roadway leads down to the tramway siding on which is an impressive train of 18 loaded wagons. (Grimsby Evening Telegraph)

The locations of underground voids and subsequent caving in of mined areas were not seen as a problem. These would simply be identified and avoided. The overburden would be removed by using a combination of tractor scraper units and a dragline with the stone being removed with the use of two medium sized face shovels. Removal to a stockpile in the yard would be by 'trackless transport'. The report concluded that the recovery of the stone was a necessity and an economic proposition.

Interestingly, within the report was a comment that 'all have admitted that the old mine should have been an opencast proposition from the start...' There is no indication so far discovered that this was ever considered when the mine was first developed. The technology in use in the Scunthorpe opencast quarries at that time comprised large shovels and draglines so this probably could have been an option. The idea would be revived in 1966. *(See Section 36. Economies and Closure).*

Only one month later a second report, this time by Mining Engineer Robert B. Beilby,[2] cast some doubt on these findings. He concluded:

- Because of roof collapses it was doubtful if good clean ironstone would be extracted
- The Tealby Limestone over the ironstone could only be removed by scrapers if it was very friable.

Otherwise it would need blasting and removal by shovel or dragline, as a separate operation

- Geological problems causing the Tealby Clay overburden to slip were likely to be encountered
- Care would have to be taken to consolidate weak ground which had subsided in order not to damage machines or put them out of action through burial

Beilby identified four small areas suitable for open casting which would produce an estimated 3.1 million tons of ironstone. Unfortunately the map with the report has not survived. However, given the subsequent developments these can be expected to have been those, or among those, shown on Fig 21.1.

Planning permission was granted for opencast working on the eastern outcrop of the whole length of Nettleton Mine, together with a much smaller area on the western outcrop, north of the mine yard, in 1957.[3] Fig 21.1 includes the dates each opencast site was worked, starting in 1956 and ending in 1968.

One site, Three North, was shown as having been worked in 1956/57 on the Mine Abandonment Plan, so work here predated the reports considered above and the planning permission. Three North could have been quarried as a test to determine the quantity of recoverable stone and inform the investigations.

In 1960 planning permission was granted for the working of sand and gravel from below the ironstone over a small area which included Three North. A further planning application in 1963 gave approval for the working of sand and gravel from below the ironstone in the Haddocks Area.[4] This name may be considered unusual but took its name from the Haddock Houses, a pair of dwellings demolished between 1887 and 1905. These were the last surviving remnant

Fig 27.2. (Top)
Fowler Challenger 4 tractor with an Onions box scraper removing overburden in Nettleton Bottom. (Roy Thomas collection)

Fig 27.3. (Bottom)
A Ruston Bucyrus 22 RB face shovel with an Aveling Barford shuttle dumper, at work in Nettleton Bottom in June 1961. A 38 RB face shovel was also used.
(Grimsby Evening Telegraph)

of Hardwick village. The name may have been a corruption of Hardwick.

From Two East and Nettleton Top Farm stone was removed by rail, sidings for that purpose being provided from Back o' the Farm. Rail transport was also used for Nettleton Bottom, a siding running south from the west end of the embankment over Nettleton Beck. The stone was taken by lorry from all the other sites. From Three North a new road ran north from the main haulage road from a point just east of the Normanby Road crossing. The earthworks for this can still be seen crossing the fields here.

Opencast ironstone production averaged around 3,500 tons per week and was extremely economical. It subsidised the underground production to the extent that the cost of stone delivered to Scunthorpe was on a par with its cost in 1936, more than 20 years earlier.[5]

The work inevitably had an effect on the landscape of this part of the Lincolnshire Wolds. A newspaper photograph showed the Nettleton Bottom quarry with a simple headline; 'Looking Down on the Moon?'[6] *(Fig 27.1)*. The overburden was stripped using crawler tractors hauling scrapers and stored for replacement as part of the restoration process. *(Fig 27.2)*. When the ironstone was exposed it was removed with the use of Ruston Bucyrus face shovels. In Nettleton Bottom it was loaded into shuttle dumpers for transfer into mine wagons. *(Figs 27.3 and 27.4)*.

As the hillsides had, in most cases, also been part excavated by mine tunnels, it was not unusual to expose former underground working. *(Fig 27.5)*.

Underneath the ore seam was a deep layer of sharp sand which was extracted by an old 24 RB dragline, loaded into AEC dumper lorries and hauled to the sand washer in the mine yard.[7] *(Fig 26.4)*. A small area of land to the north east of Three North was being worked for sand at the time the mine was closed and this, together with the sand washing equipment in the mine's yard and the road link between them, was leased to J.W. Hurdiss who worked it out subsequently.

All the land worked opencast was restored after working ceased. As they were all steep hillsides they have been restored as grassland for cattle to graze, a contrast with the arable land on the higher ground they run up to. Another clue is that they generally have a concave slope whereas the natural slopes tend to be convex or even. But what looks so much like a natural landscape belies the noise and activity that went on here to create the 'moonscapes' of the mid twentieth century.

Fig 27.4.
Loco No 8 leaving the opencast workings on the west side of Nettleton Bottom valley. It is about to enter the tunnel leading to the mines yard, about 1961. Jack Smith is the driver. (Author's collection)

Fig 27.5.
Underground mine roadway exposed by opencast working. (Author's collection)

28. The Chalk Quarry

The charge of a blast furnace consists of carefully calculated proportions of iron ore to which is added coke and, where sufficient lime is not present in the iron ore, chalk or limestone. Lime is needed as a flux to carry away the earthy materials in the form of slag. The Normanby Park steelworks at Scunthorpe needed a regular supply of chalk and, with the development of

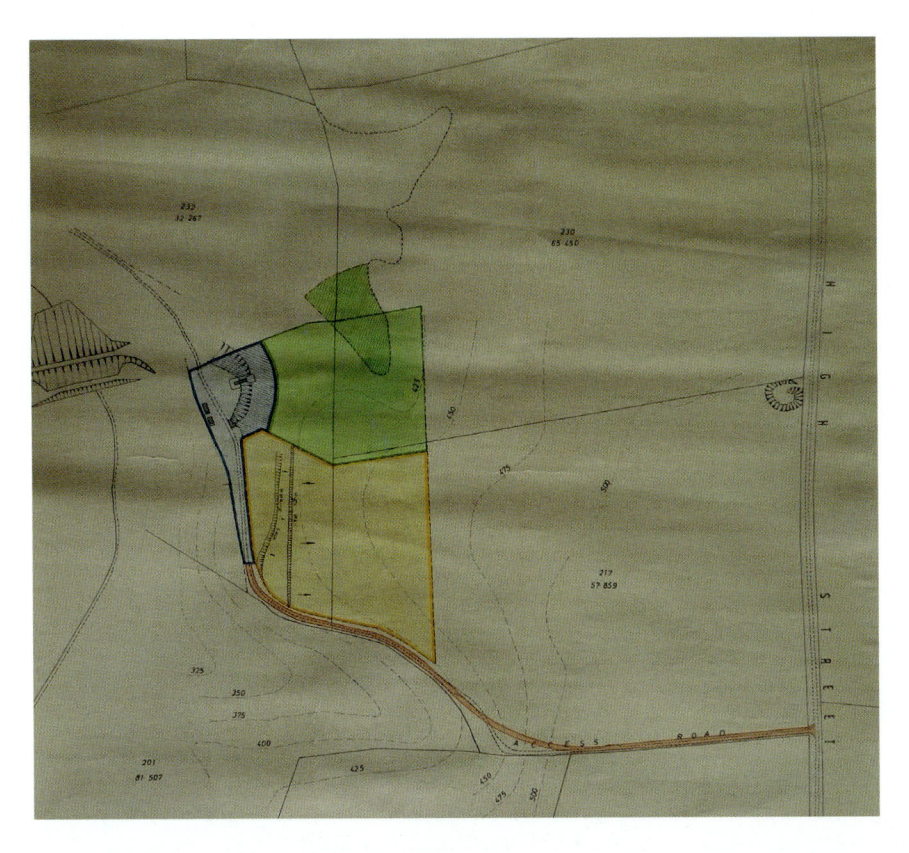

Fig 28.1.
The chalk quarry. The yellow area was the subject of the 1959 planning application, together with the blue area, for service buildings, and the brown access road. The green area was the area of the 1963 planning application, together with the triangular green area. This latter area was for the tipping of waste materials. (Extract from an undated plan in the Scunthorpe Steelworks archive, copy held by author)

the Nettleton Bottom mine, an opportunity arose to ensure a supply from a quarry in their control.

Planning applications were submitted for chalk extraction at the quarry in two phases: the southern half of the site in 1959 and the northern half in 1963.[1] *(Fig 28.1)*. The area to be worked was over the mine, the tunnels of which were to be around 100 feet below the bottom level of the chalk.

The quarry was very prominent in views from within the Nettleton Bottom valley. *(Fig 24.6)*. The scar it created was mitigated in views from the north and the south by some carefully sited tree planting. The eastern boundary was kept below the ridge line for the same reason.

The bed of chalk here was around 60 feet thick, worked in a series of five lifts, each of 12 feet in height. *(Fig 28.2)*. A Smith 21 excavator was used to dig chalk, which was then loaded into an Aveling Barford shuttle dumper for transportation to the screen. An example of the latter can be seen in Fig 27.3. The screen separated the ore from any waste material.

Quarried chalk was passed through the screen, loaded into dump trucks and taken by road to Scunthorpe. There were four loads per 12 hour shift with two lorry drivers working one shift each. Until 1963 this was done by Lysaghts but after this time it was contracted out.[2] Subsequently it was taken by lorry over the haulage road and down to Holton le Moor Sidings. About 1,000 tons per week was sent to Normanby Park works.[3]

A number of buildings were provided at the quarry. *(Figs 28.2 and 28.3)*. A compressor house provided compressed air for use in the mine below with a substation providing electricity to both mine and quarry. The south end of the substation also included a small mess room and toilet. Two chalk screens facilitated transfer of chalk from quarry to lorry and, for a short period, there was a maintenance garage for plant and machinery to the north of the substation. Mine and quarry were linked by road but also by a flight of steps rising some 50 feet from the south side of the East Main Drift to the quarry roadway above. These steps can be seen in Fig 30.8.

The quarry remained in use after ironstone production had ceased until 30 April 1971 when the British Steel Corporation, the owners from July 1968, had no more

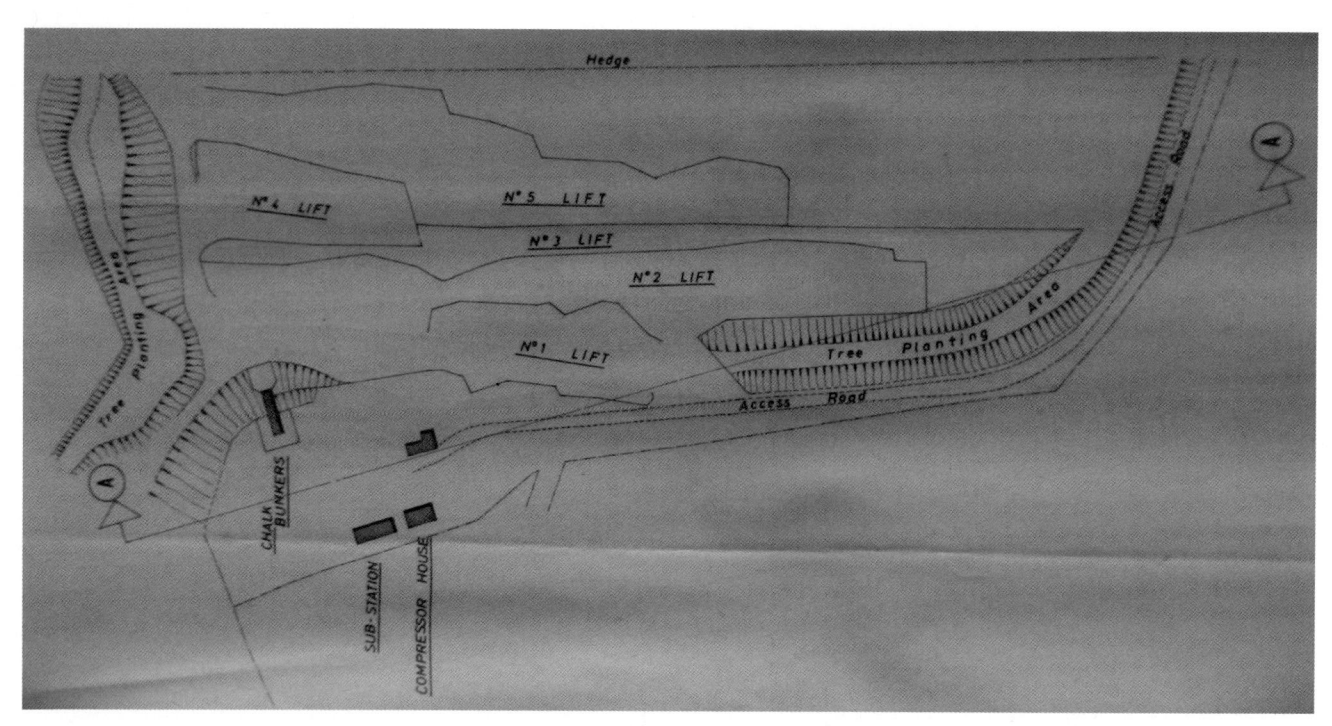

Fig 28.2.
The method of work within the quarry. North is to the left. The line above each lift number is the limit of the working face in that lift. The highest level is Lift 5 with the lowest Lift 1. The northerly chalk bunker for loading lorries is identified. The lower level structure of the second bunker is the small L shaped building nearby.
(Extract from a drawing entitled Layout of Chalk Quarry Faces and dated August 1963. From a plan held in the Scunthorpe Steelworks archive, copy held by author)

Fig 28.3.
A view of the chalk quarry from the west. The concrete faces of the East Main and the East Return Drifts into Bottom Mine can be seen to the left centre. From the left the buildings and structures are: a chalk loading bunker, the electricity sub station and mess room, and the compressor house. Behind the compressor house is the second chalk loading bunker. In the quarry, at the top right, the Smith 21 Excavator can be seen.
(David Robinson)

need for it. It appears to have been worked to a limited extent by a subsequent operator but has been out of use for some years now. There was a proposal in 1986 to use it for landfill but this did not happen. There was great concern locally about potential pollution of watercourses exacerbated by the potential instability of the mined area beneath.[4]

29. Holton le Moor Sidings

Compared with what these sidings would become in later years, in the beginning there was a minimal siding layout here. It comprised a single siding with a passing loop, one side for empties to pass and the other for loading wagons. *(Figs 29.1 and Fig 4 in Section 23. The Aerial Ropeway. See also Fig 34.1).*

No standard gauge shunting locomotive operated here. Empty timber mineral wagons would be positioned at the eastern end of the siding, clear of the loop. It is likely that these would be left with brakes on, standing at the head of a gently falling gradient. It was common to operate sidings such as these by gravity. Horse shunting was another possibility but there is no evidence of any stable here. Individual wagons would be uncoupled and allowed to run slowly down the gradient to stop under a discharge chute. When full, they would run on to be coupled together into a train for despatch to the steelworks.

The 20 ton capacity hopper, continually being filled from the aerial ropeway at 25 tons an hour initially, rising to 75 tons per hour, would need a regular supply of wagons to take the stone away. *(See Section 23. The Aerial Ropeway)*. With no extra storage capacity, any shortage of railway wagons would necessarily bring production to a halt.

Because of the limits determined by the lack of siding space for both empty trains arriving and loaded trains being taken away, use must have been made either of a loop siding within the Holton le Moor station limits or one train waiting on the main running lines while

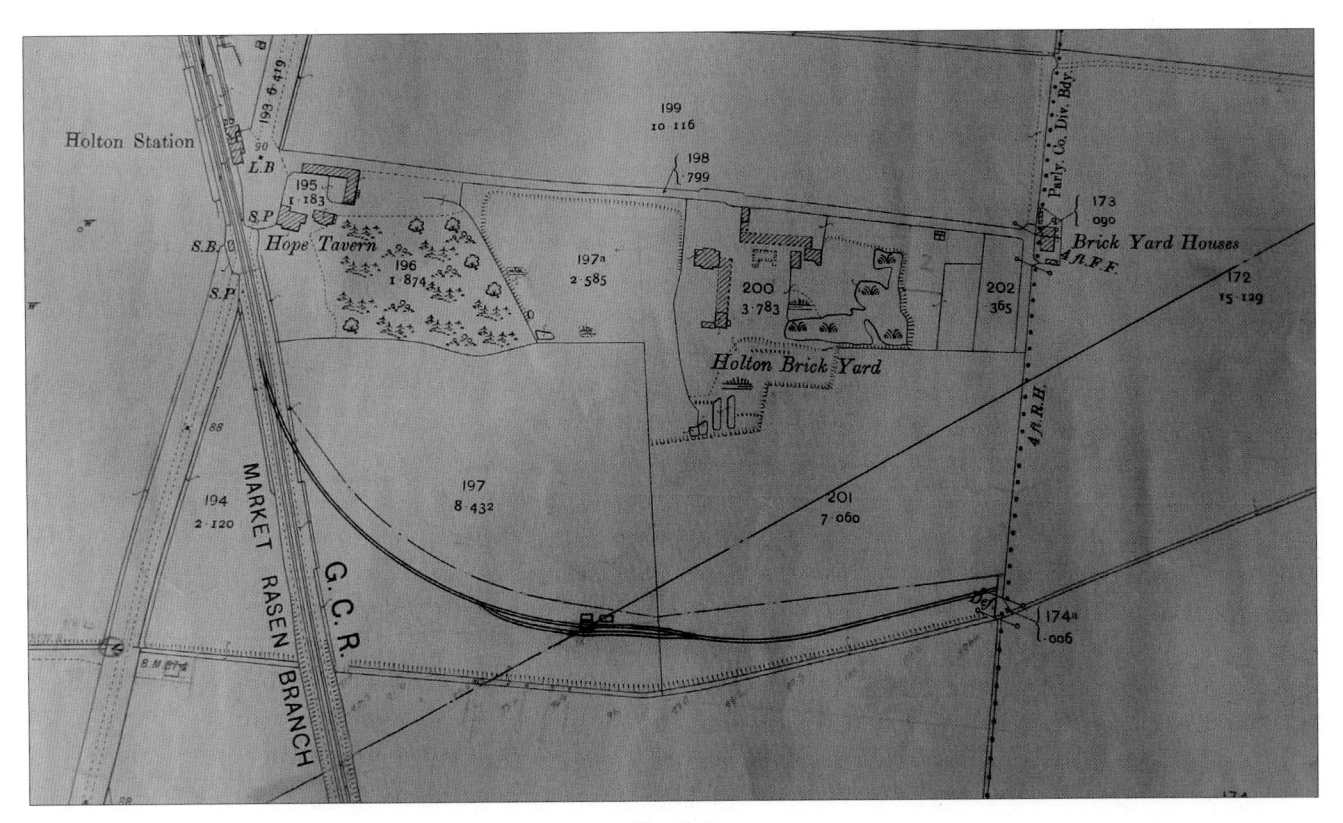

Fig 29.1.
Undated plan of the early layout of Holton le Moor sidings. Extract from a plan of Holton le Moor sidings, aerial ropeway and Nettleton Top Mine buildings, drawn on a copy of Ordnance Survey map, 1:2500, Second Edition, Lincolnshire XXXVII.8. (Scunthorpe Steelworks archives, copy held by author)

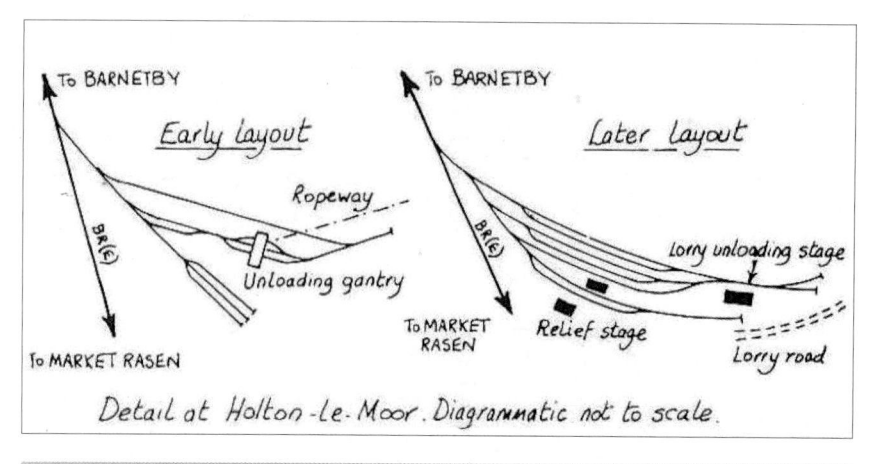

Fig 29.2. (Top)
Holton le Moor sidings before and after the opening of Bottom Mine. To the left is the layout by 1951 with additional sidings and a grading plant. To the right is the layout provided for Nettleton Bottom Mine. (From Eric Tonks, The Ironstone Quarries of the Midlands, History, Operation and Railways, Part VIII, South Lincolnshire, Runpast, 1991, p.229. With the permission of Book Law Publications)

Fig 29.3. (Bottom)
One of the fleet of six AEC Dump Trucks purchased by Lysaghts for use at Nettleton. Note the half cab. (Roy Thomas collection)

the shunting was carried out. By 1951 there had been considerable changes to the siding layout. Now there were three loops which ran under a much enlarged hopper discharging different grades of crushed stone into separate wagons. There were extra sidings too for trains to be made up before despatch. *(Fig 29.2).*[1]

In 1941 there was no office staff at Holton le Moor station. A clerk travelled every day from Moortown station and, among their duties, was to walk round the ironstone sidings to count the empty wagons waiting there.[2] This was to ensure there was a continuous supply of wagons to maintain production. In 1953 a train of empty wagons arrived every morning, Monday to Friday, from the Normanby Park Steelworks.[3]

Once positioned in the reception siding by the locomotive bringing them here, the wagon brakes would be put on. Each wagon would then be uncoupled from the rest as required. A slight fall in the level ensured that it could be eased forward into a headshunt which was level. From here it would be eased into the siding leading under the bunker, which also had a slightly falling gradient. Once in position for filling it would be braked and, when full, would continue on the falling gradient to be recoupled into a train for despatch.

The opening of Nettleton Bottom Mine with its increased production required changes at the sidings. A road replaced the ropeway and stone was

Fig 29.4. Holton le Moor sidings and the Lysaghts playing field in about 1960. Thirty-eight steel standard 16-ton mineral wagons can be seen in this view. More may be hidden behind the cricket pavilion. At the levels of production in 1957/8 about 42 of these wagons would be needed every working day. (Roy Thomas collection)

tipped into lorries at the tippler. It was then taken by road to a tipping dock at the sidings and tipped directly into railway wagons. Fig 29.2 shows the revised siding layout. A new weighbridge and mess room were also provided.

From a bunker below the tippler the ore was moved on a conveyor belt to a large storage bunker. From this the ore was dropped into dump trucks to be taken to Holton le Moor sidings. The hopper door of the bunker was operated with compressed air controlled by one man who stood on a gantry on the side of the bunker. The dumper would reverse under the hopper door so that the part of the body nearest the cab was under it. Stop blocks – old railway sleepers – were fitted for the dumper to back up to. This positioned it in the correct position so the front end of the body could be loaded first. The controller operated the hopper door to fill it. When full the controller would twice ring a bell positioned on the concrete wall adjacent to the dumper cab. The driver would then draw forward a short way and the process was repeated. Once full the controller gave a continuous ring to let the driver know that all was clear to move off.[4]

At first the delivery work from tippler to sidings was contracted out to Archer and Sharp of Scunthorpe.

Lysaghts soon purchased a fleet of six AEC Dump Truks, with single cab, for the work.[5] *(Fig 29.3)*.

Movement of railway wagons around the site continued to be largely by gravity. The sidings soon after their remodelling are shown in Fig 29.4.

30. Locomotives and Rolling Stock

LOCOMOTIVES

The mine tramway had a gauge of two feet six inches. From the beginning diesel locomotives were used for haulage in the main drifts and on the surface. Indeed, Nettleton Top Mine was one of the first in the UK to use diesel locomotives underground. This was a gas free mine and all that was required was a wash box to clean the exhaust gases of poisonous fumes. The speed limit on site was 4mph.

It was to the Lincoln firm of Ruston and Hornsby that the Mid Lincolnshire Ironstone Company, and later, Lysaghts, turned for the supply of their locomotives. Not surprising, perhaps, as they were developing a worldwide reputation for their products. A total of 12 locomotives were supplied to Nettleton between 1934 and 1961, with others being trialled under working conditions here, by the manufacturer. *(Table 5)*

Number	Model	Works No	Builder	Year	Purchased	Rebuilt	See Note
1	4wDM 16HP Class	170374	RH	1934	New	1951	a
2	4wDM 18/21HP Class	175403	RH	1935	New		b
3	4wDM 20HP Class	183429	RH	1937	New		c
4	4wDM 16/20HP Class	191680	RH	1938	New	1951	d
5	4wDM 25/30HP Class	195865	RH	1939	New		e
6	4wDM 30DL Class	224315	RH	1944	New		f
	4wDM	318748	RH	1952	On Trial		g
(4) 7	4wDM LBU Class	402439	RH	1957	On Trial 1957/8 Purchased 1959		h
(1) 8	0-4-0DM LHU Class	427856	RH	1958	New		i
(5) 9	4wDM LBU Class	432654	RH	1959	New		j
10	4wBE	2996	GB	1960	New		k
(2) 11	0-4-0DM LHU Class	435402	RH	1960	New		l
12	4wBE	6018	GB	1960	New		m
13	4wBE	6017	GB	1960	New		n
(3) 14	0-4-0DM LHU Class	435403	RH	1961	New		o
A	4wBE	3268	GB	1961	Admiralty		p
B	4wBE	3280	GB	1961	Admiralty		q
C	4wBE	3279	GB	1961	Admiralty		q
(F) C	4wBE	3277	GB	1961	Admiralty		q
E	4wBE	3267	GB	1961	Admiralty		p
(D) F	4wBE	3278	GB	1961	Admiralty		q

Table 5
Locomotives and Rail Trolleys, Nettleton Mines.

NOTES FOR TABLE 5

This list was sourced from *The Ironstone Quarries of the Midlands, Part VIII, South Lincolnshire;* Eric Tonks, 1991; *Industrial Railways and Locomotives of Lincolnshire and Rutland,* Industrial Railway Society (IRS), 2010; with subsequent revision and updating with the help of the IRS and members of the Narrow Gauge Railway Society.

RH	Ruston & Hornsby, Lincoln
GB	Greenwood and Batley, Leeds
4wDM	4-wheel; D – Diesel Locomotive; M – Mechanical Transmission
30DL	30 – the horsepower; DL – Diesel Locomotive
LBU	L – Locomotive; B – weight, in this case 4.5 tons; U – Underground work in mine with no fire hazard
LHU	L – Locomotive; H – Hydraulic transmission; U – Underground use in mine with no fire hazard
BE	Battery Electric

a 170374. Delivered to Greetwell Mines in Lincoln in 1934 and to Nettleton in 1935. Refurbished in the workshop at Nettleton and sold to the Welshpool and Llanfair Railway, March 1961. Sold October 1974 to a private owner in Herefordshire and, *c.*1992, to a private owner in Staffordshire where it remains. *(Fig 1)*

b 175403. Rebuilt in the workshop at Nettleton in 1962. Given a steam outline body and renamed CANNONBALL, delivered to Lysaghts Sports and Social Club at Holton le Moor to run on a circular track around the playing field. Sold, together with carriages and rails to a private owner in Lincolnshire in 2000 after the Lysaghts Club closed. Sold again at auction on 21 July 2012 in two Lots as 'Lot 66. Ruston 2 foot 6 inch gauge diesel locomotive c/w three 12 seater carriages and a further chassis which could be made into an additional carriage.' Sold for £3650. Lot 66A was approx 325 metres of 2 foot 6 inch rail track, sold for £3200. Present location and ownership not known. *(Fig 35.3)*.

c 183429. Sold to Millom Ironworks in 1966 for use for spare parts. Sold to J.S. Morgan and Sons Ltd, Barrow in Furness, for scrap in 1968.

d 191680 Scrapped at Nettleton for spares 1965. Frame and unreclaimed equipment sold to the Welshpool and Llanfair Railway. Sold August 2016 to a private owner, believed to be in the Stoke on Trent area.

e 195865. Placed in store inside the mine in 1966. Buried by a rock fall in 1967 and not recovered. *(Fig 30.3)*

f 224315. In 1965 this was renovated, painted red, and dedicated to use with the ambulance cars. Sold to a private collection in Hertfordshire in 1970, where it remains today.

g 318748. The prototype RH Class LBU locomotive, loaned by Rustons for underground haulage trial in January 1952. Sold to Dorman Long and Co for Kilton Ironstone mine in October 1952 and later transferred to Lingdale Mines in North Yorkshire. Subsequently scrapped at an unknown date. *(Fig 30.2)*

h 402439. From Rustons for two months trial November 1957. Returned to RH 1958 and a replacement 2YDA engine fitted February 1959 and purchased March 1959. Sold to a private collection in Hertfordshire in 1970, where it remains today. *(Fig 30.3)*

i 427856. Sold to the Whipsnade and Umfolozi Railway, now the Great Whipsnade Railway, in 1970. Overhauled by Sir Robert McAlpine and Sons. Subsequently scrapped by McAlpines at an unrecorded date. Parts probably used for the rebuild of 435403, see Note o.

j 432654. Sold to a private collection in Hertfordshire in 1970, where it remains today. *(Fig 30.3)*

k 2996. Sold 1970 to BSC Blackdene Fluorspar Mines. Subsequently sold to J.A. Lister and Son Ltd, Consett, for scrap, December 1974.

l 435402. Sold to the Whipsnade and Umfolozi Railway, now the Great Whipsnade Railway, in 1970. Overhauled by Sir Robert McAlpine and Sons. Subsequently scrapped by McAlpines at an unrecorded date. Parts probably used for the rebuild of 435403, see Note o.

m 6018. Sold to a private collection in Hertfordshire in 1970, where it remains today.

n 6017. Sold 1970 to BSC Blackdene Fluorspar Mines. Subsequently sold to J.A. Lister and Son Ltd, Consett, for scrap, December 1974.

o 435403. Sold to the Whipsnade and Umfolozi Railway, now the Great Whipsnade Railway, in 1970. Overhauled by Sir Robert McAlpine and Sons, probably using parts from 427856 and 435402, see Notes i and l. Sold to the Sittingbourne and Kemsley Light Railway, Kent, 10/1972 where it remains. *(Figs 30.4 and 30.5)*

p 3268 and 3267. Manufacture date not known. Ex Speedwell Electrics Ltd, Nottingham. Previously a torpedo carrier at Lodge Hill, Kent. Scrapped about August 1969.

q 3280, 3277; 3278; 3279. Ex Speedwell Electrics Ltd, Nottingham. Previously a torpedo carrier at Portsmouth Dockyard. 3280 scrapped about January 1969; 3277 and 3278 scrapped about August 1969; 3279 scrapped 1968.

When the mine closed redundant locomotives were stored around the site. Nos 5, 10, 12, 13 and E were retained for track lifting and underground safety works[1] but all had gone from the site by the end of 1970. Eight – five diesel and three battery – were sold on. Two of the big Rustons were cannibalised and provided spares for the restoration of the third. Three went into preservation in private collections, and others continued to find an industrial use. In addition to these, one remained at Lysaghts Playing Field and another had gone into preservation previously. At least five, maybe six, survive today. Another remains buried on site. All the details are in Table 5.

For haulage between the working faces to the main drifts horses were used in Top Mine, but with the opening of Bottom Mine three battery electric locomotives replaced them in 1960. These were supplied new. In addition, six second hand, battery electric trolleys were purchased. All nine of these electric vehicles were made by Greenwood and Batley, of Leeds. The locomotives were known as 'Greenbats' for short.

Fig 30.1. (Top left)
Loco No 1 (RH 170374) lowering tubs down to the tippler, probably in 1935. The steep siding in the foreground led down to the power house and workshop.
(Author's collection)

Fig 30.2. (Middle left)
Prototype Ruston LBU locomotive (RH 318748) on trial at Nettleton in 1952. Here for two months, it was returned to Lincoln, refurbished and sold to the Kilton Ironstone Mines in October 1952. The notice immediately above the driver's head reads 'WARNING Locos must not pass this point unless the DRIVER has set the signal to RED'.
(Author's collection)

Fig 30.3. (Bottom left)
Ruston LBU Class locomotive, believed to be works number 432654, Nettleton No 9, in 1959 at Back o the Farm. Jack Thompson is the driver. A second LBU can be seen in the background. This is probably 402439. The tunnel mouth to the right is that in which loco No 5 remains buried to this day and No 5, works number 195865, is at the extreme left. It is recognisable by the canopy over the driver's seat, a modification made in the on-site workshop.
(Author's Collection)

Fig 30.4.
Nettleton loco 14 (RH 435403) was one of three larger locos supplied for hauling stone trains from Bottom Mine to the tipping stage in 1958, 1960 and 1961. They were double ended, the cab being an optional extra. All three went to the Whipsnade and Umfolozi Railway, now the Great Whipsnade Railway, when the mine closed. Two were subsequently scrapped but this one was sold to the Sittingbourne and Kemsley Railway where it remains today.

Seen here driven by John Corcoran at Back o' the Farm, the loco is hauling the set of five man riding cars used to take miners to and from work between the welfare block at Nettleton Top and the mine at Nettleton Bottom.
(Author's collection))

The three larger Greenbats had two 7hp motors and weighed 4 tons. *(Fig 30.6)*. Essentially they comprised a large battery on a frame with a driving position at one end. Because battery locomotives are silent they acquired a reputation for causing accidents underground. Indeed, miners called them the 'widow maker', an epithet often used by miners when referring to dangerous equipment of any kind. For this reason they were equipped with a brass bell for the driver to ring as they moved and give warning of their approach.

There was a charging point for the larger Greenbats within Bottom Mine to save having to send them to the mine buildings every day. The batteries were secured by bolts and when these were removed the battery could be rolled off on small wheels. Two batteries were charged overnight and one during the day to ensure that there were always two locomotives available for work on any day.[2]

Six Greenwood and Batley, 4-wheel, battery electric vehicles were purchased second-hand from the Admiralty, via Speedwell Electrics Ltd of Nottingham where they were refurbished. These were motorised wagons rather than locomotives, known as the 'Rail Truck' by the manufacturer. Their previous use had been as torpedo carriers, four at Lodge Hill in Kent and two in Portsmouth Dockyard. Lodge Hill was one of the depots served by the 2 foot 6 inch gauge Lodge Hill and Upnor Railway. These were fitted with platforms 8 feet long by 4 feet wide with a carrying capacity of 3-4 tons. Their main use with the Admiralty was around the workshops. (3) The Lodge Hill and Upnor Railway closed in May 1961. *(Fig 30.7)*

The trolleys were probably sold as surplus to requirements to Speedwell Electrics before then since they were delivered to Nettleton in 1961. They were driven standing up, the battery and

*Fig 30.5.
Nettleton loco 14 (RH 435403) seen here in 2015 in disguise as Ivor the Engine at the Sittingbourne and Kemsley Light Railway, Kent. Edward Lloyd is the name normally given to this loco but it adopts its alter ego on special occasions. It is now driven from one end only and, because of the size of the carriages it pulls, from a standing position.
(John Corcoran)*

motor being positioned between the driver and the platform. *(Fig 30.8)*

At Nettleton the trolleys were used for the general movement of materials and equipment, although one was dedicated for the use of platelayers and another for the electricians and fitted with a cable carrier. Another was fitted with a seat and used to take the Bishop of Lincoln on a tour of the mine, and was thereafter known as the 'Bishops Carriage'.[4]

ROLLING STOCK

Wooden wagons used in Top Mine held about one ton of stone. *(Figs 30.1, 30.2 and 30.3)*. They had stout timber framing, extended to form dumb buffers, with horizontal plank sides, all strengthened with steel supports, with simple chain link coupling. Some of these were transferred from the Greetwell Mines in Lincoln when these closed; others were added and many remained in service until the 1960s. One that was transferred from Greetwell, Wagon No 20, was saved for preservation and is now believed to be that on display in the Museum of Lincolnshire Life in Lincoln.[5]

With the development of Bottom Mine new stone wagons were provided. Now steel bodied, most were long wheelbase and of three tons capacity. *(Figs 26.1 and 26.3)*. They were purchased second-hand, from where is not known. However, they proved to be too long for the corners inside the mine and had to be shortened by two feet. This was done by cutting out a central section and welding the two halves together.

All the work was carried out in the mine workshop. Some short wheelbase steel tubs of 1.5 tons capacity were also provided. For a time both the new and the older timber tubs were in use and two tipplers were in operation to serve them.[6]

The steel tubs used the Willison automatic coupling system. This was a major advantage in an operation which required every individual wagon to be coupled and uncoupled at both the loading and emptying stages. Wagons were coupled when pushed together and uncoupled easily using a hand lever set at both ends of the wagon. *(Figs 26.1 and 26.3)*

A few four-wheel flat wagons were used for carrying timber pit props from the sawmill to the mine.

The distance from the amenity and administration block at the mine yard to the mouth of Bottom Mine was almost a mile. To take miners to work a set of five-man rider vehicles was provided. *(Fig 30.4).* They were steel sided and painted with red and white diagonals. But it was not unusual to travel on benches in open tubs.

Finally, a set of three ambulance wagons were provided. Painted yellow and with fibre glass bodies, they were fitted with stretchers and first aid equipment. In 1965 Loco No 6 was renovated, painted red, and dedicated to the set as an emergency ambulance unit. *(Fig 30.9)*

*Fig 30.6. (Bottom of previous page)
A Greenwood and Batley tramming locomotive. No photographs of the large Greenwood and Batley locomotives in use at Nettleton have been found. This is very similar to them, however. It was supplied to the Llanharry Mine near Pontyclun in Wales, probably the 5 ton locomotive delivered in 1961, and now in the care of the Museum of Wales. The locomotives used at Nettleton weighed 4 tons and were fitted with a hand operated warning bell, a speedometer and a driver's seat with a back to it. The coupling system was also different at Nettleton. (National Museum of Wales)*

*Fig 30.7. (Above)
A Greenwood and Batley 4-wheel battery electric trolley, in use with the Admiralty at Chattenden in Kent in 1958. (Narrow Gauge Railway Society, D. Bailey collection)*

31. The Miners

The numbers of men employed at the two mines varied over the years. Newspapers and other records reported that in 1937 there were 160 men; in 1945, 128; 1947, 117; 1948, 148; 1961, 180; and 1968, 102. The work, especially underground, was physically hard, and men suffered from blisters and sore, hard skin on their hands.[1] A miner would usually load 13/14 tons a shift, each day for a five day week; up to 20 tons a day if robbing pillars. The wages were considered to be very good, so much so that some men went to work there for a short period to make some money before finding something more amenable to them elsewhere.[2] For others, working at the mine was something of a family tradition. John Corcoran followed his grandfather Ned Mumby, father Terry Corcoran and his uncle Jack Mumby, who all worked there for at least part of their working life.[3]

There was always a shortage of labour at the mines, compounded by turnover because many men found that they did not enjoy working underground in particular, and left for other jobs.[4] Every opportunity was taken to recruit people, and usually jobs were available to those who wanted them. There were two main problems – housing and transport. There was a lack of housing locally for the men, which meant employees lived in a variety of surrounding villages and towns. But there was also a lack of public transport links, especially at the times that men needed to be at work.

There was a variety of work available, not all of it working underground all the time. Even so, some of the surface jobs required men to work underground some of their time. Underground were miners and trammers.[5] Miners usually started their career as trammers. On the surface were office staff, electricians, blacksmiths, welders, carpenters, fitters, storemen, loco drivers, and operators of plant and machinery.

Fig 30.8. (Above)
Greenwood and Batley electric trolley crossing the embankment leading to the Nettleton Bottom Mine entrance. John Harradine driving. The long flight of steps linking the mine with the chalk quarry above can be seen on the right of this photograph.
(John Holmes, Brigg. Author's collection)

Fig 30.9. (Left)
The body of one of the ambulance cars, seen here in 2015 in use as a garden shed at Nettleton Top.
(Author)

Management required a manager and under manager, chief engineer, surveyor and mine deputies.[6]

The opening of the Nettleton mine in 1934 was a major factor in solving the unemployment problem of the Market Rasen area at a stroke. This, together with electricity and Post Office contracts as well as the need to lift the sugar beet crop provided work for every person registered with the Labour Exchange.[7] In 1938 the 160 miners were on short time, working three days a week due to a reduction in the demand for steel,[8] but in November they were back in full production.[9]

The Second World War brought some different challenges. Mining was a reserved occupation. In October 1944 a number of ironstone miners appeared at Caistor Court accused of persistent absenteeism. One, absent on 21 dates, cycled seven miles for a 6.30am start but claimed that his cycle was not always available for him. He disliked working underground and it 'made him dizzy'. He had been offered a house near to the mine but turned it down. This was not his first offence, having been fined before at Market Rasen for the same offence. He was fined again and the Chairman of the Bench said that 'the defendant must do his duty in this form of national service'. As a postscript to this case four months later, following a further Court appearance, the man was sent to prison for three months' hard labour.[10]

A second miner claimed that he was constantly unwell and that work underground brought on bad stomach trouble. He was desperate to get away from the mine and had volunteered for the Army and for work in the coalfields but had been turned down by both. Thomas Stephenson, the mine manager, told the Court that this man was a 'very good miner when he was at work'. A doctor said there were no physical reasons why he could not work, and the verdict was a fine. Two other miners were also fined, one claiming that he also had to work his 2.5 acres of land as well as help local farmers, hence he was on occasions late for work. The magistrate told him that his 'farming difficulties were doubtless very real but private considerations like this were not an answer to the charge'. He 'was a specified person and he had his duties to perform'.[11]

After the Second World War a Polish Resettlement Camp was established at the buildings of the former RAF Ludford Magna. Until 1955/56 this was home to

Fig 31.1.
Bill Portass was horsekeeper in 1961, seen here with horses Monty and Darkie, shortly before their retirement.
(Grimsby Evening Telegraph)

around 700 refugees living in Nissen huts.[12] Several men found work at Nettleton Top Mine and, without public transport, the mine had to provide a service.[13] A Commer lorry was fitted with four bench seats in the back, protected by a canvas cover, later changed to a fitted aluminium cover.

The men came out of the mine at 17.00, yellow with dust, and showered in the welfare block. The lorry first ran to Caistor and Market Rasen, returning to take the Polish workers to Ludford.

The driver started at 05.45 with runs to fetch men into work. During the day, converted to a conventional lorry, it would collect pit props from Grimsby Docks.[14]

F. Brocklesby was appointed horsekeeper on 19 August 1947. It was his 'duty to see that the horses are kept clean and well fed, and <u>no horse</u> to go to work in an unfit condition, improperly shod or

Fig 31.2.
The mine manager, Eurig Thomas, right of centre, with Josef Ivicz to his right. Josef and the two men to right and left were Hungarian refugees who came to work in the mine. (Roy Thomas collection)

without proper fitting harness including a guard for the eyes.'[15] *(Fig 31.1)*

Josef Ivicz, a blacksmith, was one of three Hungarians taken on after fleeing from the Russian invasion of Hungary in 1956. He became a British citizen in 1968.[16] When Bottom Mine opened and the office building at Top Mine became redundant, it was converted into a house, where Josef lived until being made redundant when Bottom Mine closed. *(Fig 31.2)*

In the 1950s there were three daily shifts, 06.00 to 14.00, 07.00 to 15.00 and 08.00 to 16.00. The first shift was popular as work on local farms, especially at harvest, was available to increase income.[17] Several miners mentioned this and, in 1944, there was a newspaper report that production was being lost because of absenteeism. There was a labour shortage on farms and miners were working on farms for cash in hand. Farmers and the mine managers had reached an agreement to stop the practice.[18] After 1961 there was only one daily shift underground, 07.00 to 15.00. The workshop staff worked 06.00 to 16.00, the apprentices from 06.00 to 15.00.[19]

By the time Bottom Mine opened there was a bus service, operated by Browns of Caistor. Two buses were used, one travelling south to Market Rasen, the other north to serve the Caistor area.[20] The Market Rasen bus left at 06.30, ran up the A46 to Holton le Moor and then up the mines roadway. *(Fig 31.3)*

A mine deputy was responsible for the safety of men underground on a daily basis and each one had responsibility for a particular part of the mine. He checked the safety of the roof in all working areas before men went in and around twice during the shift, and that air was circulating correctly. When pillars were being robbed he determined when the safety limits had been reached and was the last man in the area, responsible for collapsing the roof when all the

Fig.31.3.
One of the buses hired to provide a service to and from the mine for workers, seen here in 1961, standing in the mines yard. (Roy Thomas collection)

stone that could be safely got had been removed. The role of deputy was a recognised promotion from being a face worker. With responsibility came a fixed and regular wage as well as less physically demanding work. Many miners preferred to stay at the working face, however, as with piece work they had the opportunity to earn more money than did the deputy.

John Carter, as an electrician, recalled working in the south end of Top Mine after it had closed, recovering cabling, and being ordered to leave by the deputy because of a shortage of air.[21]

Apprentices were subject to the playing of practical jokes, especially when they first started. When John Corcoran started his engineering apprenticeship in 1960 he recalled being sent to the carpenters shop for a 'long stand'. He was told to stand by the stove and that he would be told when it was ready. After about ten minutes the foreman sent him back.[22] Patrick Loftus had been told of the jokes and was dreading the experience he knew he must face. So much so that when he was sent to the stores for a pair of 24 inch Stilsons he was very worried. Relief followed when he realised that there was

Fig 31.4.
Orb Cottages on Cooks Lane at Nettleton, built for miners by Lysaghts in 1944. (Dr John Esser)

The Company will obtain supplies for the Scunthorpe works mainly from the recently opened property at Nettleton Top, near Caistor.

So production was to be directed to Scunthorpe from the beginning. A very early photograph does exist, however, showing two private owner railway wagons being loaded in Holton le Moor sidings. These both carry the name 'WILLINGSWORTH'. The Willingsworth Iron and Coal Co had their steel works at Wednesbury, Wolverhampton. *(Fig 34.1)*

Top mine, as we have seen, was designed to produce 3,000 tons per week, or 156,000 tons per year and it first achieved this in 1940 and 1941, the peak years of production.

The next maximum tonnage of 173,000 tons was achieved in 1957 after opencast mining began. From then until 1962 there were year on year increases to a peak of 276,000 tons. This period saw the closure of Top Mine and the opening of Bottom Mine. The peak year of all was 1967, with almost 280,000 tons. In total 5.5 million tons of ironstone were removed in the 35 years that the mines were open. *(Table 6 and Fig 34.2)*

Fig 33.1. (Top)
The miner's basic tools, the pick and shovel. The collection seen here was being used to dig out outcropping ironstone to create the pitbank outside the mine. To the left is a tub loaded with ironstone.
(Caistor Heritage Trust)

Fig 33.2. (Middle)
Two miners using pneumatic compressed air picks, inside Bottom Mine in 1965. Although very heavy the men are holding the pick with one hand, the other supporting the compressed air pipe. They are standing on boards temporarily attached to the tub to give them the height to work the face. Beyond them are additional boards, inclined to catch falling stone and direct it into the tub. This would reduce the time required to dig fallen stone from the roadway, increasing output for the mine and wages for the men.
(Author's collection)

Fig 33.3. (Bottom)
The trial of a coal cutting machine, probably early in 1961. The auger cut a circular hole in the face but reduced the stone to a fine powder. Jim Wilkinson is the fitter seen here. (Roy Thomas collection)

Fig 34.1. (Left)
Private owner wagons at Holton le Moor sidings, taken when the permanent way was very new. The Willingsworth Iron and Coal Co had their steel works at Wednesbury, near Wolverhampton. (Author's collection)

Table 6. (Below)
Nettleton Mines: Ironstone Production, 1934 to 1969.

Fig 34.2. (Overleaf)
Nettleton Mines: Ironstone Production, 1934 to 1969.

Year	Tonnage	Notes
1934	3,280	
1935	53,250	
1936	58,978	
1937	96,514	Compressed air drills installed
1938	97,724	
1939	145,158	
1940	160,451	
1941	155,924	
1942	138,677	
1943	147,411	
1944	132,761	Taken over by J. Lysaght
1945	111,351	
1946	99,821	
1947	91,099	
1948	129,260	
1949	141,941	
1950	146,108	
1951	142,047	
1952	144,550	
1953	132,580	
1954	130,916	
1955	124,939	
1956	143,492	

1957	173,500	Opencast working begins
1958	177,609	
1959	203,125	
1960	209,276	Bottom Mine begins production
1961	264,578	Top Mine closes
1962	276,624	
1963	218,315	
1964	206,390	
1965	232,163	
1966	245,608	
1967	277,777	
1968	205,969	Bottom Mine closes and opencast ends
1969	21,236	From stock clearance and restoration work
TOTAL	5,440,402	

Nettleton Mines Ironstone Production, 1934–1969

Nettleton Mines Ironstone Production, 1934–1969

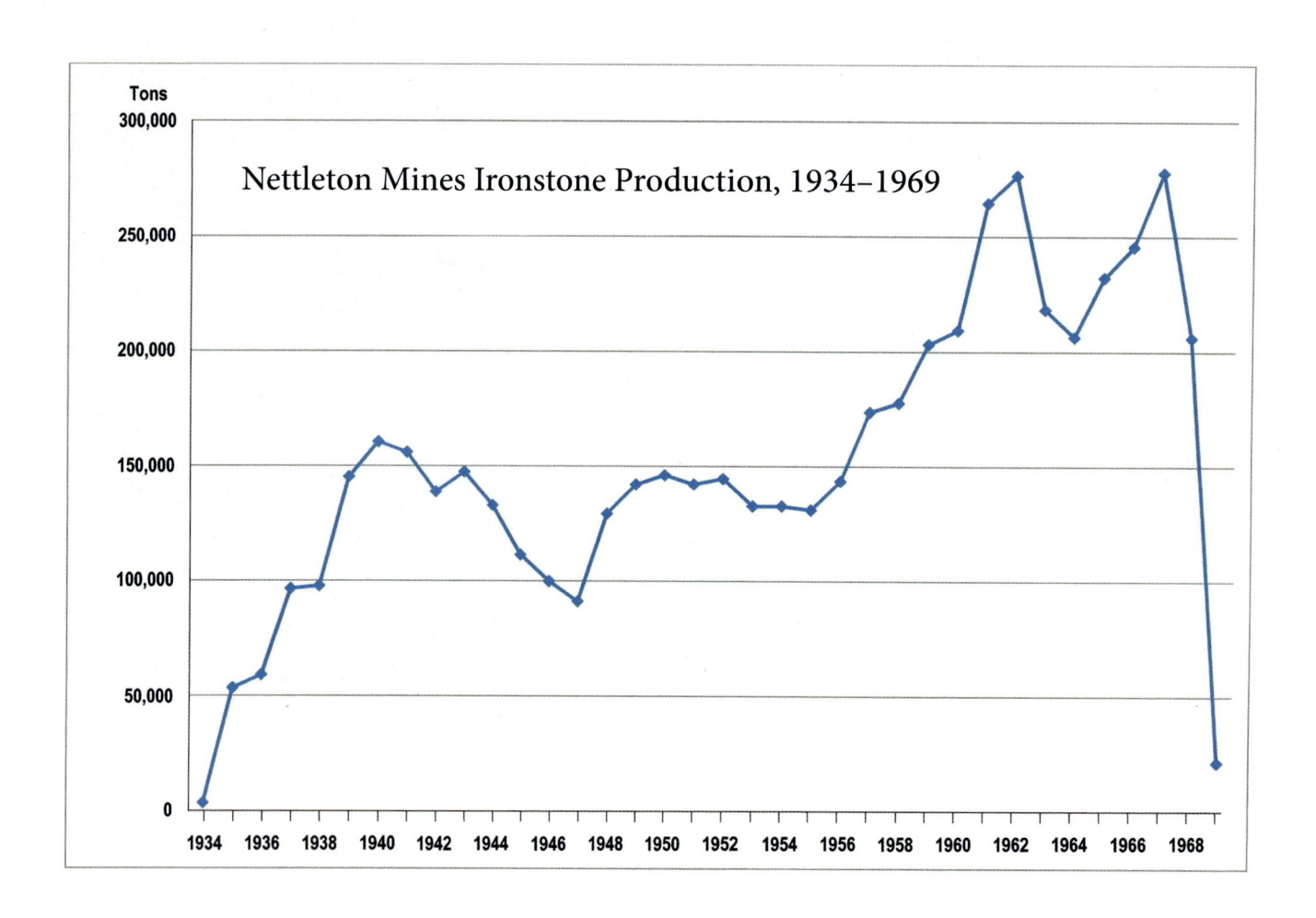

35. Lysaghts Sports and Social Club

Eurig Thomas was appointed as the mine manager at Nettleton in 1956, coming from the Irthlingborough ironstone mine in Northamptonshire. A keen sportsman, he encouraged the formation of the Lysaghts Sports and Social Club with its playing field adjacent to Holton le Moor sidings in the same year. Facilities for football, rugby, cricket and bowls were provided, together with a pavilion. *(Fig 29.4)*

Ten years later, in 1966, a new two storey clubhouse was built. Here was a large hall, bar and catering facilities.[1] *(Fig 35.1)*. The £5,000 cost was met largely with an interest free loan of £4,000 from the Scunthorpe management. This can be seen now to have been an indication of confidence in the future of the mine, made at a

Fig 35.1.
The clubhouse in 1995. The railway track laid around the playing field can be seen in the grass running away from the photographer. (Author)

Fig 35.2.
A tug o war competition under way on the playing field. Workers at the mine included here are Charlie Havercroft, Frank Favill, Albert Brocklesby, David Smith and Fred Barks. (Roy Thomas collection)

Fig 35.3.
Cannonball and its carriages on the Lysaghts Playing Field. RH 4wDM, 175403 was built into Cannonball form by Jack Mumby, Bill Maund, Russell Thomas and John Corcoran with the help of other tradesmen, welders, blacksmith and the mine machine shop. The driver is Jack Mumby. (Author's collection)

time when change was in the air and economies were being actively considered. *(See Section 36. Economies and Closure).*

The playing field and club was an important social centre for the area. Regular entertainments included parties, dances and bingo. It was also the venue for visiting entertainers, providing an opportunity to see celebrities of the day in the area. The singer Clodagh Rodgers and snooker players Alex (Hurricane) Higgins and Ray Reardon are among those remembered by local people.

The annual gala was well attended with sports, demonstrations and entertainment. *(Fig 35.2)*. In 1962 a circuit of around 500 yards of redundant railway line from the mine was laid around the outside of the playing field for the use of Locomotive No 2, rebuilt in a 'wild west' form and named 'CANNONBALL' with carriages created from redundant mine tubs. *(Fig 35.3. See also 30, Locomotives and Rolling Stock, for the locomotive details).* A lean-to shelter was provided at the rear of the cricket pavilion, forming a tunnel for the train to run through on its circuit. The train was out of use after 1965, but in 1980 was repaired and

Fig 35.4.
Lysaghts Club Snooker Trophy, later given to the Bowls Club. Made by Roly Clark of Caistor, incorporating shoes from the last three horses used underground at Nettleton Top mine, the award dates start in 1986 and end in 2009. (Dr John Esser)

refurbished to run again regularly.[2] By 1995 it was again out of use but would be occasionally pushed out of its shed for display.

The Lysaghts club disbanded in March 2000. Known to the end as Lysaghts Club, it still had former miners among its members. Its relatively isolated location and ageing membership, together with poor public transport links and the changing social circumstances that began to affect many rural pubs and clubs at that time caused its closure. The bowls club continued until about 2013, using a trophy made originally for snooker competitions in the clubhouse. *(Fig 35.4)*. The clubhouse was demolished in 2003 but the ground remained in use as the home of the South Kelsey Cricket Club until 2014.

36. Economies and Closure

In 1960 when Bottom Mine opened there must have been a feeling of optimism for the future, at least for the predicted 40-year life of production. But the 1960s were a period of change in the UK steel industry as it was in so many other industries. Nationalisation of the UK steel industry was under way and the ownership of the mine was vested in the British Steel Corporation in July 1968.[1]

An internal report by Lysaghts January 1966 considered the future of the Nettleton Mines and recommended drastic changes.[2] This report recommended:

- increasing the opencast operation to include all of the northern end of the former Top Mine, east of the Nettleton/Normanby road;
- have a self draining stack of some 20–30,000 tons of ironstone adjacent to the lorry road to Holton le Moor sidings;
- lead the stone, by road, to a stockpile to be established at Flixborough Dock. This would be available in about 12 months with the completion of mining in that area;
- aim to close the underground mine by mid to late summer 1966;
- lead the chalk from the chalk quarry by dumper and establish a stockpile at Holton le Moor sidings;
- organise a boring programme to establish the extent of stone workable by opencast methods to the north and west of the former Top Mine.

A justification for these proposals was not included but it is clear that exposing a stone bed and taking 100% of the ore using machinery was much more economically efficient than extracting 80% of the ore underground using a large number of men wielding hand held picks.

In February 1966 the mine manager gave his reply to this report. He stated that a decision on the future of Nettleton Mines was required in the immediate future as development in the underground and surface workings was at a critical stage. To achieve the necessary economies in the cost of production it was vital to mechanise the workings to the maximum possible degree.[3]

Speaking at the opening of the John Lysaghts new Clubhouse at Holton le Moor clubhouse on 14 September 1966,[4] Sir Douglas Bruce-Gardner, Chairman of GKN Steel, Lysaghts parent company, said that Britain imported 50% of the iron ore it used. The trend was to use bigger ships and improve ports to handle them as economies were needed in transport costs.[5] So shortly after Bottom Mine had gone into production the future of mining here was under review and drastic economies were being considered.

Closure of the mine was announced in March 1968.[6] It was said that nearly half of the 110 workers would lose their jobs. In fact, 42 men were made redundant in April 1968 as underground mining ceased. The last shift underground ended at 5.00pm on Friday 29 March.[7] *(Fig 36.1)* All were offered employment in the mines and quarries at Scunthorpe but only two or three took up the offer.

Opencast mining continued together with the subsequent restoration work, as did production at the chalk quarry. In February 1969 the British Steel Corporation announced the final closure of all but the chalk quarry and redundancy for some 60 men.[8] The reason given, by Mr John Darragh, mines manager, Scunthorpe, was that:

> There was too much capacity chasing demand and with some of the quarries in the Scunthorpe area at only 65% utilisation, it was logical and economic to reduce a multiplicity of units and step up production in what were left. Some of the mines in the Scunthorpe area

Fig 36.1.
A last day photograph of the men working underground. This is believed to be the last shift on Friday 29 March 1968 when this photograph of 38 of the 42 men being made redundant was taken. Underground working ceased from Monday 1 April 1968. (Author's collection)

were only single shift, one or two were double shift. The ultimate aim would be to have less mines but working round the clock. That, he said, was rationalisation.

Stating that the ore reserves in the Scunthorpe area were ample for at least the next 40 years, Mr Darragh said planning for the future envisaged a certain amount of imported ore. One of the disadvantages of Nettleton ore was that it had a high silica content, which meant that more lime had to be used.

Regarding the Nettleton limestone production, Mr Darragh said that Normanby Park would still continue to take about 1,000 tons a week'

Predictably the men themselves were concerned about their future. Some had worked at the mine for a long time; John Starbuck began work at Top Mine in 1935, 34 years before; Fred Goulsbra and Joe Wheatley for 22 years and John Smith, 14 years, are examples quoted in the report.

All workers were informed on 5 February 1969 that the production of ironstone would cease on 28 February 1969 and from that date all operations would be directed towards the restoration of the site and clearance of plant, equipment and stores. It was expected that the services of all the existing personnel would be required for at least six months from the date production ceased. Individual redundancy notices would be issued towards the end of that period and as necessary thereafter.[9] All work was completed by the end of August when all but the chalk quarry closed. The future of the chalk quarry was dependent upon the requirements of the Anchor Scheme at Scunthorpe. This was a major modernisation of the steel works during the late 1960s. Eleven men were retained to work in the quarry but by 1971 they were also redundant as need for the chalk quarry ended.

THE WALESBY SHAFT

37. A Study of the Walesby Shaft

This is the reprint of an article on the Shaft which appeared in Lincolnshire History and Archaeology, Vol 42, 2007, by the same author. It is relevant to include it in this book as it was, apart from boreholes, the only occasion other than at Claxby and Nettleton where shafts and adits were dug into the Claxby Ironstone. The opportunity has been taken to include some very minor amendments and an additional figure.

From 1868 to 1981 there was an ever present demand for ironstone mined in Lincolnshire, to feed ironworks at Scunthorpe and in the early years, south Yorkshire, north Nottinghamshire and west Derbyshire. Leases for land to be quarried in the county tended to be for relatively small areas of land with the result that there was a need for mining companies to be looking to extend their areas of work and, where possible, exploit new areas. If an area was deemed likely to have substantial deposits then surveying and exploratory work would take place to determine the quality and quantity of ore and hence the opportunity for a new mine.

On the western edge of the Lincolnshire Wolds the Claxby Ironstone Mine had operated from 1868 to 1885. Mining was not to take place again here until the nearby Nettleton Top Mine opened in 1934. However, after the First World War investigations took place at Walesby, north of Market Rasen, into the potential of an underground mine by the Frodingham Iron and Steel Co. *(Fig 37.1)* These took the form of two shafts, one a horizontal adit into the hillside from a location north of Otby Lane in the village and a vertical shaft down into the hill from a site to the north of Walesby Hill, the road from the village up onto the top of the Wolds. Both are on private land with no public access but both are visible from the adjacent roads.

The investigation of the history of these works came about as the result of a chance find of a vertical geological section entitled simply The Walesby Shaft. It transpired that there was some oral history of the investigation and this included an understanding of the site of the vertical shaft together with some memories of the adit into the hillside. The site manager had stayed at White Hart in Market Rasen and was driven to Walesby each day in a horse drawn vehicle. The men employed were from the north east of England, presumably bringing mining experience with them. In addition, when the vertical shaft was first capped it was covered with a timber cover and children dropped stones down through cracks in the woodwork.

An enquiry at the BGS (British Geological Survey) revealed that their borehole records show that the vertical shaft was put down in 1928 as a trial by the Frodingham Iron and Steel Company. Roach Ironstone was found at a depth of 101 feet (30.78m) and was 10 feet (3.05m) thick. Claxby Ironstone was found at a depth of 175 feet (53.34m) and was 22 feet (6.71m) thick. They have no record of any adit. A series of 12 further boreholes were drilled in the Walesby area between April and November 1943 by the Appleby Frodingham Iron and Steel Co to prospect the Claxby bed.

The shaft site is located on the north side of Walesby Hill (TF143 932). The site is marked by a spoil heap, now covered by hawthorn scrub. The spoil heap is the result of the digging of the shaft and is about 30m x 10m and about 1.3m high. The site of the shaft is marked by a concrete slab at the south end, 15 feet (4.6m) square. The shaft may well still exist below this. *(Fig 37.2)*

The geological section reveals that the shaft was 175 feet 9 inches (53.6m) deep. For the first 58 feet 6 inches (17.8m) it was driven through chalk, and eight

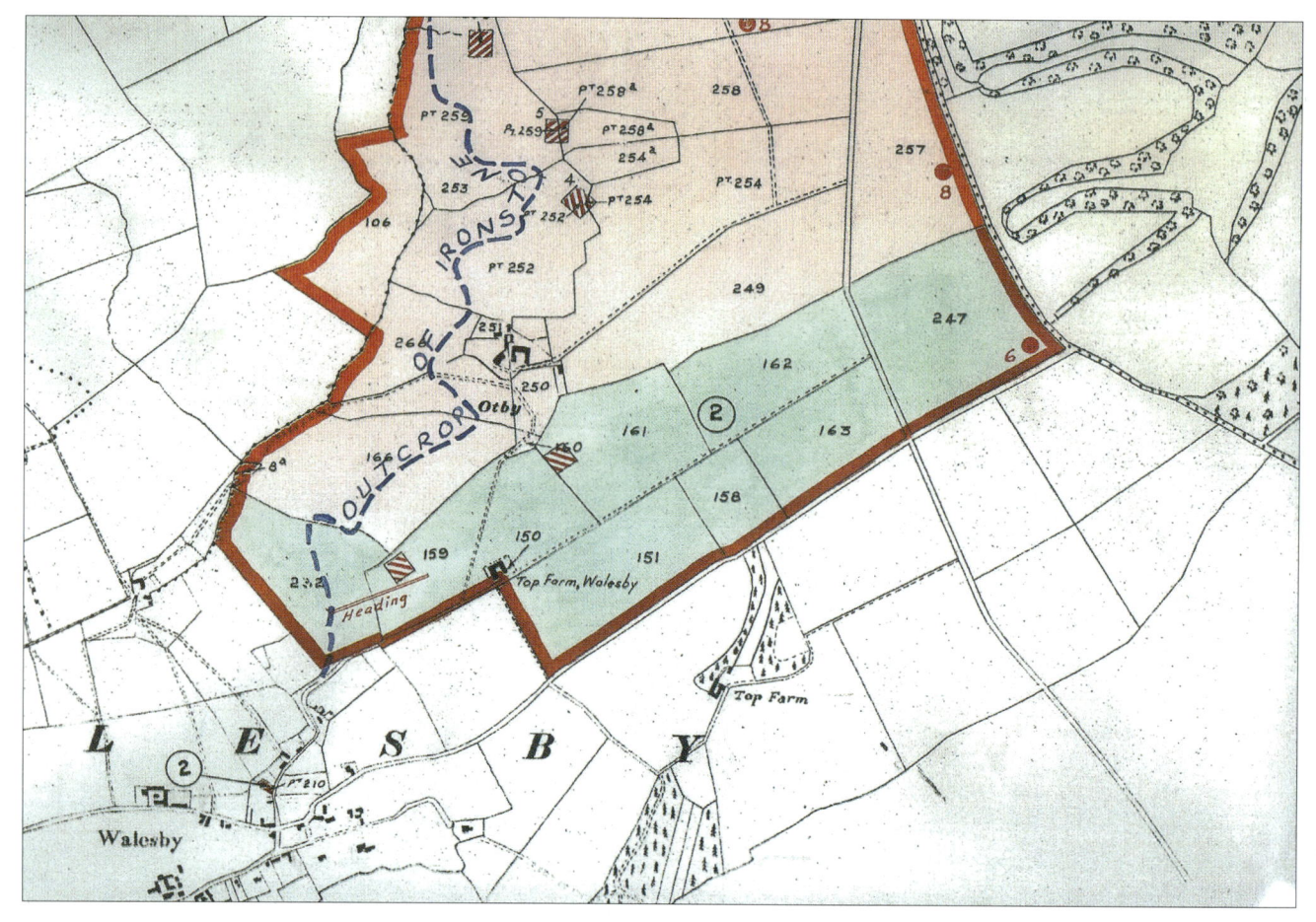

Fig 37.1.
Extract from a plan showing the area leased by the Frodingham Iron and Steel Co (sic), in green. The red line probably defines the area within which they were interested in taking a lease. The red dots are boreholes. The meaning of the hatched red squares is not known. The horizontal heading, which was Heading No 1, can be seen in the bottom left of the leased area. The vertical shaft was in the northern apex of Field 158.
(Scunthorpe steelworks archive, copy in author's collection)

feet (2,4m) square, lined with timber boards. At 63 feet (19.2m) they struck water and to a depth of 80 feet (24.4m) this section, reduced to seven feet (2.1m) square, was double timbered. From here the shaft became circular, at a diameter of six feet (1.8m). At first timber lined with steel rings on the inside, this gave way to a steel tube and, for the final 60 feet (18.3m), again timbered but, seemingly, without the steel rings. Roach Ironstone, of a quality not normally worked, was encountered between 91 feet (27.7m) and 101 feet (30.8m) and two beds of Claxby Ironstone were encountered at the base of the shaft, one of seven feet (2.1m) in depth above one of 12 feet, (3.6m) separated by two feet (60cm) of clay.

A search of the ground north of Otby Lane reveals a cutting into the steep scarp slope of the hillside with spoil creating an embankment around the lower end where it had been tipped down the hillside. (TF134 929) *(Fig 37.3)*. In line with the cutting, up the hill, a line of what appear to be shallow pitfalls can be discerned. The cutting and pitfalls appeared to be in line with the base of the shaft, a situation confirmed by an air photograph of 1971 held by the County Councils Heritage Environment Record. The cutting, pitfalls and spoil heaps are also clearly seen on Google Maps.

Confirmation of the existence of the adit came from a search of the records held by Corus in Scunthorpe.

This reveals that the adit, described as Heading No 1, was dug horizontally for a distance of 112 feet (34.1m) on the surface and for 479 feet (146m) underground. Furthermore, what was described as Heading No 2 was dug horizontally eastwards from the base of the vertical shaft for a distance of 217 feet (66.1m). Unfortunately, the drawings are not dated. However, two dates appear on the sections, one on each. For Heading No 1 the date 'Oct 7th 1919' appears at a point 357 feet (108.8m) in from the tunnel mouth. On that for the vertical shaft the date 'Oct 26' is written at a point 82 feet (25.0m) down from the surface. *(Fig 37.4)*

Heading No 1 was seven feet (2.1m) in height and was driven into the hillside at the point where the ironstone outcropped on the hillside. Heading No 2 was six feet (1.8m) in height. The latter started from the foot of the shaft and rose to follow the centre of the ironstone layer. In both Headings sumps, going down, and risers, going up into the roof, were dug at regular intervals to determine the geology. A geological section has been added to the section of Heading No 1 and this shows that the stone bed is corrugated, the shaft alternating between driving through ironstone and sand with sandstone boulders.

The geology demonstrates why the establishment of a mine here was not to be an economic proposition. The Heading could not follow the steep corrugations of the ironstone so half of what would have been produced would have been waste. The site, by contrast, would have been excellent. Sidings served by a branch from the Lincoln to Grimsby line, 3km to the west, would have run across level fields. Heading No 1 lay on about the 275 feet (83.8m) contour of the hillside from where the stone would fall to the railway around the 200 feet (61.0m) contour below.

As to the discrepancy with the dates it may be that the shaft and headings were being dug in 1919 and that the date of 1928 perhaps relates to the deposition of the record with BGS.

Fig 37.2.
The concrete capped vertical shaft with the spoil heap beyond, in February 2007. (Author)

Fig 37.3.
The view westwards from above the site of the mouth of Shaft No 1 showing the cutting into the hillside. February 2007 (Author)

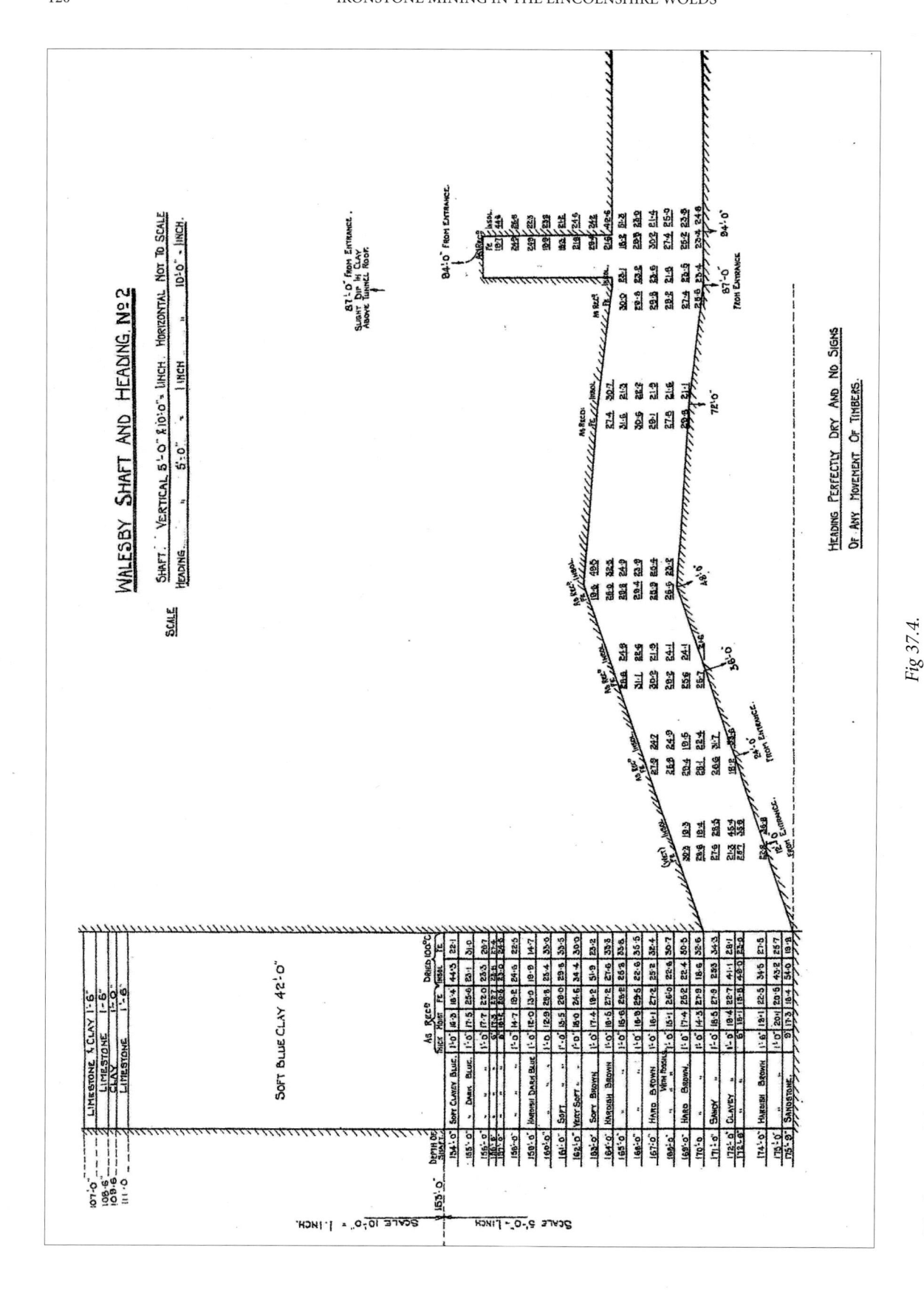

Fig 37.4.
The bottom of the shaft and the start of Heading No 2. The Claxby Ironstone has been carefully recorded, lying between the 153 feet datum and that of 175 feet. Note how the heading rises into the centre of the bed and that at 87 feet the first of the risers has been driven into the roof to prove the thickness at this point. (Authors collection)

POSTSCRIPT

*Fig 38.1.
Nettleton Mine visit, Heritage Open Days, 17 September 1995. Over 200 people turned up. (Author)*

38. Postscript

The most complete set of surviving evidence of the history of mining in Lincolnshire can be found at Nettleton. It is all in private ownership and several buildings are still in use. Only a little of this evidence is in public view. That not in use, such as mine entrances, earthworks and roadways is under threat of loss through decay, vandalism and a lack of economic use. Those elements will continue to decay and there is a risk that safety issues will require their loss.

For many years now there has been public interest in the history of mining here. Tours of the Claxby and the Nettleton Mines sites and remains have taken place several times beginning in 1995 and still remain popular today. The most remarkable was the Nettleton tour for Heritage Open Days on 17 September 1995 when around 200 people turned up! *(Fig 38.1)*

Fig 38.2. The, now closed, tunnel to take the public footpath, now the Viking Way, underneath the embankment in Nettleton Bottom valley, seen here in January 2015. (Author)

on its route south from Nettleton village, winding upwards through the Nettleton Bottom valley to reach the Nettleton to Normanby le Wold road by Acre House. This passed through the Bottom Mine embankment in a tunnel created for the footpath when the embankment was built.

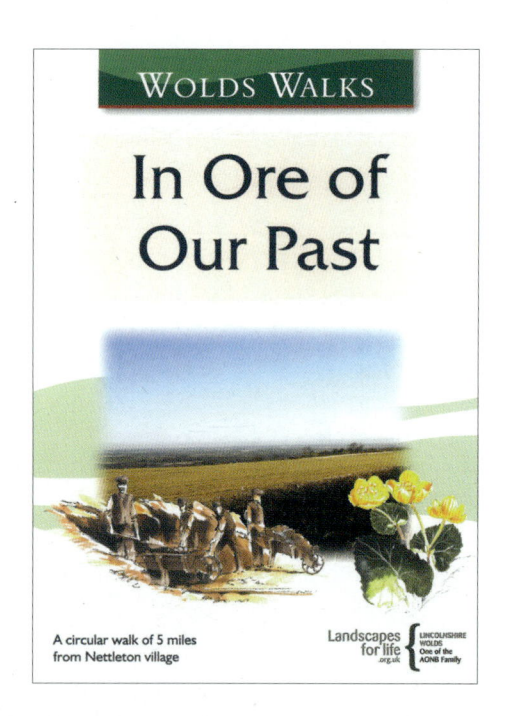

The tunnel in the embankment survives. Safety concerns due to its deteriorating condition caused it to be closed in 1998. Investigations were made into its repair by a small working group under the guidance of the Lincolnshire County Council and the Lincolnshire Wolds Countryside Project with the Society for Lincolnshire History and Archaeology but the estimated cost of £100,000 proved to be too much. *(Fig 38.2)*. The footpath was diverted and today passes the three drift entrances to Bottom Mine. A walk through the tunnel did give an impression of what the mine was like but an impression can still be gained by looking through the steel mesh screen that closes it off.

The difficulty is always the access. All of the Claxby Mine site, the Walesby Shafts and most of the Nettleton Top and Bottom Mines sites are on private land with no public access. The generosity of the landowners has been the only reason that visits have been allowed to take place.

The former mine roadway between Nettleton Top and Nettleton Bottom was for over 20 years a Permissive Path through the Environmental Stewardship scheme, but this agreement has now ceased. Permanent public access is available along the Viking Way footpath,

Fig 38.3. (Top left)
Wolds Walks leaflet and heritage trail, first published 2002.
(Lincolnshire Wolds Countryside Service)

Fig 38.4. (Above)
Nettleton Village Hall, Drop In Day, 10 January 2015
(Author)

Fig 38.5 (Opposite page)
Claxby Mine, Geology walk, Heritage Open Days on
11 September 2016 (Lincolnshire Wolds Countryside Service)

The research work undertaken at that time was not wasted, however. The popular circular walk, 'In Ore of Our Past', the Nettleton Mines Heritage Trail, was created in 2001. *(Fig 38.3)* The car park and the first interpretation boards were provided for this on Nettleton Hill and it remains a popular spot from which to take circular walks in this part of the Wolds.

The most recent event, and the one that has led to the publication of this book, has been the Down Your Wold project started in 2014. The Mining Heritage of the Lincolnshire Wolds Project was a community initiative which brought together a group of local people to raise the profile of what had happened. This was done with a Drop In Day (Fig 38.4), and a mixture of talks and visits. *(Fig 38.5)* This led to research projects; the recording of oral history;[1] photographs and documents.[2] The result has been a successful touring exhibition *(Fig 38.6)*, newspaper articles, local radio and television programmes, and this book, to ensure that the history is recorded, the landscape changes understood and that the history will not be lost.

Fig 38.6.
Former miners at the launch of the touring exhibition display, Caistor Heritage Centre, 5 March 2016. Back row, left to right, Joe Willisch, Victor Brocklesby, Bill Maund. Front row, left to right, Patrick Loftus, John Corcoran, Roy Thomas
(Linda Oxley)

NOTES AND REFERENCES

1. Introduction
1. Squires, Stewart, 2007, 'The Underground Mines of Lincolnshire', in J. Howard and D. Start (eds), *All Things Lincolnshire, a collection of papers and tributes to celebrate the 80th birthday of David N Robinson, OBE MSc*, Lincoln, Society for Lincolnshire History and Archaeology, 2007, pp 203-210.
2. Frank Henthorn, PhD, *Letters and Papers concerning the establishment of the Trent, Ancholme and Grimsby Railway, 1860-1862*, Lincoln Record Society, 1975, pxvi.

3. Geology
1. Swinnerton H.H. and Kent P.E., *The Geology of Lincolnshire*, Lincolnshire Naturalists Union, Second Edition, 1976.
2. Robinson, David, April 1971, 'Nettleton Iron Mine', *Lincolnshire Life*, pp 30-33.
3. G.D. Gaunt, T.P. Fletcher and C.J. Wood, *Geology of the country around Kingston upon Hull and Brigg*, London, HMSO, 1992, pp 130-131.
4. Nikolaus Pevsner, John Harris and Nicholas Antram, *The Buildings of England, Lincolnshire*, Penguin Books, Second Edition, 1989.
5. *Leeds Mercury*, 9 November 1872.

4. Archaeology
1. Lincolnshire HER. Claxby Parish, HER Numbers 50143, 51943, 51944, 51949, 51953.
2. *Lincolnshire Chronicle*, 19 August 1892
3. E. Mansel Sympson. *Lincolnshire*, Cambridge University Press. 1913, reprinted 2012, p86.
4. Everson, Taylor and Dunn, *Change and Continuity, Rural Settlement in North-West Lincolnshire*, London. HMSO, 1991, pp 1, 2, 7, 10.
5. *Stamford Mercury*, 11 June 1869.
6. Lincolnshire HER. Nettleton Parish, HER Numbers 50190, Hardwick DMV and 50191, West Wykeham DMV.

5. Landowners and Prospectors
1. *Frodingham Ironstone, Letters, notes and observations concerning the discovery and exploitation, Part one, 1858 to 1860*, Les Wells, Scunthorpe, 2006.
2. Marling was the process of improving the quality of poor sandy soils by spreading clayey soil over it.
3. *Stamford Mercury*, 8 June 1860.
4. *Stamford Mercury*, 15 June 1860.
5. *Stamford Mercury*, 22 June 1860.

6. In the Beginning
1. Ordnance Survey, 1:2500 County Series Second Edition, Lincolnshire, XXXVIII.9.
2. Plan of Ironstone Mines worked in the Parishes of Normanby, Nettleton and Claxby, Dated 1872 but updated with the workings to 1885, Copy with the author, from the British Geological Survey. BGS ref KP7531.
3. Lincolnshire Archives Ref YARB 5/9/7.
4. *Stamford Mercury*, 22 November 1867.
5. G. Hurst, *Great Central East of Sheffield, Vol 1*. Milepost Publications, 1989. p.73.
6. Stewart Squires, *The Lincoln to Grantham Line via Honington*. Oakwood Press. 1996, pp 105-125.
7. Copy of Lease, Lincolnshire Archives, Reference YARB 5/9/8.
8. Copy of Tracing Shewing (sic) the Quantity of Land Occupied by the Works and Tramways at the Claxby Ironstone Mines, October 1867, John Fraser, Leeds, Civil Engineer, Lincolnshire Archives, Reference YARB 5/9/6.
9. Lincolnshire Archives, YARB 5/9/6.

9. Surface Works and Buildings
1. Ordnance Survey, 1:2500 County Series First Edition, Lincolnshire, Sheets XXXVII.12 and XXXVIII.9.
2. Sheet XXXVII.12 was surveyed in 1886 and published in 1887. Sheet XXXVIII.9 was surveyed in 1887 and published in 1888. The survey date is the year that the superintendant made his final examination of a ground survey that would have taken place before this date. Such details as the railway lines would be added or deleted by him on his inspection. The former survey ignored sheet boundaries but the final inspection was confined to them. Hence changes here would reflect changes that had taken place between the dates of the final inspection and if there were differences either side of the boundary they would appear on the published maps. Hence, there were two tipping docks in 1886 but the rail access to them had changed by 1887. (Correspondence with Rob Wheeler, Secretary to the Charles Close Society).
3. *Lincolnshire Chronicle*, 21 May 1927.
4. *Lincolnshire Chronicle*, 21 May 1927.
5. Tramplates were a form of early rail, commonly used on tramroads in the late eighteenth and early nineteenth centuries. They were short sections of angled rail, around 3 feet long. Bolted together they provided a railway where the flange was on the rail rather than the wheel and the wheels were contained within the flanges.
6. *Lincolnshire Chronicle*, 21 May 1927.

10. Railway Siding and Incline
1. *Lincolnshire Chronicle*, 3 December, 1927.
2. Personal correspondence, Chris Padley, 2 October 2000.
3. Working Timetable for the Manchester, Sheffield and Lincolnshire Railway, Hull and Lincoln Branch, and Timetable of Iron Ore Trains between Ardsley

and Holton, via Keadby, National Railway Museum, ALS4/132/A/5, pp 56 and 58.
4. Ordnance Survey, First Edition 1:2500 map, Sheet XXXVII.8, published 1887.
5. Stewart Squires, *The Lincoln to Grantham Line via Honington*, Oakwood Press, 1996, p.120.
6. *Stamford Mercury*, 4 February 1870.

11. Calcining
1. *Stamford Mercury*, 22 November 1867.
2. *Stamford Mercury*, 21 July 1871.
3. *Lincolnshire Chronicle*, 21 May 1927.
4. Historic England, Rosedale East Mines, Scheduled Ancient Monument List Entry Summary.
5. *Stamford Mercury*, 26 August 1872.

12. The Miners
1. *Stamford Mercury*, 4 November 1870.
2. *Stamford Mercury*, 1 September 1871.
3. Leverington and Birch. 'Claxby Ironstone Mine', *Industrial Archaeology Newsletter*, Vol 3. No 2, 1968, pp 9-10.
4. Rex C. Russell and Elizabeth Holmes, *Two Hundred Years of Claxby Parish History*, Claxby Parish Council, 2002, p.43.
5. *Grimsby Evening Telegraph*, 21 November 1972 and 25 January 1973.
6. *Lincolnshire Chronicle*, 21 May 1927.
7. *Lincolnshire Chronicle*, 3 April 1896.
8. Rex C. Russell and Elizabeth Holmes, *Two Hundred Years of Claxby Parish History*, Claxby Parish Council, 2002, p.9.
9. The former school, on Pelham Road, is now the Viking Centre, a hostel for groups involved in field studies and outdoor pursuits.

13. Accidents
1. Compiled from information collected by Rex Russell and the author from a variety of published sources, mainly local newspapers.
2. *Stamford Mercury*, 31 December 1869
3. *Stamford Mercury*, 1 April 1870
4. *Stamford Mercury*, 8 April 1870
5. *Stamford Mercury*, 25 May 1870
6. *Stamford Mercury*, 21 July 1871
7. *Stamford Mercury*, 4 August 1871
8. *Stamford Mercury*, 18 August 1871
9. *Stamford Mercury*, 25 August 1871
10. *Stamford Mercury*, 10 May 1872
11. *Stamford Mercury*, June 1872
12. *Stamford Mercury*, 26 July 1872
13. *Stamford Mercury*, 27 December 1872
14. Eric Tonks, *The Ironstone Quarries of the Midlands, History, Operation and Railways, Part VIII, South Lincolnshire*, Runpast, 1991, p.224
15. John Wrottesley, *The Great Northern Railway, Volume II. Expansion and Competition*, Batsford, 1979, pp 126-127.
16. Plan of Ironstone Mines worked in the Parishes of Normanby, Nettleton and Claxby, dated 1872 but updated with the workings to 1885, copy with the author, from the British Geological Survey, BGS ref KP7531.

14. The Strike of 1872
1. *Stamford Mercury*, 26 August, 2 and 9 September 1872.

15. 1871 Census
1. *Stamford Mercury*, 7 February 1873.
2. *Lincolnshire Chronicle*, 21 May 1927.

16. Production
1. G. Hurst, *Great Central East of Sheffield*, Vol 1, Milepost Publications, 1989, p.73.
2. Lincolnshire Archives, Yarborough Estate Account Book, YARB 5/9/6.
3. Lincolnshire Archives, YARB/5/9/10.
4. *Stamford Mercury*, 12 March 1875.
5. Squires, Stewart, 2010, 'The Greetwell Ironstone Mines', *Lincolnshire History and Archaeology*, Vol 45, pp 55-6.
6. *Stamford Mercury*, 21 December 1877.
7. *Stamford Mercury*, 17 February 1882.
8. *Lincolnshire Chronicle*, 21 May 1927.
9. *Stamford Mercury*, 7 February 1873.
10. *Lincolnshire Chronicle*, 27 May 1875.

17. Closure and After
1. Report by Lysaghts dated February 1943. Copy held by author.
2. Personal conversation with John Brant.

18. Claxby Parish Church
1. *Stamford Mercury*, 23 June 1871
2. Ordnance Survey, 1:2500 County Series First and Second Edition, Lincolnshire, XXXVIII.9.

19. Early Proposals
1. Eric Tonks, *The Ironstone Quarries of the Midlands, Part VIII, South Lincolnshire*, Runpast Publishing, Cheltenham, 1991, p.227.
2. *Hull Daily Mail*, Wednesday 8 March 1905
3. Ordnance Survey 1:10560 County Series Second Edition maps, 1907, Lincolnshire Sheets XXXVII.NE and XXXVII.NW.
4. Plan signed B. Ramsden, Greetwell, Lincoln and annotated *Sent March 29 1906. Duplicate of plan sent April 1906*. Author's collection.
5. Squires, Stewart, 2010, 'The Greetwell Ironstone Mines', *Lincolnshire History and Archaeology*, Vol 45, pp 55-67.
6. British Geological Survey; BGS ID: 472813: BGS Reference: TF 19NW47.
7. Undated plan showing trial holes, plotted on a composite of the OS Second Edition 1:2500 maps, all published 1906, XXXVII.4, XXXVII.8, XXXVIII.1, and XXXVIII.5. Plan held at Scunthorpe steelworks archive, copy held by author.

20. In the Beginning
1. The Mid-Lincolnshire Iron Co Ltd changed its name

to the Mid-Lincolnshire Ironstone Co Ltd in July 1885. However, they used the title 'The Mid-Lincolnshire Iron Coy Ltd' on their steam locomotive, delivered to the Greetwell Mines in 1911 and Mid-Lincolnshire Iron Co Ltd on the reports at footnotes 2, 3, and 6 below. Tonks, *The Ironstone Quarries of the Midlands. History, Operation and Railways. Part VIII. South Lincolnshire*, Runpast Publishing, Cheltenham, 1991, pp 213-214, 220 and 223.
2. File copy of Progress report on work at the site, by the Mid-Lincolnshire Iron Co Ltd, dated 27 Jan 1930. Copy held by author.
3. File copy of Progress report on work at the site, by the Mid-Lincolnshire Iron Co Ltd, dated 23 Aug 1930. Copy held by author.
4. *Lincolnshire Echo*, 9 February 1939. Thomas Stephenson, 'the manager of the ironstone mine at Nettleton', was fined for a traffic offence on the road from Market Rasen to Caistor.
5. *Lincolnshire Echo*, 10 September 1934
6. File copy of report on work at the site, by the Mid-Lincolnshire Iron Co Ltd, dated 3 June 1937. Copy held by author.
7. Plan of Nettleton Mine, dated 14 March 1941. Copy held by author.
8. *Mine & Quarry Engineering*, May 1944, http://www.dmm.org.uk/minequar/4406-02.htm.

21. Underground
1. Drift No 2 is identified on some surviving plans as 'North No 1 Main'. To avoid any confusion the original terms have been used in this book.
2. Monty and Darkie were the last two, joining Duke, Shorty, Jack and Laddie living in retirement on site. With complete closure in 1969 all the survivors were bought by local people.
3. Fred Wright, oral history.
4. Kenneth Sharp, oral history.
5. The base was unscrewed and filled with calcium carbide in pellet form. A reservoir at the top of the lamp held a small amount of water which, by the use of a tap, was allowed to flow into the carbide chamber below. The water reacted with the carbide to form acetylene gas, fed to a burner to produce a flame. The latter was focused by a shiny reflector to give a bright white light.
6. Not all ironstone mines were entirely gas free. An explosion of gas in Lingdale Mine in Cleveland, 24 August 1953, killed eight miners.
7. Tailby, Alan R., *A Parish Camera, Nettleton, Holton le Moor, Caistor, Grasby*, self published, 1994, p.49.
8. Kenneth Sharp, oral history.
9. *Nettleton Mine, Support Rules, Coal Mines (Support of Roof and Sides) Gen. Regs. 1947*, (4A). Lincolnshire Archives, MISC DEP 316/4/2.
10. Kenneth Sharp, oral history.
11. Kenneth Sharp, oral history.
12. Nettleton Top Mine, undated plan, Author's collection.
13. Nettleton Top Mine, Working Plan of the Mine as completed up to August 1961. Author's collection.
14. Tailby, Alan R., *A Parish Camera, Nettleton, Holton le Moor, Caistor, Grasby*, self published, 1994, p.49.
15. *Lincolnshire Echo*, 9 February 1938.
16. Correspondence with owner, email dated 22 January 2015.
17. Nettleton Top Abandonment Plan, 4 August 1961, Copy held by Author.

22. Surface Works and Buildings
1. Eric Tonks, *The Ironstone Quarries of the Midlands, History, Operation and Railways, Part VIII, South Lincolnshire*, Runpast, 1991, p.228.

23. The Aerial Ropeway
1. *Lincolnshire Echo*, 29 January 1947.
2. *Lincolnshire Echo*, 24 February 1947.

24. Development
1. BGS Borehole logs.
2. Extension of the Nettleton Mining Area, preliminary report by Durnford and Lee, Mineral Valuers, Consultant Mining Engineers and Surveyors, Doncaster, for John Lysaghts Scunthorpe Works, dated 1 April 1955. (Author's collection)
3. In his early career Eurig Thomas worked as a coal miner in Wales. Obtaining management qualifications, he moved to the Irthlingborough ironstone mine in Northamptonshire, from where he came to Nettleton in 1956. (Roy Thomas, personal conversation)
4. Lincolnshire County Council, *Review of Mineral Sites*, January 1996. Copy held by author.
5. Eurig Thomas, interviewed 17 August 1995.
6. Bill Shaw, oral history.
7. Report, *Future Developments at Nettleton Mine*, dated 14 January 1961. (Author's collection)
8. Eric Tonks, *The Ironstone Quarries of the Midlands, History, Operation and Railways, Part VIII South Lincolnshire*, Runpast, 1991, p.232.
9. The new rails were of 60lb and 40lb per yard in weight, compared with 30lb per yard rail used for Top mine. Eric Tonks, *The Ironstone Quarries of the Midlands, History, Operation and Railways, Part VIII South Lincolnshire*, Runpast, 1991, p.228 and p.232.
10. Report dated 7 June 1957, *Nettleton Project*, by John Lysaghts Scunthorpe Works Limited.

25. Underground
1. Mine report, 27 October 1961. Copy held by author.
2. Summary of Mining at Nettleton, undated, probably 1964. Copy held by author.

26. Surface Works and Buildings
1. Conversation with Roy Thomas.
2. The tubs were fitted with the Willison Automatic Coupling, a system that ensured that tubs became coupled up immediately they were pushed together.
3. Drawing of workshop layout by John Corcoran, copied to author in May 2015.

4. Undated and untitled plan showing water supply arrangements, Copy of that in Scunthorpe Steelworks archives, held by author.
5. John Corcoran, email to author.
6. Plan, Arrangement of Welfare and Office Block for Nettleton Mine, John Lysaghts Scunthorpe Works Ltd, 25 May 1959. Copy held by author.
7. Plan, John Lysaghts (Scunthorpe Works) Ltd, Nettleton Mines, September 1960. Copy of that in Scunthorpe Steelworks archives, copy held by author.
8. Eric Tonks, The Ironstone Quarries of the Midlands, History, Operation and Railways, Part VIII, South Lincolnshire, Runpast, 1991, p.232.

27. Opencast Working
1. Report dated 7 June 1957, *Nettleton Project*, by John Lysaghts Scunthorpe Works Ltd. Copy held by author.
2. Report dated 9 July 1957, *Nettleton Mining Area*, by Robert B. Beilby, Mining Engineer, for John Lysaghts Scunthorpe Works. Copy held by author.
3. Report dated January 1996, *Environment Act 1955: Review of Mineral Sites*, Lincolnshire County Council. Copy held by author.
4. Report dated January 1996, *Environment Act 1955: Review of Mineral Sites*, Lincolnshire County Council. Copy held by author.
5. Summary of Mining at Nettleton. Undated report of c.1961 included within mine papers in the Roy Thomas collection.
6. Grimsby Evening Telegraph, cutting undated but probably June 1961.
7. John Corcoran, email to author, 19 May 2015.

28. The Chalk Quarry
1. Lincolnshire County Council, Review of Mineral Sites, January 1996, copy held by author.
2. John Carter, oral history and interview with author.
3. David Robinson, 'Nettleton Iron Mine', *Lincolnshire Life*, April 1971.
4. www.bbc.co.uk>history>dblock>page

29. Holton le Moor Sidings
1. Eric Tonks, *The Ironstone Quarries of the Midlands, History, Operation and Railways, Part VIII, South Lincolnshire*, Runpast, 1991, p.230.
2. Joan Shacklock, joined LNER as girl clerk during war, article in *Evening Telegraph* special publication, 26 February 2001, p.27.
3. *British Railways Eastern Operating Area (Western Division) Working Time Table, from 21st September, 1953, until further notice, Lincoln District*. British Railways Working Timetable Reprints. Reprinted 2014.
4. John Corcoran, interview with author.
5. John Carter, interview with author.

30. Locomotives and Rolling Stock
1. Eric Tonks, *The Ironstone Quarries of the Midlands, History, Operation and Railways, Part VIII, South Lincolnshire*, Runpast, 1991, p236

2. John Carter, interview with author
3. D Yeatman, *The Lodge Hill & Upnor Railway, Industrial Railway Record*, No 12, December 1966, Industrial Railway Society, pp277-292
4. Eric Tonks, *The Ironstone Quarries of the Midlands, History, Operation and Railways, Part VIII, South Lincolnshire*, Runpast, 1991, p235
5. Eric Tonks, *The Ironstone Quarries of the Midlands, History, Operation and Railways, Part VIII, South Lincolnshire*, Runpast, 1991, p235
6. John Corcoran, interview with author.

31. The Miners
1. Bill Shaw, oral history
2. Kenneth Sharp, oral history
3. John Corcoran, by email to author
4. Ken Clark, oral history
5. A Trammer was responsible for maintaining a supply of empty mine wagons – trams – to miners at work, and for removing the full ones.
6. John Corcoran, oral history
7. *Lincolnshire Echo*, 13 September 1934
8. *Lincolnshire Echo*, 25 August 1938
9. *Lincolnshire Echo*, 26 November 1938
10. *Lincolnshire Echo*, 10 February 1945
11. Unknown newspaper, 14 October 1944
12. polishresettlementcampsintheuk.co.uk
13. Derek Favill, oral history, his father Frank was the lorry driver
14. Derek Favill, oral history, his father Frank was the lorry driver
15. Letter of appointment of F Brocklesby, Lincolnshire Archives, 316/5/2
16. *London Gazette*, 26 March 1968
17. Bill Shaw, oral history
18. *Lincolnshire Echo*, 25 August 1944
19. John Corcoran, oral history
20. John Carter, interview with author
21. John Carter, oral history
22. John Corcoran, personal conversation with the author
23. Patrick Loftus, personal conversation with the author
24. John Corcoran, personal conversation with the author
25. John Corcoran, oral history
26. *Lincolnshire Echo*, 10 September 1934
27. *Lincolnshire Echo*, 17 January 1935
28. Report by Mid LincolnshireIron Co Ltd, 3 June 1957. Author's copy

32. Accidents
1. *Lincolnshire Echo*, 9 September 1935. He was buried at Nettleham, near Lincoln. This may indicate that he had formerly worked for the Mid Lincolnshire Iron Co at their Greetwell Mines and transferred to Nettleton when the latter closed. Many men from Nettleham worked at the Greetwell Mines.
2. Alan R Tailby, *A Parish Camera, Nettleton, Holton le Moor, Caistor, Grasby*, 1994, p52

3. *Market Rasen Mail*, 16 November 1940
4. Fred Wright, oral history
5. Accident plans, Tata Steel archives, copies held by author

33. Compressed Air Picks
1. Letter from the Mid Lincolnshire Iron Co Ltd, Lincoln, to John Lysaghts, dated 14 September 1937, Authors collection.
2. Letter from the Mid Lincolnshire Iron Co Ltd, Lincoln, to John Lysaghts, dated 30 June 1938, author's collection.
3. David Jackson, oral history.

35. Lysaghts Sports and Social Club
1. *Market Rasen Mail*, 17 September 1966.
2. Caistor Memories Facebook page, posted 6 October 2012.

36. Economies and Closure
1. Eric Tonks, *The Ironstone Quarries of the Midlands, History, Operation and Railways, Part VIII, South Lincolnshire*, Runpast, 1991, p227
2. Nettleton Mine – Potential Opencast Iron Ore Reserves, R Girdham, for Lysaghts Scunthorpe Works, 21 January 1966
3. Letter dated 9 February 1966, to Sir Douglas Bruce-Gardner, Bt, Chairman, GKN Steel Co. Lysaghts Scunthorpe Works, from WE Thomas, Mine Agent. Lysaghts had become part of GKN Steel in 1961. (copy held by author)
4. Swedish iron ore was being imported to Lysaghts via their Trent wharf at Flixborough in the 1930s and after the Second World War. (Caldicott, Arthur, *Life on the Trent and Humber Rivers*, Richard Kay Publications, 1995, pp 26, 27 and 35
5. *Market Rasen Mail*, 17 September 1966
6. *Lincolnshire Chronicle*, 15 March 1968
7. Unidentified newspaper report, 7 February 1969
8. *Lincolnshire Times*, February 14, 1969
9. Notice, British Steel Corporation, 5 February 1969, copy held by author.

38. Postscript
1. The oral history recordings of John Carter, John Corcoran, Derek Favill. David Jackson, Patrick Loftus, Kenneth Sharp, Bill Shaw and Les Wilkinson are available at the Caistor Heritage Centre.
2. Documents and photographs were copied and returned to their owners. Digital copies are available through the Caistor Heritage Centre. Additional documents are available at the Lincolnshire Archives and the National Archives at Kew.

BIBLIOGRAPHY

A. Relating to mining at Claxby and Nettleton

A Parish Camera, Nettleton, Holton le Moor, Caistor, Grasby, Alan R Tailby, The Author, 1994.

Aspects of Life and Work in Nettleton in the C19, Nettleton WEA, 1980.

Nettleton Iron Mine, DN Robinson, Lincolnshire Life, April 1971.

Nettleton Mines, Stewart Squires, in *The Lincolnshire Wolds,* pp 67-68, Editor David Robinson, Lincolnshire County Council, 2009.

Two Hundred Years of Claxby Parish History, Rex Russell and Elizabeth Holmes, Claxby Parish Council, 2002.

The Ironstone Quarries of the Midlands, History, Operation and Railways, Part VIII, South Lincolnshire, Eric Tonks, Runpast, 1991.

B. Relating to ironstone mining and quarrying in Lincolnshire, not included above

Lincolnshire Towns and Industry, 1700 to 1914, Neil Wright, History of Lincolnshire Committee, Volume XI, 1982.

The Appleby Ironstone Mine, M.G. Upton, Lincolnshire Industrial Archaeology, Vol 6, No 4, 1971.

The Greetwell Ironstone Mines, Stewart Squires, in *Uphill Lincoln II,* Survey of Lincoln, 2010.

The Greetwell Ironstone Mines, Stewart Squires, Lincolnshire History and Archaeology, Vol 45, 2010, Society for Lincolnshire History and Archaeology.

The Lincoln to Grantham Line, via Honington, Stewart Squires, Oakwood Press, 1996.

The Underground Mines of Lincolnshire, Stewart Squires, in *All Things Lincolnshire, a collection of papers and tributes to celebrate the 80th birthday of David N Robinson OBE MSc,* Society for Lincolnshire History and Archaeology, 2007.

INDEX

Page numbers in **bold** refer to illustrations

Acre House Farm 21, **23,** 26, 28, 29, 31, 122
Adwick Junction, South Yorkshire 43
AEC Dump Truk 92, **96,** 97
aerial ropeway 65, **71,** 75-77, 80, **85**
ambulance car 99, **104**
ambulance room 16, 88, **109**
ambulance wagons 103
Anchor Scheme 116
Andrews, Rev S W 59
antique cells 22
Appleyard, William, Claxby mineworker 55
archaeology 20, 22
Archer and Sharp 97
Ardsley, South Yorkshire 15, 28, 43, 45
army battlefield training 22, 59
Arnett, H, Nettleton mineworker 108
Aveling Barford Shuttle Dumper **91,** 93

Back o' the Farm 69, 80, 82, **101**
Baker, Claxby mineworker 50
Baker, George, Claxby mineworker 56
Balderson, John, Claxby mineworker 55
Balderson, Joseph, Claxby mineworker 55
Baldock, James, Claxby mineworker 57
Baldock, John, Claxby mineworker 56
Baldock, Thomas, Claxby mineworker 50, 50, 52
Barks, Fred, Nettleton mineworker **113**
Barkston, ironstone mining 13
Barnetby, railway station 43, 75
Bassingthwaite, John, mines surveyor 21
Basson, Thomas, Claxby mineworker 56
Baxter, Edward, Claxby mineworker 56
Baxter, John, Claxby mineworker 56
Beales, Thomas, Claxby mineworker 50, 43, 49
Beilby, Robert B, mining engineer 90, 91
belemites 16, **21**
Belfield, George, Claxby mineworker 49, 50
Bellamy, Charles, Claxby mineworker 55
Bellamy, Henry, Claxby mineworker 56
Bellhouse, George, Claxby mineworker 55
Benniworth Haven 20
Bessemer, Sir Henry, steelmaking inventor 13
Bilton, George, Claxby mineworker 55
Birchnall, William, Claxby mineworker 57
Blackdene Fluorspar Mines, Co. Durham 99
blast furnace 19, 92
Blewitt, Thomas, Claxby mineworker 57
Booth, Benjamin, Claxby mineworker 56
bord and pillar, mining method 29, 31, 65

boreholes 32, 58, **78,** 79, 117, **118**
Borril, Nettleton mineworker 108
Bowman, John, Claxby mineworker 56
Bowman, Richard, Claxby mineworker 56
Bradford, Leeds and Wakefield Railway 53
Bray, Edwin, railway contractor 28
Breckley, George, Claxby, mineworker 56
Bristow, Claxby, blacksmith 37
British Geological Survey 32, 92, 117
British Steel Corporation 15, 81, 93, 115
Brocklesby, Albert, Nettleton mineworker **113**
Brocklesby, F, Nettleton horsekeeper 105
Brocklesby, Victor, Nettleton mineworker **113**
Brookes, William **27,** 28, 29
Browns of Caistor, bus company 106
Bruce-Gardner, Sir Douglas, baronet, Berkshire 115
Burman, H, Nettleton mineworker 108
bus service 106, **107**
Button, James, Caistor builder 45
Buxton, John, Claxby mineworker 49, 50

Caistor church 20
Caistor Grammar School 20
Caistor High Street 16, 28, 58, 79, **84**
Caistor Petty Sessions 68, 105,
Caistor RDC Housing Committee 108
calcining 28, 37, 38, 43, 44, 54
calcining kilns 50, 51
Cannonball, locomotive 99, **114**
carbide lamps 66, **69**
Carlton Scroop, ironstone mining 13, **14**
Carr, John George, Claxby mine manager 49
carstone 16, **19,** 29
Carter, John, electrician 107
Caythorpe, ironstone mining 13, **14,** 43, 49
chalk bunker **94**
chalk quarry 15, 19, 58, **80, 81,** 83, 92-95, **93, 94,** 108, 115, 116
Chalmers, Dr, of Caistor 28, 49, 51
Chant, J T, druggist of Caistor 24
chute 44, 95
Clark, Roly, of Caistor **114**
Clark, Thomas, Claxby mineworker 56
Claxby village 20, 45
Claxby cells **23**
Claxby ironstone 16, **19, 20,** 117, 118, **120**
Claxby ironstone field **18,** 65
Claxby Mine 13, 15, **18,** 21, 24, 25-60, 117, **123**
Claxby, St Mary's church **21, 51,** 59
Claxby Terrace **47, 48**

Claxby Wesleyan Chapel 53
coal cutting machine 83, 109, **110**
Colsterworth, ironstone mining 13, **14**
compressed air picks 83, 93, 109, **110**, 111
Corcoran, John, engine driver **101**, 103, 107, 108, **114**, **123**
Corcoran, Terry, Nettleton mineworker 103
cottages 15, 19, 45, **47**, **70**, **107**, 108
Coulbeck, John, Claxby mineworker 57
Coulson, John, Claxby mineworker 49, 50
Cowley, George, Claxby mineworker 56
cross cut tunnel **83, 84**

Darby, Abraham, ironmaster 13
Darragh, John, mine manager 115, 116
Davy Lamp 66, **69**
daylight hole 32, 35, 68
Denton, ironstone mining 13
deposits of iron ore in Britain 16, **17**
deputy, mine employee 54, 56, 66, 106-108
Dewhirst, John, Claxby mineworker 50, 51
Dinsdale, Jeffery, Claxby mineworker 56
Dixon, T J, landowner, Holton le Moor 24, 61
Donington on Bain 20, 24
drift 28, **29**, **31**, 32, **34**, 35, 36, 39, 40, 44, **62**, 63-69, **71**, **72**, **79**, **80**, 80-81, **81**, 83, 85, 87, **94**, 100, 109, 122

Easton, ironstone mine 13, **14**
East Rosedale mine, North Yorkshire 44
Eimco Rocker Shovel **84**
Ellick, George, Claxby mineworker 50
England, W H, West Yorkshire Iron and Coal Company, 52
Evratt, George, Claxby mineworker 55
explosives 22, 29, 33, 35, 39, 40, 65, 68, 109,

Faith, David, Claxby mineworker 55
Farmery, Eric, under manager **84**
Favill, Frank, Nettleton mineworker 108, **113**
Firth and Co., iron and steel makers 28, 53
Firth, William **26**, 28
Foster, John, Claxby mineworker 44, 50, 51, 57
Fowler Challenger 4 tractor **91**
Fowler, James, Louth architect 20, **21**, 60
Fox, William, Claxby mineworker 55
Foxley, John, Claxby mineworker 57
friendly societies 52
Frodingham Iron and Steel Co. 117, **118**
Frodingham ore 19, 24, 28,
Frow, Samuel, Claxby mineworker 55
Fulbeck, ironstone mining 13, **14**

geology 16, **19**, 60, 64, 79, **81**, 91, 117, 119, **122**
geological cross section 19

geomorphology at Claxby 19
gloomy cave of disaster 15, 49, 50, 52
Godbold, William, Claxby mineworker 56
Goulsbra, Fred, Nettleton mineworker 116
Great Northern Railway 43, 53
Great Whipsnade Railway, Bedfordshire 99, **101**
Green, William, Claxby mineworker 56
Greenwood and Batley 99, 100, 101, **102**, **103**, **104**
Greetwell, ironstone mining 13, **14**, 25, 57
Griffin, Richard, Claxby mineworker 50, 52
Grimsby Docks 105

Haddock Houses, Nettleton 91
Haggswood Junction, South Yorkshire 43
Hand, Charles, Claxby mineworker 56
Hand, Edward, Claxby mineworker 56
Hanson, Ted, Claxby mineworker 57
Hardwick Deserted Medieval Village 22, 92
Hargraves, Mrs & Son 28
Harlaxton, ironstone mining 13, **14**
Harradine, John **104**
Hart, William, Claxby mineworker 57
haulage drift 32, 65
Havercroft, Charlie **113**
Hayward, Ezekial, Claxby mineworker 57
helmet lamp 66, 85
Heritage Open Days **121**, **122**
Highfield House 69
Hill, John, Claxby mineworker 55
Hill, Richard, Claxby mineworker 55
Hitchcock, Thomas, Claxby mineworker 56
Holton le Moor 45, 62, 99
Holton le Moor, proposed site of iron works **26**
Holton le Moor railway sidings 28, 40, 43, 75, 81, 87, 88, 93, 95-97, **95**, **96**, **97**, **110**, **111**, 115
Hope Tavern, Holton le Moor 49
horses 32, 36, 39, 40, 43, 65, 66, **69**, 70, 95, 100, **105**, **114**
horsekeeper 70, **105**
Houghton, William, Claxby mineworker 55
Hubbart, David, Claxby mineworker 56
Hunstanton Formation 16
Hunt, Benjamin, Claxby mineworker 49, 50
Hurdiss, J W 92

incline 28, 37- 44, 50
'In Ore of our Past' 123
internal layout, 7 The Terrace, Claxby
iron ore 20, 24, 28, 44, 61, 64, 92, 115
iron ore, deposits in Britain 16, **17**
iron works, proposed site in Holton le Moor **26**, 28
Irthlingborough Ironstone Mine, Northants 113
Ivicz, Josef, Nettleton blacksmith **106**, 106

INDEX

Ivor the Engine **102**
Jackling, William, Claxby mineworker 55
Jackson, William, Claxby mineworker 56
Jenkinson, William, Claxby mineworker 57
Johnson, Bill, Nettleton engine driver **85**

Keal, William, Claxby mineworker 50, 51, **51**, 56
Kidd, Charles, Claxby mineworker 55
Kilton Ironstone Mine, Teeside 99, **100**

Lacey, Francis, Claxby mineworker 55
Lacey, William, Claxby mineworker 57
lamps, 66, **69**, 85
Leadenham, ironstone mining 13, **14**
Lilley, James, Claxby mineworker 55
Lingdale Mines, North Yorkshire 99
Lincoln, ironstone mines 13, 24, 44, 99, 102
Lincoln, John, Claxby mineworker 55
Lincoln, Tom, Claxby mineworker 56
Lincolnshire Wolds Countryside Project 122
Llanharry Mine, Mid-Glamorgan **103**
Lloyd, Edward, locomotive **102**
locomotive 65, 66, 71, 80, 81, **85**, 88, **92**, 95, 96, 97-102, **100**, **101**, **102**, **103**, 114
Lodge Hill and Upnor Railway, Kent 101
Loftus, Patrick 107, **113**
London and North Eastern Railway 75
Lowe, Job, Claxby mineworker 56
Lower Tealby Clay 16, 65, 91
Ludford Magna, RAF station 105, 108
Lysaghts, John, iron and steel makers, 15, 58, 62, 63, 65, 75, 77, 79, **107**
Lysaghts playing field **97**, 99, 100, 109, **109**, 113, **113**, 114, **114**
Lysaghts Sports and Social Club, 99, 113-115, **113**

Maddison, Richard Claxby mineworker 50, 52
Mammoth, Mr, mining engineer 52
man-riding cars **101**
Manchester, Sheffield and Lincolnshire Railway 28, 43
Market Rasen **84**, 105, 106, 117
Markham, John, Claxby mineworker 56
Markham, Philip, Claxby mineworker 56
Marsden, John Woodhead, mining engineer 28
Marshall, George, Claxby mineworker 56
Martin, J, Nettleton mineworker 108
Maund, Bill, Nettleton mineworker **114**, **123**
McAlpine, Sir Robert, and Sons 99
Mid Lincolnshire Ironstone Company 15, 57, 61-63, 65, 70, 75, 97, 108
Middle Rasen 54, 55
mine abandonment plan 53, 69, 91
mine deputy 54, 56, 66, 106, 107, 108

mine manager 45, 47, **49**, 52, 53, 65, 80, **84**, 88, 105, **106**, 108, 113, 115,
mine rescue demonstration **109**
miners' houses **47**, 108,
Monks Abbey Mine, Lincoln 44
Morgan, J S and Sons, Barrow in Furness 99
Mower, Charles, Claxby mineworker 56
Mumby, Jack 103, **114**
Mumby, Ned **69**, 103
Museum of Lincolnshire Life, Lincoln 102
Musk, Charles, Claxby mineworker 55

Needham, William, Nettleton mineworker 108
Nettleton Bottom Mine 15, **18**, 22, 63, 79-88, **90**, **91**, 92, **92**, 93, **96**, **104**, **109**
Nettleton church **21**
Nettleton Top Mine 13, 15, **18**, 22, 28, 32, 47, 58, 61-77, 87, 88, 89, **95**, 97, **104**, 105, 108, **114**, 122
Nettleton village 15, 20, 45, 55
Newsham Abbey, near Brocklesby 21
Normanby le Wold 20, 22, 26, 45, 54, 55
Normanby Park steelworks 77, 92, 93, 96, 116

offices 22, 36, 37, 70, 71, 72, 87, 88, 103, 106
Onions box scraper **91**
opencast working 13, 65, 89-92, **90**, **91**, **92**, 108, 110, 112, 115
Orb Cottages 15, **107**, 108
Osgerby, Robert E, Claxby mineworker 56
Osgodby 49
Owston, R 24

Padley, George, Claxby mineworker 55
Palmer, Edward, Claxby mineworker 57
Palmer, Nathan, Claxby mineworker 57
Parker, George, Claxby mineworker 55
Paynel, Joseph, Claxby mineworker 56
Pearce Roe, J, ropeway inventor 75, 76
Pearson, Reginald H, consulting engineer 77
pecten shells 16, **21**
Pelham Arms Inn 51
Peniston, William, Claxby mineworker 57
pick and shovel 35, 109, **110**
piecework 36, 54
Pilkington, Ernie, welder 108
pillar and stall, mining method **29**, 31, 65, 66
pinch bar **42**, 43
Pinder, Charles, Claxby mineworker 56
pit bank 64, **64**
Plaskitt, Harry **63**
Polish Resettlement Camp 105, 108
Portass, Bill **105**
Portsmouth Dockyard, Hampshire 99, 101

powder house 29, **32**, 35, **36**, 39, 40, 58
power house 71, **71**, 72, **74**, **100**
production, ironstone 13, 15, 43, 44, 47, 53, 57-59, 64, 74, 79, 80, 92, 95, 96, **97**, 105, 106, 109-112, 115, 116
quarry, chalk 15, 19, **80**, **81**, 83, 92-95, **94**, **104**, 115, 116
quarry, ironstone 15, 22, 28, 29, 60, 65, 89, **90**

Radcliffe, Geoff **109**
Ramsden, B 62
red chalk 16
retaining wall **36**, 37, 38, **41**, 65, **79**,
Rimington, John, Claxby mineworker 57
roach stone 16
robbing 31, 65, 66, 103
Robertson, R 108
Robinson, John, Claxby mineworker 55, 56
Robinson, Jonathan, mine agent 47, 51, 54, 56
Roseby, John, mining engineer 24, 28
Ruston Bucyrus, machinery manufacturers, Lincoln **91**, 92
Ruston and Hornsby, diesel engine makers, Lincoln, 65, 72, **74**, 81, 97, 99, **100**
Ryder, Eddie 63

Saley, John, Claxby mineworker 57
sand and gravel 28, 57, 58, 91, 92
sand washing 88, **89**, 92
Saunby, Thomas, Claxby mineworker 56
Scunthorpe, ironstone mining 13, 90, 115
Scunthorpe steelworks 15, 16, 19, 92, 93, 110, 118
Second World War 22, 58, 59, 105
Selby, Joseph, Claxby mineworker 57
Shacklock, Jim **63**
Sharp, Mr, shopkeeper 47
Shaw, John Arthur **63**
Sittingbourne and Kemsley Railway, Kent 99, **101**, **102**
Skelton, David, Claxby mineworker 55
slag, iron production **23**, 92
Smith 21 Excavator 93, **94**
Smith, David, Nettleton mineworker **113**
Smith, Jack **92**
Smith, John, Claxby mineworker 55
Smith, John, Nettleton mineworker 116
Smith, Norman, Nettleton mineworker 108
Smith, William, Claxby mineworker 55
smithy **35**, 36, 37, 70, 71, **74**, 78,
Society for Lincolnshire History and Archaeology 122
South Kelsey Cricket Club 115

South Witham, ironstone mining 13, **14**
Southwell, John, Claxby mineworker 49, 50, 51, 55
Speedwell Electrics Ltd 99, 101
Spilsby Sandstone 16, **36**, 38
stables **35**, 36, 58, 70,
Stainby, ironstone mining 13, **14**
Starbuck, John, Nettleton mineworker 116
Stephenson, John, Claxby mineworker 57
Stephenson, R, Nettleton mineworker 66, 68
Stephenson, Thomas, mine manager 65, 105
Stordy, George, Claxby mineworker 56
Storr, K 108
strike, miners' 44, 53
Sturdy, William, Claxby mineworker 55
sub-level caving 83, **84**
Sumner, Revd M H 15, 50, 52
surface works and buildings 26, **33**, **34**, 35-40, **37**, 69, 70-74, **86**, 87-88, 103

Tealby Limestone 16, **36**, 38, 90
Tealby Series 16
Temple, James, Claxby mineworker 55
Temple, Samuel, Claxby mineworker 55
Thistleton, Rutland, ironstone mine 13
Thomas, Eurig, mine manager 80, **106**, 113
Thomas, Gilchrist 13
Thomas, Roy, **123**
Thomas, Russell **114**
Thompson, Jack **100**
tipping stage or dock **36**, 37, 38, 44, 62, 63, 97
tippler **62**, 63, 64, 70, 71, 72, **73**, 75 76, 80, 87, **88**, 97, 103
Tole, Thomas, Claxby mineworker 55
trammer 66, 103
tramplate **35**, 37
tramway 27, **31**, 32, 36, 37, 40, 43, 44, 66, **83**, 88, **90**, 97
travelling drift 32
Trent Ironworks, Scunthorpe 13
trial holes 13, **61**, 62, **62**, 63
tubs 32, 38, 64, 66, **69**, 71, 72, **73**, 76, 80, 87, **100**, 103, 109, 114
tub standage 68
Turner, Emma, of Caistor 49

Upper Tealby Clay 16

ventilation shaft 28, **30**, **32**, 32-35, 58, 63, 65, 68, **82**, 85
Viking Way **121**, 122
village school, Claxby 15, 45, **46**, 49

Wakefield 43, 45
Walesby 117
Walesby shaft 13, 15, 16, **18,** 117-120, **118, 119, 120**, 122

Walker, George, Claxby mineworker 50, 52
Walls, Christopher, Claxby mineworker 50
Watson, James, Claxby mineworker 57
Weardale, Co. Durham 49, 54, 56
Weldon, Ernest, Nettleton mineworker 108
Wellebourne, Jesse Claxby mineworker 55
Welshpool and Llanfair Railway, Powys 99
West Wykeham Deserted Medieval Village 22
West Yorkshire Iron and Coal Company 15, 28, 43, 52, 53, 54, 57, 59
Wheatley, Joe Nettleton mineworker 116
Whipsnade and Umfolozi Railway, Bedfordshire 99, **101**
white chalk 16
Whiting, William, Claxby mineworker 57
Wilkinson, James, Claxby mineworker 50
Wilkinson, Jim **110**
Willingsworth Iron and Coal Co, Staffordshire 110, **111**
Willisch, Joe **123**
Willison automatic coupling system 103
winding drum 39, **40**, **41**, 42, 43, 44, 58
winding house **40**, 43
Winn, Rowland 24, 28
Wolds Walks leaflet **122**
Woolsthorpe, ironstone mining 13, **14**
working timetable 43
workshop 70, 71, **71**, 72, **74**, 87, 88, 99, 101, 103, 106, 108
Wright, Fred, Nettleton mineworker 108
wrought iron rail **35**, 36

Yarborough, Earl of 26, 28, 57, 60
Yarborough Estate **26**, 47, 58, 60